IT Auditing

More than ever, technology is indispensable to business operations and record-keeping, so people skilled in computer automation – IT Auditors – have become an essential part of the financial audit team.

This book is a comprehensive guide to the IT Audit discipline and to the impact of abstraction on businesses. Developments including Robotic Process Automation (RPA) and Artificial Intelligence (AI) mean that businesses are moving from a physical world to an abstracted digital world, increasing reliance on systems, their design, their implementation and on those that oversee and maintain these systems – often parties outside the businesses' control. Though the implications of these shifts go far beyond IT Auditing, this book focuses on what IT Auditors need to know in this new environment, such as

- How to understand abstracted services and appropriate internal business controls
- How to evaluate situations where physicality has been replaced by abstracted services
- How to understand and adapt to the impact of abstracted services on objectives, operations, decision-making, and Risk Management, including changing risk profiles and introducing new risks.

In the wake of the Certified Public Accountant (CPA) Evolution project, this book will be an essential resource for readers seeking CPA certification, as well as for business leaders and Risk Management professionals who need to understand the benefits and challenges of ever-increasing automation and its concurrent abstraction of physical reality.

Jerald M Savin is Founder, President, and CEO of Cambridge Technology Consulting Group, Inc., which specializes in Automated Business Software, including assessment, selection, implementation, and troubleshooting, Data Architecture, IT Auditing and Compliance, and Judicial Expert Witness Testimony. Jerald has taught at UCLA Extension for 30+ years, the UCR Graduate School of Business for ten years, and California State University Northridge for nine years' teaching courses in Information Systems, IT Auditing, and general IS classes.

IT Auditing

The Practitioner's Guide to Reliable
Information Automation

Jerald M Savin

Routledge
Taylor & Francis Group

NEW YORK AND LONDON

Designed cover image: Getty Images

First published 2025
by Routledge
605 Third Avenue, New York, NY 10158

and by Routledge
4 Park Square, Milton Park, Abingdon, Oxon, OX14 4RN

Routledge is an imprint of the Taylor & Francis Group, an informa business

© 2025 Jerald M. Savin

Library of Congress Cataloging-in-Publication Data
Names: Savin, Jerald, author.
Title: IT auditing : the practitioner's guide to IT audit /
Jerald M. Savin.
Description: New York, NY : Routledge, 2025. | Includes
bibliographical references and index. |
Identifiers: LCCN 2024036854 (print) | LCCN 2024036855
(ebook) | ISBN 9781032689333 (hbk) | ISBN 9781032678665
(pbk) | ISBN 9781032689388 (ebk)
Subjects: LCSH: Information technology—Auditing. |
Information technology—Management.
Classification: LCC HD30.2 .S288 2025 (print) | LCC HD30.2
(ebook) | DDC 004.068—dc23/eng/20241112
LC record available at https://lccn.loc.gov/2024036854
LC ebook record available at https://lccn.loc.gov/2024036855

ISBN: 9781032689333 (hbk)
ISBN: 9781032678665 (pbk)
ISBN: 9781032689388 (ebk)

DOI: 10.4324/9781032689388

Typeset in Times New Roman
by codeMantra

Contents

Figures

Preface – IT Auditing

Chapter Contents

Intended Audience

While the primary audience for this book is IT Audit practitioners and students, do not let the word *Audit* discourage you from considering this book. This book's content applies to IT Professionals, to Business Owners and Managers, to Financial Auditors and other types of Auditors as well. Why such a wide audience? The answer lies in two major areas.

First, the increasing role of automation in business and the increasing amount of intelligence of that automation. AI and the ability to automate tasks across multiple systems, that is, Robotic Process Automation (RPA), are recent additions to business automation. They convert manual activities to automated activities and do so more intelligently.

Second, businesses depend on automation to consistently process their business transactions. Businesses expect their activities, such as sales, purchasing, and manufacturing, to happen the same way repetitively and for the automation to accommodate specific variations. This expectation may be expressed in the words 'dependable' or 'reliable'. In other words, businesses rely on or they depend on automation to get things done right. How is this possible? Because of the Controls, the Internal Controls, built into the automation. These Controls are the proverbial 'guardrails' to reduce the chances of something inappropriate occurring if not completely preventing inappropriate actions.

Increasing Automation

Automation is an ever-increasing aspect of our professional and personal lives. As this book is being written, ChatGPT, a Large Language Model (LLM), has sucked the air out of the room. Is it here to help us? Is it here to hurt us? Or will we be both helped and hurt by it? A tech commentator suggested, we may be overestimating AI in the short term and underestimating AI in the long term. The commentator went on to say that "AI isn't going to take your job, but someone who knows AI will" [Erik Qualman, email blog, February 18,2024]. While we can only guess about the impact of intelligent automation on us and our businesses, the impact is sure to occur and is sure to be significant. The only thing we do not know is the nature and extent of the impact. Most likely, the outcomes will be both positive and negative. Early adopters will capture AI's benefits first while later adopters will be catching up.

Automation has already changed many industries as diverse as farming, manufacturing, communications, navigation, and so on. Have you used automation today … to get to work, to look up material, to get materials online, to get lunch, to shop, to navigate heavy traffic at the end of your day, to get news, to decide what to watch on TV. The list is nearly endless. Automation is already ubiquitous.

Besides dependability and reliability, why do businesses automate?

- To be more productive, that is, to effectively scale to larger transaction volumes.
- To be more efficient, that is, to better utilize materials and resources.
- To be more effective, that is, to have fewer errors and greater precision.
- Or maybe just to be able to sleep at night, to be away from the business (for whatever reasons) and not have to worry about the business spinning out of control.

Taken collectively, these reasons focus on more success, greater effectiveness, greater efficiency, and greater profit, making this book appropriate for Business Executives, Business Owners, IT Professionals as well as current and aspiring IT Auditors.

The Origins of IT Audit

IT Audit originated from the recognition by financial auditors that the records upon which they rely for their professional opinions regarding the 'fairness' of financial statements are generated and maintained by computerized systems. These records depend upon data stored in databases that are managed by computerized application software. Hence, questions about 'fairness' ultimately rest on data accuracy, data correctness, data completeness, data timeliness, and data integrity. If these automated systems generated data that lacked integrity, the financial statements would be compromised and their auditors would be forced to expand their examinations.

To find the origins of business automation, look back to Great Britain post-World War II and, of all things, the Lyons Tea Shops. This appears to be the first application of computer technology to business. Lyons used the computer to calculate product costs and payroll [—https://www.sciencemuseum.org.uk/objects-and-stories/meet-leo-worlds-first-business-computer, and https://www.computerhistory.org/timeline/computers/]. In the decades since, automation moved from individual Accounting Modules to automated Accounting and Distribution systems to fully integrated Enterprise Business Software. Somewhat in parallel, IBM was working on opportunities to apply computing to manufacturing, especially inventory controls for NASA's Man on the Moon program, circa 1968. SAP arrived in the United States with its Dow Chemical's contract in 1988 bringing a fully integrated accounting, distribution, and manufacturing system to the United States. [See https://www.sap.com/about/company/history/1981-1990.html.]

Automation was clearly part of business by the 1960s and 1970s and was fully on this path before Gartner coined the acronym ERP in 1990s. ERP, Enterprise Resource Planning, focused on the capabilities of these systems and their integration. Integrated systems spelled the end of individual modules and customers looking for 'Best of Breed' solutions.

Mandate for 'An Adequate System of Internal Controls'

As computerized systems became more involved in business transaction processing and financial recordkeeping, financial regulations increased. Among the most significant recent government regulations was the Sarbanes-Oxley Act of 2002 (SOX). SOX mandated the following for businesses registered with the SEC:

- Businesses must have an *adequate* system of Internal Controls (Section 404a).
- The Chief Executive Officer and the Chief Financial Officer, or their equivalents, are responsible for having such a system in place (Sections 302 and 404a).
- Financial Auditors are required to examine the business' system of Internal Controls and issue an opinion on the adequacy of these controls (Section 404b).

Technically, SOX applied only to businesses registered with the SEC; however, these requirements inevitably became the standard for private and non-registered businesses as well.

As emphasis on Internal Controls increased, so did attention to business risk and Risk Management. COSO, the Committee of Sponsoring Organization of the Treadway Commission, codified the definition of Internal Controls in its *Internal Control – Integrated Framework* in 1992, a decade before SOX:

> **Internal control is a process**, effected by an entity's board of directors, management, and other personnel, designed to provide **reasonable assurance regarding the achievement of objectives** related to operations, reporting, and compliance. [bold type added by author for emphasis]
>
> —COSO, Internal Control – Integrated Framework,
> COSO, May 2013, p. 1

COSO's second major publication was *Enterprise Risk Management – Integrated Framework*, which was first published in 2004 and subsequently updated in 2017 as *Enterprise Risk Management – Integrating with* Strategy *and Performance*. These did for Risk Management what COSO did for Internal Control pushing both Internal Controls and Risk Management to the forefront of business management.

Bad Things Happen

From technology's beginnings, technologists looked for ways to reduce failures and increase system integrity. One of the simplest mechanisms was making backup copies so that if the original copy was destroyed or compromised, the backup copy could be restored bringing the system back to its previous state. This was a simple, effective remedial process. These practices were adopted not out of concern for Internal Controls or Risk Management, necessarily, but as a simple recognition that things break, and these were prudent actions (for IT Professionals to keep their jobs). These were easy ways to be a hero.

Around the Clock Operations

More and more processes are automated. The automation encompasses more parts of the business. The automation became more intelligent, even before AI. And businesses were operating longer hours. For example, items can be purchased online around the clock. International businesses became businesses on which 'the sun never sets'. In other words, automation allowed many aspects of business to operate outside what used to be called 'traditional business hours,' that is, 8:00 am to 5:00 pm, or 10:00 am to 09:00 pm. Not to be ignored are manufacturers, and other businesses, that operate 24 hours a day, with second and third shifts.

The cumulative effect of these changes raises the importance and significance of IT Audit beyond just financial reporting. Businesses needed assurance that their systems were operating as they expected them to operate consistent with and enabling the Enterprise to achieve its business objectives dependably and reliably.

Thank Yous

Books are a labor of love and collaboration. This book is no different. It is based on more than 40 years of experience in business and teaching. The final push included special assistance from Mark Ruppert, an Internal Audit colleague, Dr. Daeeun 'Daniel' Choi and Dr. Yue 'Jeff' Zhang, fellow Professors at CSUN, and Anne Gani Sirota, my very special partner and proofreader. Thank you, your input and insights are greatly appreciated. Also Thank Yous to my students at CSUN, UCLA Extension and UCR. They helped me bring clarity and understanding to the classroom and this book.

Chapter 1

Introduction to IT Auditing

Chapter Contents

Introducing IT Auditing

As early as the mid-1960s, there were individuals in businesses responsible for 'auditing' computerized business systems. The EDP Auditors Association (EDPAA) [Electronic Data Processing Auditors Association] began as a 'band of brothers' (to borrow a movie title), a group of individuals with similar jobs that were becoming increasingly critical to their respective employers. The group was formally incorporated in 1969. In 1976, the EDPAA formed an educational foundation, the Information Systems Audit and Control Association (ISACA), to undertake significant research regarding IT governance and controls. [– https://isacala.org/lachapterinfo/] Early IT Auditors relied on the EDPAA's *Control Objectives*, which ultimately became ISACA's *Control Objectives for Information and Related Technology* (COBIT). The Canadian Institute of Chartered Accountants had a similar publication that was also widely used.

IT Auditing has been an essential part of financial auditing since financial records became computerized. IT Auditing as a discipline was practiced both in the CPA profession and in industry, especially in businesses with significant computer automation.

The CPA Evolution Initiative

In 2018, a joint initiative of the American Institute of Certified Public Accountants (AICPA) and the National Association of State Boards of Accountancy (NASBA)

DOI: 10.4324/9781032689388-1

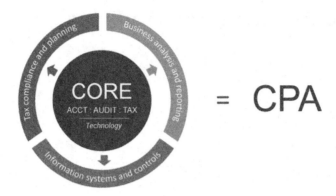

Figure 1.1 CPA Evolution Initiative Model Matrix. Reproduced with permission of AICPA-CIMA. https://www.evolutionofcpa.org/.

was launched. It was called The CPA Evolution Initiative. Its purpose was to review and update the educational requirements and practice realities of the public accounting profession. It was a belated recognition that automation and automated systems were essential to business processes and to financial recordkeeping and reporting. Enterprises, non-profits, and businesses of all sizes and their owners and Auditors relied on the information generated by and maintained in these systems. The integrity of the systems, the integrity of the processes, and the integrity of the Data were critical to effective operation, to effective decision-making, and to accurate financial reports ... and have been for more than five decades. The CPA Evolution initiative was a long overdue acceptance of reality.

While the focus of the CPA Evolution Initiative is on transforming the CPA licensure model, its significance extends beyond the licensure model. CPA Evolution focuses on the skills and competencies that are required of professional accountants today. The results of the Initiative are summarized in Figure 1.1.

- At its highest level, the CPA Evolution Initiative includes Technology as a core competency alongside the traditional competencies of Accounting, Auditing, and Tax. This says that accountants and Auditors need Technology skills and competence to be effective accountants, Auditors, and tax planners and preparers.

  From a historical standpoint, SAS 70, the predecessor of today's System and Organization Controls (SOC) Reports, was initially issued in 1992, 30 years prior to the CPA Evolution project. The Institute of Internal Auditors (IIA) released its first Global Technology Audit Guide (GTAG) on *Information Technology Risk and Controls* in 2005, more than 15 years before the Evolution Initiative. The goal of this guide "... was, and is, to provide an overview of the topic of IT-related risks and controls". [—The Institute of Internal Auditors, *Information Technology Risk and Controls*, 2nd edition, p. 2.]

For decades before the CPA Evolution Initiative, Professional Accountants and Auditors were already accustomed to working with technology and understood its essential roles in business and finance.

- The Evolution Initiative created three disciplines:
  - Business Analysis and Reporting (BAR)
  - Tax Compliance and Planning (TCP)
  - Information Systems and Controls (ISC)

- BAR recognizes that analytics and business reporting are essential parts of the work of Accountants and Auditors.
- TCP recognizes that CPAs are also reliant on automated systems for tax preparation and planning. The days of manually prepared tax returns are long gone.
- A new third discipline, ISC, was created by the Initiative.

  The subject matter content of the ISC discipline is the Business Information Systems that process business transactions and the Internal Controls surrounding Infrastructure and Applications and embedded within Applications.

  Examples of Enterprise Business Information Systems are Enterprise Resource Planning (ERP) systems, Customer Relationship Management (CRM) systems, Human Resources/Human Capital Management (HRM/HCM) systems, Payroll systems, Inventory Management systems, etc. Enterprises depend on these systems to operate.

IT Auditing is the third discipline. IT Auditing extends beyond just the systems and the controls to the environments on which businesses depend.

Hence, this book is essential knowledge for all Accountants and Auditors regardless of their professional activities, regardless of whether they are external or internal Accountants or Auditors.

Professional Standards – IT Audit Frameworks and Resources

Every profession has its professional literature and standards. IT Auditing is no different. Its authoritative literature includes:

- *COBIT®* published by ISACA
- GTAGs published by The IIA
- Various audit standards, guides, and papers published by the AICPA

To this list, other resources can be added, such as:

- *ITIL®*, originally the Information Technology Infrastructure Library, is published by Axelos Ltd. ITIL® was originally developed by the United

Kingdom Government's Central Computer and Telecommunications Agency (CCTA) in the 1980s. ITIL began as BS 15000 for IT Service Management. It was adopted by the Internal Standards Organization as ISO 20000.

For a quick overview of ITIL® consider *What is IT Infrastructure Library (ITIL)?* at https://www.ibm.com/topics/it-infrastructure-library.

ISO 20000 is the international standard for Information Technology Service Management (ITSM). The difference between ITIL® and ISO20000 is the difference between a practice framework and a practice standard. ITIL® is the framework and ISO 20000 is the standard.

In addition to these professional resources, a variety of publications are available, each drilling into different aspects of IT Auditing to varying degrees.

Please refer to Appendix 1 for a cross-reference between COBIT® and ITIL® and ITIL® and COBIT®. Both frameworks have items in common and differences. COBIT® and ITIL® were designed for slightly different purposes and audiences; hence, even the elements in common contain differences; however, the common themes and the differences are broadly identified.

Internal Controls in Context

America has a kneejerk reaction to Internal Controls. The kneejerk reaction is to oppose anything that limits or restricts our ability to do things … including our ability to screw up. (Said only partly in jest.)

However, businesses rely on controls to ensure consistent products and services without the blink of an eye. Why? How do you feel when you buy a product or service that isn't up to your expectations? Letdown? Do you pick another product or supplier next time? This is the painful reality for businesses.

Controls ensure uniformity and consistency. Without uniformity and consistency, every purchase would be a surprise, and highly available, high-quality, highly reliable products and services would not exist.

Business Owners and Executives have said 'you can implement controls … BUT don't do anything that limits their ability to do whatever they want to do'. Yes, there is some poetic license, but this was the message of a client in slightly more opaque language.

Businesses readily embrace controls when they increase efficiency and/or reduce cost. But what about protecting the integrity of business processes and business systems? Yes, generally businesses are in favor of controls that improve business processes, limit defects and errors, and ensure that businesses achieve their objectives.

The two sides of control: Ensuring uniformity and consistency versus somehow limiting freedom of choice or freedom of opportunity. Internal Controls are not the enemy of innovation, maybe they are the guardrails of innovation.

Changing IT Environment

The Information Technology (IT) environment is constantly changing in subtle ways, and in some not-so-subtle ways, which IT Audit must consider.

The biggest challenge today is Artificial Intelligence and its benefits and liabilities. Following closely behind is the change from Physical Assets to Virtual Services. This change is summarized in a single word, Abstraction. The essence of abstraction is that physical assets and services are replaced by digital services. Instead of dealing with physical servers and applications, software, Customers and their Auditors deal with services provided by Cloud Service Providers (CSPs).

What was once a physical asset under the control of its owner is now a service provided by a third party under the control of the third party. This change is hugely significant for IT Auditors and Businesses as well. If something fails, who do you yell at, whose 'throat do you choke'? In the case of CSPs, 'a single throat to choke' has become a marketing mantra, but does it work?

Enterprises are transferring control of key Infrastructure to third parties. Yes, the third parties may have greater skill and depth than a business typically has, but the third parties have their own agenda, their own priorities, which may not align with the priorities of their Customers. This non-alignment or potential misalignment may be neither obvious nor explicit. After Enterprises adopt cloud services, they are operationally dependent on their service providers. When a service is interrupted, do the service providers step into the breach, and handle the business operations when their services fail? Hardly. In any number of situations, CSPs' services have failed. Granted the service providers work to restore their services as soon as possible, for a variety of reasons … but … what happens to their Customers? Say, for example, a CSP is hosting an airlines' aircraft systems, crewing systems, and reservation systems and the service fails. Does the hosting provider send people to the airport(s) to help the airline explain why its flights were cancelled. Very, very unlikely.

Businesses are reliant on third parties for essential services that can bring their operations to a standstill. Yes, financial arrangements may reduce the financial impact of outages, but these arrangements do not address the businesses' standing in the marketplace with their Customers.

Granted this is a worst-case scenario. Service providers may have more technical skill, competence, and experience than their Customers; however, the Customer is ultimately dependent upon a resource over which they have little knowledge, insight, and control. As the responsibility for infrastructure, applications, and services shifts from businesses to their service providers, the skill, competence, and experience of the business declines. How will this void be filled? The institutional answer is SOC reports, which will be subsequently covered in a separate chapter. SOC reports are great but where is the expertise within the Customer enterprise to evaluate these reports? 'Shared

Responsibility', which will be discussed below, is another significant aspect of cloud service agreements. Is the Customer's knowledge and skill sufficient for the Customer to fulfill its responsibilities?

This change impacts the skills and knowledge required of Auditors, which reminds us of the CPA Evolution Initiative.

In summary, CSPs abstract their Customers' previous physical assets and processes. This change impacts IT Audit in several ways: It extends concerns to the Auditee's service providers, the Auditee's dependence on third parties for basic business operations, and potentially results in less technical expertise in Auditees.

Chapter 2

IT Audit's Big Questions

Chapter Contents:

Introduction to IT Auditing

Checklists are a common auditing tool. They help ensure that specific areas and topics are covered adequately and may dictate outcomes. They are helpful, especially for the uninitiated. But, to some degree, they undermine thinking. Auditors

DOI: 10.4324/9781032689388-2

become reliant on their checklists. The successful completion of a checklist does not ensure a successful audit, which is their intended purpose.

During the middle of the initial wave of Sarbanes-Oxley Act (SOX) compliance, an internal bank IT auditor was confronted by a reasonable request from its financial audit firm for the bank's backup and recovery procedures. Not an unreasonable request, except, the bank had multiple systems, multiple databases, multiple data centers and transactions were replicated across multiple systems, multiple platforms, and multiple data centers. When the Internal Auditor asked why the External Auditor was asking for the backup and recovery procedures, the External Auditor was surprised and merely repeated the request. From the beginning, the Internal Auditor suspected the External Auditor was driven by checklists and was oblivious to the bank's business continuity procedures, which were extensive, as would be expected. The request was resolved the following day when the External Auditor returned and requested the Backup and Recovery documentation again because it was on the audit firm's checklist. Nothing was requested about the bank's extensive business continuity architecture and procedures because that was not on the checklist.

Fast forward to today, checklists are updated. But how current are the checklists given new technologies and new methods? Checklists are points-in-time documents. They need to be regularly reviewed and updated to reflect changing conditions.

Why mention this? Because the focus of this book is less on specific risks and controls and more on general principles and guidance that are remain relevant regardless of the specifics of individual situations, such as the emergence of Generative Artificial Intelligence (AI) and its impact on businesses.

Underlying IT Audit Principles

The intention of this book is to focus on enduring, underlying principles, the principles upon which the checklists are based instead of on the checklists themselves.

With the previous circumstances in mind, what are major issues that IT Auditors confront when assessing systems and controls? In the vernacular, what are the underlying IT audit principles on which businesses and it audit rely?

As technologies develop, morph, and mature, the Big Questions persist. The forms, the formats, and the mechanisms may change, but the basic, underlying principles endure. They persist even though the degree and type of automation changes. While these changes do not impact the basics, they may change the Risks and the nature of appropriate Internal Controls based on the new Risks.

As this book is being written, AI is on the cusp of a massive impact on business and society. How will AI change IT Auditing? Among the most concerning questions today are the impact of AI on society and closer to home on our careers. What will the job market look like five or ten years from now? Will we all be on the beach with nothing to do? (with its positives and negatives) See Figure 2.1.

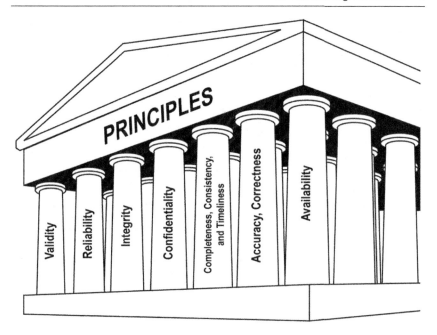

Figure 2.1 Basic IT Principles.

When talking about Business Risks and Internal Controls, basic principles generally boil down to at least the following principles and major questions:

- Availability

  What can interfere with the availability of infrastructure, systems, applications, Data, and IT services?

  Note: Availability is not only an on-and-off function; it also comes in degrees.

- Accuracy, Correctness

  What can cause inaccuracies and/or incorrectness?

  Note: Accuracy and Correctness may be used interchangeably because they are similar ideas but from different perspectives. Accuracy is computational while Correctness is representational. Accuracy generally relates to numbers, and to numeric values. Preciseness is a related concept to Accuracy. In other words, how Precise must a value be to be accurate? Consider financial statements that are considered accurate even though they are rounded to the nearest millions of dollars.

  Correctness, on the other hand, is representational. Does the item in question fairly or truly represent what it is supposed to represent or is it misleading? Does it misrepresent what it is supposed to represent? An alternate definition of Correctness is 'free from errors'. In this use case, criteria determine the nature and severity of errors.

- Completeness, Consistency, and Timeliness

  How can Data or information become compromised by incompleteness, inconsistency, or time-related issues? While these might be considered separate items, they are combined here because their absence (i.e., incompleteness, inconsistency, or inappropriate timing) can be misleading.

- Confidentiality

  How can confidentiality be compromised? What are the business and compliance issues related to confidential information, especially if it becomes compromised? This principle also includes Privacy as a subset of Confidentiality.

- Integrity

  How can the integrity of a system, an application, or Data be compromised?

- Reliability

  How can a system, an application, or Data become unreliable, undependable, or unusable?

- Validity

  Is the business Data or information valid? Invalid Data means the Data or information is somehow inaccurate or misleading, which can lead to suboptimal if not outright bad decisions.

- Fitness

  Is the Data 'fit for its intended purpose' [—Thomas C Redman, *Data Driven: The Field Guide*, Boston: Digital Press, 2001, p. 73] or is it inappropriate or misleading? The last principle is Data specific, whereas the other principles are generic IT principles.

These questions can also be viewed from an IT Risk perspective:

- What Risks does IT bring to an Enterprise, especially risks that did not previously exist, or risks that change minor inconveniences into significant disruptions or failures because of the automation?
- What Risks are associated with IT Products and Services?
- What Risks are associated with IT Infrastructure, which may be referred to as Enterprise Architecture (EA) Risks?
- What Risks are associated with Enterprise Application Software?
- What Risks are associated with Enterprise Data?
- What IT Risks are associated with outsourced products or services?
- What Cybersecurity Risks are there and how are they changing?
- How do new technologies impact IT Risks?

Each of the questions above deals with Availability, Accuracy/Correctness, Completeness, Consistency, Timely; Confidentiality; Integrity; Reliability; Validity; and Fitness to varying degrees.

Failure often comes up in the discussion of these questions. Failure often refers to a total, complete breakdown. However, the more insidious side of failure are partial failures and inconsistent failures, which mean the system works correctly some of the time, maybe most of the time, but not all of the time. Disruptions come in degrees ranging from minor to total failures. The most obvious less than total failures are slowness, degradation, or latency.

These principles, IT-related questions, are important in two audit contexts:

- Business Context

  These questions ultimately relate to business objectives, to the achievement of business objectives, and to situations that interfere with the achievement of these objectives. The Business Context is business benefit centric, i.e., achieving business objectives.

- Compliance Context

  Compliance extends beyond business benefits and considers the implications and risks associated with non-compliance. In an extreme case, a business might lose its ability to operate, i.e., be shut down by outside forces, such as losing the ability to take credit cards because of significant Payment Card Industry Data Security Standard (PCI-DSS) violations or losing its business license because of a compliance failure.

These basic principles are considered below in sequence realizing that they are interrelated, not necessarily independent of each other. They work together in the provision of IT Resources and Services as required by the Enterprise to achieve its business goals and objectives.

Underlying IT Audit Principles in Detail

Availability: Infrastructure, System, Application, Data

Availability is often defined in terms of operating hours. Traditionally, 8:00 am to 5:00 pm Monday through Friday or 10:00 am to 9:00 or 10:00 pm Monday through Saturday were the norms with different practices on Sundays. Today operations are more likely to be 24 hours a day, 7 days a week, 52 weeks a year. In other words, businesses and their systems are operating continuously, hence are continuously available. Consider police and fire departments, utilities, hospitals, hotels, and online retailers. They are constantly open for business. Banks are an interesting combination. Their branch offices are typically open 'banker's hours'; however, Customers can go to their ATMs at any time of the day or night and withdraw or deposit money, while the retail side of the bank is closed.

Availability is not exclusively an issue of available versus non-available. Service levels may fluctuate, and systems may be intermittent, which can drive consumers and technicians crazy. We take our car to the garage to be fixed and the mechanic says everything is working just fine except the problem continues. Or we have Internet connectivity issues, but the instruments do not indicate line errors leaving the Customer dissatisfied and the engineer with uncertainty.

Availability can be continuously available, continuously not available, or the more troublesome alternatives, diminished capability, disruptions with no obvious explanations. Consider Internet Availability: High-speed availability, Customers are happy; medium-speed availability, Customers are frustrated; and low-speed availability, Customers are dissatisfied.

Closely associated with Availability are Reliability and Dependability. Uneven Availability means Enterprises cannot rely on, or depend on IT Assets, Services, and Data because their Availability is less than needed. In terms of general expectations, we have come to expect subsecond responsiveness from our systems without interruptions or degradations.

There is an exception, a 'get out of jail' card, for Availability and Continuity. The exception is intentional outages. Circumstances occur where systems must be taken offline, typically for repair or maintenance. When these outages are announced in advance, they do not count against Availability.

'High Availability' systems are specifically designed to minimize latency and outages through redundancy and fault tolerance. While an ATM system that is out of service for maintenance is inconvenient, slowness in an air traffic control system for any reason could be catastrophic.

Accuracy, Correctness: What can Cause Process Inaccuracies and/or Inaccurate Data?

Accuracy encompasses multiple criteria, including correctness, preciseness, and accurately representing situations as opposed to being misleading. Examples include order accuracy, employee time record accuracy, asset value accuracy, automated process operation accuracy, item description accuracy, item availability accuracy, and so on.

Accuracy is a numeric construct and may involve precision. Consider the weight of precious metals or the linear measurement of material that must fit precisely between two points where fractions of an inch are critical. At the other end of the spectrum, consider the financial statements of large corporations, which are rounded to the nearest million dollars (000,000). The company's public accountant's opinion is that these statements 'present fairly, in all material respects'. These are widely divergent examples of accuracy.

Another use case is product descriptions. Are the product descriptions accurate? The descriptions may include words and images. Do they accurately represent the products? Are the descriptions correct? Or are they misleading? Does the product look like the image? Does the product work as described? Is the color of the product close to but not the same as the picture?

Hence, Accuracy and Correctness are similar but different depending on circumstances. Maybe the best test of accuracy and correctness is whether the Data 'presents fairly' the circumstances.

Completeness, Consistency, and Timeliness: Is the Data Complete, Consistent, and Timely?

Completeness, Consistency, and Timeliness could be part of Accuracy, but these characteristics extend beyond a traditional definition of Accuracy.

Completeness asks, is the Data complete? Business Data is a byproduct, maybe even the product, of business processes. Business Processes are normally multistep. Looking at Data in a business process, it should be complete up to a given point in the process, but it is not complete with respect to the entire business process. This is generally inconsequential if the duration of the process is measured in seconds, but if the business process extends over days, weeks, or even years, then the question of completeness might arise.

Consider online shopping. Customers put items in their shopping carts. If the cart is abandoned, the system may empty the shopping cart, which means the Customer must start over next time, or the system may preserve the shopping cart. In the second case, the Customer can delete items, purchase items, or save items for a future purchase. Whatever occurs, the Data is complete at every step in the process but incomplete over the life of the purchase. Hence, the process can be complete at each point in the process but incomplete with respect to the entire process, which means the Data may be both complete and incomplete depending upon timing, which means completeness and timeliness can be interrelated.

In financial analyses, timeliness is extremely important. Partially complete transactions may be identified as pending or they may be disregarded depending on the circumstances. An incomplete sale is excluded from revenue, while unpaid sales are included in revenue and accounts receivable. In the first case, the sale is incomplete; in the second case, the sale occurred, and the revenue is recognized, but the supplier has not yet been paid.

Consistency means that similar processes behave similarly and that Data from similar business processes will be similar or consistent with each other.

When talking about consistency, consider Master Data Management (MDM). MDM emphasizes consistent identifiers for master Data, such as Customer IDs, Vendor IDs, Item IDs, Location IDs, and so on. Imagine a Customer that deals with different parts of a large Enterprise. What are the chances that the Customer ID will be the same in all places? If a central authorization authority is used to grant IDs, the chances are higher; but if different places use different business systems, then it is unlikely that the Customer ID will be the same in different places. This difference makes consolidating Data difficult because the same Customer is identified differently in different systems, i.e., Customer IDs are not consistent. Both the Enterprise and the Customer could suffer from this difference. For more information about this topic, consult DAMA's *DAMA-DMBOK2*, https://www. dama.org/cpages/body-of-knowledge. [DAMA-DMBOK2 was originally published in 2018. A Revised Edition was released in March 2024, which included significant changes to DAMA-DMBOK2.]

When it comes to external Data, Data that originates outside of the Enterprise's systems, the quality of the external Data is completely out of the hands of the Enterprise. Data Quality may be dictated by a contract, such as a Service Level Agreement (SLA). Even so, Data aggregators do not necessarily guarantee the quality of their Data. There may be unintentional deficiencies in the Data. This issue is important when external Data is combined with internal Data and the combined Data is used for decision-making. Data assessment and verification becomes important during Data Importation. For example, consider the A.K.A. (also known as) section of a credit report. You may be surprised by what is in that section; it is at least worth a chuckle. From where did the inaccurate Data come?

The point is that Completeness, Consistency, and Timeliness are essential and involve multiple challenges, i.e., things may not be nearly as straightforward as might be expected.

Process Integrity and Data Integrity can easily be reduced. From the IT Audit perspective, process, and Data completeness, consistency and timeliness may require special assessments and treatments.

Confidentiality: How Can Confidential Information be Compromised?

Confidentiality deals with Data. The Data may be confidential because of regulations, such as privacy regulations, or it may be confidential because of attorney-client privilege or healthcare privilege may apply, or it may be confidential because the business considers the Data proprietary, such as product formulas, bills of materials, Customer lists, or any other Data the business does not want to be published. Two terms that apply to confidentiality are Privacy and Trade Secrets.

Because Confidentiality and Privacy are often discussed in the context of Cybersecurity, the detailed discussion of Confidentiality is postponed to that chapter.

For IT Auditors, the issues are knowing the circumstances regarding the confidentiality of the Data, the Enterprise's policies, procedures, practices, and standards related to the handling, preserving, accessing, and distribution of Confidential Data, and the repercussions associated with compromising Confidential Data.

Integrity: How Can System Integrity, Application Integrity, or Data Integrity be Compromised?

Integrity involves at least two dimensions:

* Process Integrity
* Data Integrity

Are Processes executed as they were designed and implemented? Does the business' Data, regardless of its sources, have integrity over its lifecycle? Do the Processes achieve their objectives? Do the Data accurately reflect reality? Hence, Integrity could be defined as design conformance and/or as accuracy, consistency, and suitability.

For IT Auditors, Process and Data Integrity are major concerns. What can compromise these elements? What policies, procedures, and practices reduce the likelihood that Integrity will be compromised and if compromised how quickly will the compromise be discovered and remediated? When the question of 'how long' arises, consider the cybersecurity concept of 'dwell time'. It is one thing if the attacker is in your systems once; it is another thing if the attacker has been in your systems for an extended period of time before being discovered.

Process Integrity will be discussed further in the chapter on Enterprise Business Systems, and Data Integrity will be discussed further in the chapter on Auditing Data.

Reliability/Dependability: How Can Systems, Applications or Data Become Unreliable, Undependable?

Can the systems, can the applications, can the Data be relied upon, can they be depended on? If not, what is causing the unreliability, the undependability?

A leading reason for automation is reliability, that the same action will occur the same way with the same outcome repeatedly. As the sayings go, that's why Enterprises 'spend the big bucks' so management and owners can 'sleep at night'. The worst thing for executives and owners is a call in the middle of the night that operations are malfunctioning or stopped. A primary justification for automation is continuous, consistent operations, especially eliminating random mistakes.

For IT Auditors, this gets to the question of the Enterprise's policies, procedures, practices, standards, and assets that ensure the Integrity, Reliability, and Dependability of its systems for both operations and decision-making. What constraints or guardrails were implemented to reduce Risk and ensure the Enterprise achieves its Objectives, which in this case are reliable operations and reliable Data.

Validity: How Can the Data and Information in Business Systems be Validated?

Validity is verification. What mechanisms are present to confirm that transactions, operations, and Data are valid? The big IT Audit questions regarding Validity include the following:

- Is the business' Data valid?
- How is validity confirmed or verified?

How are businesses assured that their decisions are based on Data that are appropriate, relevant, and reasonable?

An Alternate Perspective – IT Risk Management

An alternate approach is to ask similar questions from the perspective of IT's impact on the Enterprise (Figure 2.2).

Enterprises are dependent on Manual and Automated processes, which have different characteristics, advantages, and disadvantages. The big advantage of Manual processes is the ability of a person to adjust a procedure to a situation, whereas Automated procedures shine in their consistency and the ability to scale. The big disadvantage of Manual procedures is random mistakes, whereas

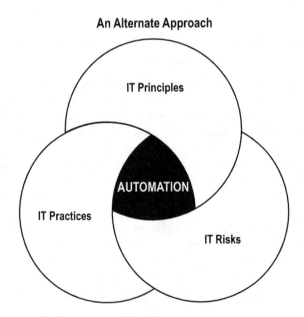

Figure 2.2 An Alternative Approach.

automated processes repeat the same mistakes continuously until the automation is corrected. Yes, Automated processes can break, but the problem can be recognized and addressed promptly.

Random errors are a different story. They can be difficult to identify and troubleshoot. They may lack obvious solutions. Remember taking your car to the garage to be fixed and being told that the mechanic didn't find anything wrong with the car. The problem is intermittent errors or in technical language random errors.

Essential aspects of automation are its design, configuration, and implementation. Automation operates continuously according to its design, configuration, and implementation. Often subsequent problems can be traced back to the system's design, or its configuration, or its implementation. In these cases, the system needs to be revised to deal with the problem. Once the problem is remediated, the system is fully functional working appropriately, predictably, and continuously.

Risks and remedial controls in Manual processes focus on control procedures that ensure correct behavior and identify and remediate incorrect behavior, including minimizing random errors. In contrast, Automated processes may need to be re-designed, re-configured, and/or re-implemented. With more 'intelligent' systems, this concern may diminish as 'self-healing' mechanisms make necessary adjustments. Think of autopilot systems or speed or pressure regulators that respond to their environment. They 'self-correct'. These systems may also avoid situations that would otherwise cause errors, such as finding alternate routes to avoid heavy traffic.

The introduction of new Automation introduces a new set of Risks that did not previously exist. The new Automation may have advantages and disadvantages over the previous existing situation. The new Automation may exacerbate existing Risks; however, it may also reduce existing Risks, which is generally why businesses acquire new technology to accentuate the positive and eliminate the negative. For example, consider the unknown Risks associated with AI. Granted there will be Risks. The problem is we just do not know what those Risks will be. AI may turn out to be a boon when one is looking for information, has writer's block, or is checking coverage or comprehensiveness of an article or report, or a bust if AI provides incorrect or inappropriate information. So, a technology, such as AI can be both a boon and a bust.

To summarize,

- IT may introduce new Risks.
- IT may amplify existing Risks.
- IT may reduce or eliminate existing Risks.

Risks can change. They can decrease over time as automation becomes more self-adjusting, and more self-correcting. The gold standard for Quality Control is a mechanism that identifies defects as they occur and automatically adjusts to correct them when they occur instead of having to subsequently re-work items or have Customers return items because they were incorrect.

IT resources can be packaged as products, such as computers, peripheral devices, storage devices, software, or as services, such as cloud services, technical support, repair services, design services, construction services, production services, and so on. Accordingly, Risks that IT introduces into a Business can be product-related or service-related. In either case, the Risks may not exist prior to the introduction of Automation. The obvious caveat is that Risks routinely exist, and Automation is typically introduced to reduce these Risks. However, Automation can introduce new Risks as well as reduce or amplify existing Risks.

Besides Process Risks, Automation can introduce Data Risks, can compromise Data, which can be the result of unremediated Process Risks. Either way, Data Risks need to be evaluated and corrected as appropriate.

Another aspect of Automation is its dependability until it is not dependable. What does this mean? Consider reliance on something that is generally but not completely reliable. Machines break; Automation breaks. Regularly or intermittently? The break may range from minor annoyances to major service disruptions, which may be momentary or longer lasting. Responding effectively and timely is critical. The objective is to contain the interruption, quickly resolve the interruption, and resume normal operations.

Minor annoyances, if tolerable, may be ignored, but situations that threaten significant disruption are generally addressed for economic or social reasons, ranging from cost to reputation damage.

IT Product-Related Risks

IT Product-related Risks are associated with things that malfunction. Products are designed and implemented to provide specific capabilities. They are dependable to the extent that they provide their capabilities reliably, consistently, and timely. As noted above, a major distinction between Manual and Automated processes is randomness. Manual procedures tend to be affected by random mistakes, ignoring intentional acts, while automated processes tend to operate continuously as they were designed, configured, and implemented with a greater degree of accuracy and certainty. If there is a catch here, as mentioned above. It is initial misdesign, mis-configuration, or misimplementation, which causes errors. The good news is that these errors are often easily identified and resolved, more easily than intermittent random errors, especially when a pattern is not obvious.

IT Products, whether hardware or software related, have the Risk of unintended consequences. IT Products may incorrectly calculate numbers. Products may produce wrong results. Products and Services may fail to live up to their promises. How bad is it? Gartner conjured up the idea of a Hype Cycle. Admittedly for a slightly different purpose, but just the idea of hype as a factor in IT Products and Services is unsurprising. Similar ideas include 'good enough to ship' and 'minimally viable product' (MVP). In a hypercompetitive market, the urge to gain market share may be irresistible; hence, Products and Services are only good enough to ship, or just 'half-baked', with the potential for errors, mistakes, and deficiencies. Do Enterprises want to bet their existence on 'half-baked' Products and Services? Do Customers want to be forced to rely on 'half-baked' Products and Services?

IT Infrastructure-Related Risks

First and foremost, IT Infrastructure is the foundation. If that foundation isn't appropriate, the entire Enterprise can be at Risk. Major systemic infrastructure Risks include:

- Availability:

    A 24-hour world requires 24-hour infrastructure, infrastructure that is continuously operational, and continuously available, even if it is not actively used 24 hours a day. The days of being able to shut things down, for whatever reason, are mostly gone.

    In Global Enterprises, divisions in different time zones may have limited hours, say daytime hours; however, from the Enterprise's perspective, the systems are constantly in operation supporting the various divisions as they turn on and off around the globe.

- Dependence and Reliability:

    A 24-world world depends on a 24-hour infrastructure, which is reliably available to serve the Enterprise and its Customers.

    This dependency extends beyond just Infrastructure to the Enterprise's applications, databases, communications, and services, basically everything.

    Fault Tolerance is a critical design factor. In fault-tolerant environments, failures are confined, and alternate assets and processes take over to ensure continuous operations. This will be discussed further below.

- Appropriateness:

    Are the Infrastructures appropriate for the Enterprises' needs and objectives? To borrow a concept from COBIT, does the Infrastructure 'align' with the needs, objectives, and expectations of the Enterprise? Appropriateness means a specific Infrastructure is required, not just any Infrastructure.

- Time:

    As Enterprises grow and change, their infrastructure, applications, and Data need change as well. What once served Enterprise objectives may no longer serve those objectives. Hence, Enterprises need to regularly assess their Infrastructure and upgrade and replace it as needed.

The good news in a cloud environment is that this requirement falls to the service provider and likely the robustness of the cloud services may substantially exceed the Enterprise's requirements.

Enterprise Business Software-Related Risks

Today, Enterprise Business Software is deeply intertwined in business. Businesses depend on their automation. It is the centerpiece of an Enterprise, managing operations, and recording Enterprise transactions. Could a world-class online retailer function today without automation? Obviously, Not. To sustain large continuous operations, businesses require business process automation to operate. This necessity increasingly applies to small and mid-size businesses as well.

Besides the dependency Risk, automation must be configured appropriately and installed appropriately. Failing in either area can render systems less effective. Also, significant customization to commercial Business Software can create a worst-case scenario whereby the system gets 'frozen' in the past unable to keep up with the inevitable patches and updates commercial developers release. These changes need to be assessed and revised as needed.

Because customization can end up standing in the way of software maintenance, the choice to customize should be carefully evaluated during system selection and implementation before deciding whether customization is the best option or the only option.

Outside IT Services-Related Risks

Increasingly businesses are looking for outside IT resources to augment or replace in-house IT resources. The obvious examples are cloud-based services and outsourcing in general. In both situations, businesses are looking for outside IT Services that can be essential to their operations.

The big question: What Risks do the outside resources bring into the Business? And how does the Business manage those Risks? One option is System and Organization Controls (SOC) reports, which are covered in a separate chapter.

A significant outsource Risk is any Activity or Service that involves Administrative access to business systems. These high-privilege accounts give the outside party Administrative access to systems. This is especially concerning if that access is to critical Infrastructure. A good practice is to grant outsiders, and insiders as well, two accounts. One account is used for activities and services they perform that *do not require* administrative access. The second account is the high-privilege account, which should be closely monitored. One can go as far as disabling the account and requiring its users to schedule time when the account will be active and ask them to document what they did while using the high-privilege account, basically limiting the damage they can do.

Outsourced Products and Services share the risk of dependence on third-party providers for essential resources. The problem: Will the third party be a dependable supplier? Will their Products and Services be appropriate now and in the future? Even large businesses lose interest, change priorities, and/or fail. Consider the telecommunications industry's shifting priorities from basic telephone services to content providers, for example. What happens to the supplier's Customers? A happy ending is not guaranteed.

IT Services, like IT Products, may fail to live up to their promises, and may fail to deliver the expected results. Entering the IT Services market is a very low bar. In the extreme, a person can hang out a shingle in front of their garage advertising IT Services. Their services may be superb but how would businesses know? At the other end of the spectrum are established IT Services firms. One would think they are a shoo-in, but Services involve people, and the IT Services industry is especially porous. Countless projects start with a specific group of people. Before long, substitutions occur often because the individuals providing the services move to other firms or other ventures. Ensuring a steady supply of competent personnel can be a challenge even for well-established IT Services firms. This does not imply that having in-house resources is necessarily any easier.

Open-Source Products and Services are another interesting use case. Open-Source Products offer advantages and disadvantages. Among the disadvantages are maintenance, support, and sustainability, which means support for these Products and Services can decline over time. One approach to shielding Businesses from dependence on uncertain Open-Source resources is to hire in-house expertise and support. The Business assumes responsibility for maintaining these Products or Services, lessening, if not eliminating, the Business' dependence on third parties. This is particularly the case with large Businesses that rely on Open-Source Product and Services, such as Linux or Apache, for example.

In many cases, the major advantages are cost containment and cost reduction, especially when IT is not part of the Enterprise's core mission.

Regardless of the situation, the Enterprise needs to at least assess the Risks and determine appropriate responses to those Risks. For these Risks, no single answer exists. Risk Tolerance and Risk Appetite will affect the remediation strategies adopted.

New Technology-Related Risks

Every new technology poses new challenges, such as AI, Data Analytics, Intelligent Automation, and so on. AI is particularly intriguing. Its impact and implications on humanity will be profound, likely surpassing previous technical innovations.

The details and narratives regarding these technologies will change, but the Big Questions will remain: Access, Appropriateness, Availability, Integrity, and Reliability. New technologies mean Enterprises need to have active Risk

Assessment programs in place. 'One and Done' is not viable. Enterprises need to constantly re-evaluate Risk, especially as new technologies emerge and become essential for businesses' effectiveness, efficiency, and competitiveness.

IT Audit Considerations

From the IT Audit standpoint, business objectives control everything. As businesses' objectives are established, the question of inherent Risks can be addressed followed by the question of suitable remediation. Whether the underlying issues relate to Availability or Dependence or another factor, the Enterprise is obligated to define its objectives and then assess the Risks of not achieving those objectives and potential remediation strategies. No single answer exists; 'no one-size that fits all'.

For IT Auditors, explicit statements of Business Objectives, Risks, and Controls are essential. Lacking such clarity, IT Auditors may become advisors assisting the Enterprise in the definition and formulation of its Business Objectives, Risks, and Controls. Only with explicit statements are IT Auditors in a position to assess the adequacy, appropriateness, and suitability of Internal Controls.

Standard Operating Practices to Address IT Risk

Against this background, IT has a variety of standard IT controls. Often if IT is asked about its controls, IT merely shrugs its shoulders and replies that these are things IT does to avoid having a 'bad day'. They are generally accepted standard IT operating practices.

The point of these procedures or practices is to minimize IT problems. Things that are mechanical fail. For example, spinning hard drives have a life span. The good news is that the life span of hard drives probably exceeds their replacement cycle. Solid state drives are an alternative, but they also have a 'duty cycle'.

Against the backdrop of IT Audit's Big Underlying Principles, Figure 2.1, IT already has remedial practices in place to ensure that things go normally, which is discussed in the chapter on Basic Good IT Practices.

Chapter 3

IT Risks and Internal Controls

Chapter Contents:

IT Risk Management

COSO, the Committee of Sponsoring Organization of the Treadway Commission, introduces Enterprise Risk Management as follows:

> Every choice we make in the pursuit of objectives has its risks. From day-to-day operational decisions to the fundamental trade-offs in the boardroom, **dealing with uncertainty** in these choices is a part of our organizational lives. [Bold type added by author for emphasis.]
>
> —*COSO-ERM-Presentation-September-2017*,
> COSO, slide 9

DOI: 10.4324/9781032689388-3

Risk Management is all about making decisions in the presence of 'uncertainty'. The decisions may be daily operational decisions, or they may be strategic decisions with significant long-term implications.

Uncertainty is a measure of doubt regarding outcomes. In this case, the uncertainty involves the intersection of business objectives and technology, specifically IT-related technology. IT Risk Management recognizes the impact of IT automation. IT-related Technology presents two use cases:

- IT-related Technology can amplify, reduce, and/or change *existing* Business Risks.
- IT-related Technology can introduce *new* Business Risks, Risks that did not previously exist.

To illustrate these two use cases, consider picking inventory items. With manual picking, a person has an item description and/or location and/or item number. The picker goes into the warehouse and retrieves the item based on this information. In the case of automated picking, items are retrieved based on location and item number.

In the first use case, pickers may accidentally, or intentionally, pick the wrong items, assuming the Data is correct. If the Data is erroneous, the picker may be able to compensate for the errors and still pick the correct items. In the case of automated picking, the pick is determined by the Data. If the Data is incorrect, the pick will be incorrect. In the future, intelligent automation *may be able to compensate* for Data errors, such as evaluating the item's name or appearance to confirm the pick.

As automation becomes more intelligent, it may become more accurate than manual picking, and in the process, eliminate both unintentional and intentional errors. At least for now, individuals have an intelligence advantage over machines when it comes to adjusting for misinformation, but machines have a clear volume and scalability advantage over people.

The advent of new computer hardware, or software, or IT services brings new and different Risks into the Enterprise, such as the following:

- Concentration of Data (more eggs in one basket). New Enterprise Business Systems collect more Data and in doing so concentrate more Data in their Data storage facilities. The concentration of Data is both a business operations risk and a cybersecurity risk.
- New business systems provide new features and functions. The new features and functions introduce new Risks to established business operations. Accordingly, the new features and functions need to be evaluated in terms of their impact on the achievement of Enterprise's Business Objectives.
- Likewise, new IT Services introduce new Risks into the Enterprise which also need to be evaluated in terms of their impact on the business.

The Technology challenge is balancing new Risks with new Opportunities the technologies bring to Businesses, especially in the areas of Availability, Accuracy, Consistency, and the ability to Scale, to handle more transactions, more quickly.

IT Internal Controls

For the uninitiated, one way to approach Internal Controls is to work backward.

Q: Why Internal Controls?	A: To remediate or reduce Risk.
Q: What Risk?	A: The Risk the Business will not achieve its Business Objectives.
Q: What are Biz Objectives?	A: The Business Objectives are the goals, targets, results, outcomes, aspirations, and expectations the Business wants to achieve.

Remember COSO's definition of Internal Control:

Internal control is a *process* ... to provide *reasonable assurance* regarding the *achievement of objectives* relating to operations, reporting, and compliance. [Bold type added by author for emphasis.]
—*Internal Control – Integrated Framework*, COSO, May 2013, p. 1

Internal Controls are specifically designed to **reasonably ensure** the Enterprise will accomplish its Business Objectives. Note that Internal Controls only provide **reasonable assurance**, not absolute assurance. Internal Controls are appropriate, but they do not guarantee the Business Objectives will be achieved. Risks and Controls only make sense in terms of the Business' Goals and Objectives. Different Goals and Objectives mean Different Risks and Controls.

In the previous example of item picking, the Enterprise's objective is to pick items correctly. The Risk is that the picks are incorrect. In the case of raw materials, an incorrect pick could delay manufacturing; in the case of sales, an incorrect pick could result in wrong items being sent to Customers, increasing returns and eroding trust.

Reasonable Assurance means appropriate Internal Controls reduce Risk, but they are not a panacea.

COSO categorizes IT Internal Controls into three separate groups each with its own challenges:

- General IT Controls
- Application Controls
- End-User Controls

General IT Controls are Internal Controls related to the following broad topics:

- IT Governance
- IT Management
- IT Asset Acquisition
- IT Asset Management, including but not limited to IT Infrastructure
- IT Development Programs and Projects
- IT Service Delivery
- IT Personnel Competencies, Roles, and Responsibilities
- IT Policies, Procedures, Practices, and Standards
- Continuous Improvement of IT's Products and Services

The essential elements of General IT Controls are the management of IT, its Products and Services, and the environment in which these Products are selected, developed, and implemented and through which Services are delivered. *General IT Controls* often overlap with standard IT Operating Procedures. Standard procedures develop over time often in response to specific problems, such as Data loss, system failure, unavailability, etc.

With respect to frameworks, COBIT addresses General IT Controls across all five domains. ITIL does not have a specific topic for General IT Controls; they are spread throughout ITIL.

Application Controls are controls woven into application software in contrast with General IT Controls that affect the environment in which the Business Applications reside.

Sticking with inventory picking, application controls are the measures built into the software that control the picking process. These controls may be part of Inventory Control, or Warehousing Systems, or embedded in ERP (Enterprise Resource Planning) systems, such as identifying item numbers and locations prior to picking regardless of whether the picking is manual or automated.

Applications are software specifically designed to automate business operations including handling large volumes of transactions more accurately than human systems can. Hence, woven into the automation are a myriad of controls to assure accuracy and completeness to reduce the likelihood of errors and to increase system dependability and reliability.

COBIT addresses Application Controls in DSS06 Business Process Controls. ITIL does not have a similar subtopic.

End-User Controls are controls related to end-user-developed software. The problem with end-user developed application software is that the development occurs outside of IT's normal software quality assurance policies, procedures, and practices. User-developed software circumvents design, development, implementation and quality control standards, not intentionally, but users typically are not aware of or schooled in these controls.

Spreadsheets are a good example of this problem. End-users constantly use spreadsheets to track Data, to calculate outcomes, and to make decisions based on these analyses without the oversight provided by IT methodologies. This means end-user-developed software could inject errors into business process automation and business decision-making. Suppose a spreadsheet erroneously tells the factory to make a million widgets when in fact only a thousand widgets are needed.

In the early stages of Sarbanes-Oxley (SOX) implementation, Auditors sent spreadsheets offshore for examination and verification. After the initial wave of SOX compliance, interest in End-User Controls faded. Application Controls matured shifting efforts away from End-User Controls; however, the advent of new development technologies, such as Low-Code No-Code platforms and code written by Artificial Intelligence (AI), may re-invigorate interest in End-User controls. These platforms give End-Users increased ability to create business process applications outside of IT and its traditional software development controls. With more opportunities, End-User Controls may require more attention in the future.

Internal Controls can be classified as:

* Preventive Controls
* Detective Controls
* Corrective Controls

Preventive Controls concentrate on preventing bad things from happening.

Detective Controls detect bad things happened either contemporaneously or after-the-fact.

Corrective Controls correct the bad results caused by bad things happening.

The initial wave of SOX compliance emphasized Detective Controls. Soon after initial compliance, the effort shifted from Detective Controls to Preventive Controls. Consider the maxim, an ounce of prevention is worth a pound of cure.

Current IT controls include a mix of Preventive controls, such as fault tolerance and border security including firewalls and Intrusion Detection and Prevention solutions (IDS/IPS); and Detective controls, such as monitoring software and reconciliation processes; and Corrective controls, such as systems backups and disaster recovery plans. While preventive controls may be superior to corrective controls, a layered approach to controls means Businesses do not rely on a single control but rather a group of related controls to reduce Risk.

Testing IT Internal Controls

A primary responsibility of IT Audit is to determine or confirm the effectiveness of an Enterprise's system of Internal Controls. This includes three different types of tests:

* Determining the suitability, adequacy, or appropriateness of the Design of Internal Controls.
* Testing the Effectiveness of the Internal Controls to remediate the Risks identified.
* Confirming the Continuous Operation of the Internal Control throughout the period being examined.

This third type of test focuses on the question of whether Internal Controls *operated continuously* without interruptions during the period being audited.

All three tests are backward-looking tests; however, the implication is that if the design is appropriate, if the internal controls were effective in the past, especially during the relevant time period, then they will continue to be effective in the future. The problem of course is that Internal Controls can be overridden, i.e., turned off or just plain ignored. Also, the control environment can change requiring a revision in the Internal Controls for them to remain effective. Internal Controls that are effective intermittently are problems. Why weren't the internal controls continuously in effect? Under what circumstances can Internal Controls be off or ignored and why?

Design Test

Generally, if Internal Controls are not properly designed, they will not accomplish their objectives. Hence, the first test of Internal Controls is the determination of the appropriateness or suitability of the Design for the situation. Or will the Internal Control Design adequately remediate Risk if properly configured and implemented?

Since Risk Remediation/Reduction is the central theme, Tests of Design only make sense in the context of Enterprise Business Objectives and the Risks of not achieving those Objectives. Hence, Enterprise Business Objectives are the foundation for Internal Control Design.

Consider the interaction between Business Objectives and Design in the following situation. IT is asked to provide continuous power for a Business' servers. IT concludes that to provide continuous power for an extended amount of time, a power generator will be required along with a giant tank of diesel fuel to allow the generator to operate for at least a month without outside electricity. While this may seem excessive, a former client had giant autoclaves, which required continuous power to prevent the ovens from cooling, which would cause the brick lining to crumble. So once the autoclaves were turned on, they had to remain on. IT goes to management and requests a million-dollar budget for the project. Management was not expecting anything in this range. In response, management asked IT for less expensive options. Without going into the back-and-forth discussion, management and IT ultimately settled on batteries for less than $100,000. The alternative selection provided continuous power for the servers for a day or two but that was all. If the outage extended beyond these limits, the servers would shut down.

This example highlights the interaction between Business Objectives and Design. When faced with the financial realities, the Enterprise scaled back its Business Objectives, and the Design changed accordingly. The project was scaled back to a financially appropriate amount, hence, the intersection of planning and financial constraints; the ideal was adjusted for reality.

This example illustrates two problems:

- Developing a Design that reflects Enterprise Objectives, and
- Adjusting the Design based on other factors, such as cost or feasibility

The takeaway: Business Objectives and Controls do not exist in a vacuum; they are interdependent. In this example, the Enterprise scaled back its Business Objectives given costs. Often, there is no single answer with respect to Objectives and Controls, but a range of choices within which the Enterprise selects choices that are 'best' or 'better' depending on the situation.

Design is not singular, but an accommodation to competing necessities. Ultimately the question of appropriate Design depends on and reflects the Enterprise's Business Objectives, which may be adjusted for a variety of factors.

Given these variations, a Test of Design may pose a variety of audit questions.

- Does the Design reflect, is it consistent with Business Objectives?
- Were Business Objectives adjusted to reflect business constraints?
- Does the Design appropriately remediate the risks at least conceptually?
- Is the Design an established 'good' or 'best' IT practice?

For a variety of reasons, the Author suggests moving from 'best' to 'good' because 'best' is not necessarily singular. 'Best practices' are often asserted to compel compliance. 'Good Practices' may be more realistic. Typically, a variety of answers or approaches are available and while one may stand out, there is still more than a single approach available, and an Enterprise may prefer different good practices for specific reasons. The AICPA's System and Organization Controls Reports (SOC Reports) uses the term 'suitable' instead of 'appropriate' or 'adequate' for evaluating Internal Control Designs.

In this book, 'adequate', 'appropriate', and 'suitable' are used interchangeably for the purpose of evaluating Internal Control Design.

Effectiveness Test

The Test of **Effectiveness** is just that. Did the Internal Controls remediate the Risks as intended? Were they Effective? For non-auditors, this is the easiest concept to grasp. One might argue this is the ultimate test. If it is not effective, regardless of the reasons be it Design or Implementation or something else, the Internal Controls are not remediating Risks, which is their purpose.

Furthermore, an appropriate Design that is improperly implemented will most likely be ineffective.

In-Effect Test

On the surface, this test may seem redundant until an Internal Control is determined to be periodically circumvented or in the worst case was never implemented. Does this happen? Unfortunately, yes.

The Test of Implementation of an Internal Control over a **Span of Time** may be interpreted in two ways:

- First, the Internal Control was continuously in effect since its inception.
- Second, the Internal Control was operating effectively during the time period being audited without regard for before or after that time period? This is a narrower span of time.

If the Internal Control can be turned off and on, then the Internal Control may not have been continuously in effect. As noted elsewhere, intermittent is a difficult situation for Auditors. This raises the questions of How and Why. For what purpose was the Internal Control turned off? Was turning the Internal Control off a necessity, a matter of convenience, to allow fraudulent activity, or something else?

In summary, Tests of Design ask *can* the Internal Control reduce Risk while Tests of Effectiveness ask *did* the Internal Control reduce Risk.

Internal Control Failure

If an Internal Control is determined to be ineffective, the obvious question is: Why?

- Was the Design inadequate, inappropriate, or unsuitable?
- Was the Internal Control improperly configured?
- Was the Implementation inappropriate or deficient?
- Was the Internal Control operating intermittently, meaning it was on and off at different times?
- Did the effectiveness of the Internal Control degrade over time?

This latter situation can occur for a variety of reasons. Did the environment in which the Internal Control operates change? Did Business Objectives drift? Did new Risks arise?

To say an Internal Control is not effective does not mean there is a single answer although the answer may come down to one or two words: Constantly versus Intermittently. However, Internal Controls may be ineffective for a variety of reasons, and these deficiencies may work in combination with each other to erode control effectiveness.

Effectiveness is not necessarily an on or off, good or bad situation. Effectiveness can involve degrees of effectiveness, where the Internal Control is mostly effective but not effective in all situations. This could be a Design issue or an Implementation issue. From the IT Audit perspective, regardless of the reasons or the duration, the Internal Control is not completely effective.

Ultimately the situation may break down to the collision of an unmovable object and an irresistible force, i.e., something that must be done but is prohibitively expensive. These are the cases where Enterprise Objectives and Internal Controls collide and ultimately result in compromises, which must be evaluated by IT Auditors.

Deviations

Deviations occur. They are departures from the actions prescribed by an Internal Control; they are effectiveness failures. SSAE 18 describes deviations as follows:

> .25 If the practitioner designed and performed tests of controls to rely on their operating effectiveness and identified **deviations** in those controls, the practitioner should make specific inquiries and perform other procedures as necessary to understand these matters and their **potential consequences**. [Bold type added by author for emphasis.]
>
> —AICPA Statement on Standard for
> Attestation Engagements, 18, April 2016, p. 54

Departures from the prescribed actions of Internal Controls may occur. In those situations, Auditors need to understand the frequency and significance of these deviations and ultimately answer the question of whether the Internal Control is effective or not. Said differently, were the Deviations of sufficient significance to conclude that the Internal Control did not achieve its Risk remediation objectives? If this threshold is not met, then the Internal Control is effective.

SSAE 18 equates deviations and misstatements. [—AICPA Statement on Standard for Attestation Engagements, 18, April 2016, p. 56.] Hence, Deviations are potential misstatements of Internal Control assertions. See SSAE 18 section A18 for Qualitative factors IT Auditors may wish to consider when evaluating the impact of Internal Control deviations. [—AICPA Statement on Standard for Attestation Engagements, 18, April 2016, p. 75.]

Risk and Control Matrices (RACMs)

One method for analyzing and documenting Internal Controls is a **Risk and Control Matrix (RACM)**. RACMs can be used to develop Internal Controls and to assess their Suitability and Effectiveness.

Properly used, RACMs explicitly show consistency of Business Objectives, Risks associated with the achievement of these Objectives, and the Internal Controls designed to remediate these Risks. RACMs can also be used to identify the tests required to confirm the Suitability and Effectiveness of Internal Controls. Figure 3.1 shows a basic format for RACMs.

Cntrl Nmbr	Business Objectives	Risks to Achievement of Objectives	Internal Controls	Types	Principles	Test Procedures	
Ctrl_00	1) 2) etc	1) 2) etc	1) 2) etc	1) 2) etc	1) 2) etc	1) 2) etc	Design
			1) 2) etc	1) 2) etc	1) 2) etc	1) 2) etc	Effective
Ctrl_01	1) 2) etc	1) 2) etc	1) 2) etc	1) 2) etc	1) 2) etc	1) 2) etc	Design
			1) 2) etc	1) 2) etc	1) 2) etc	1) 2) etc	Effective
Ctrl_02	1) 2) etc	1) 2) etc	1) 2) etc	1) 2) etc	1) 2) etc	1) 2) etc	Design
			1) 2) etc	1) 2) etc	1) 2) etc	1) 2) etc	Effective

Figure 3.1 Risk and Control Matrix.

Notice the numbering scheme. It is designed to explicitly connect Objectives, Risks, Controls, and Tests. The numbering scheme allows for multiples as well as connecting related elements. For example, there may be multiple Business Objectives. A Business Objective may have multiple Risks. A Risk may have multiple Controls. And Internal Controls may have multiple Tests. The numbering scheme is designed to connect Business Objectives, Risks, and Internal Controls consistently and to allow for multiple elements.

The RACM identifies:

- The Business Objectives for a given business process, situation, or domain.

  There may be a single Business Objective or there may be multiple Business Objectives.

- The Risks are the potential obstacles to achieving the Business Objectives.

  As with Business Objectives, multiple Risks may exist.

- The Internal Controls are the methods adopted to remediate, i.e., to reduce, the Risks.

  As with Objectives and Risks, multiple Internal Controls may be involved. A single Internal Control may not adequately remediate the Risks.

  In cybersecurity, for example, the expression 'Belt and Suspenders' is used to describe multiple countermeasures. 'Belt and Suspenders' is also a reasonable metaphor for multiple Internal Controls, where the organization does not rely on a single Internal Control but a set of Internal Controls to remediate a Risk.

- For each Internal Control identified, there are three types of tests:
  - Test(s) of Design
  - Test(s) of Effectiveness
  - Test(s) of Continuous Operation (In-Effect)

- In Figure 3.1, there is also a column for Test Procedures.
- In actual practice, a column for Test Results will also be present.

Being consistent among Business Objectives, Risks, Internal Controls, and their Tests can be challenging. Disconnects between Business Objectives, Risks, Internal Controls, and Test of Controls can easily occur. These disconnects include the following:

- Inconsistent Business Objectives and Risks
- Inconsistent Risks and Controls
- Inconsistent Tests of Controls

The most common inconsistency is confusing a Test of Effectiveness for a Test of Design. Yes, Tests of Effectiveness are, from a practical standpoint, the ultimate test of Internal Controls, but Tests of Effectiveness are no substitute for an affirmation that the Internal Control's Design is suitable or appropriate or adequate.

Furthermore, Tests may not address the suitability and/or effectiveness of an Internal Control. Mistakes can occur at any point in this interrelated continuum.

In practice, RACMs often include provisions for Domains, Authors, Preparation Dates, Examination Dates, and additional columns for types of controls, priority, importance, comments, and more. What appears in Figure 3.1 are the basics. Any Enterprise or IT Auditor is free to add additional columns as needed; however, the basics remain:

- Business Objectives
- Risks to Achievement of Business Objectives
- Internal Controls
- Tests of Internal Controls

RACMs in Practice

To get an idea of what RACMs look like in practice, consider the following examples. These examples were simplified to focus attention on the essential parts of RACMs and the consistency among these parts.

- Domain: General IT Control > Infrastructure > Continuous Operations [Provided for context]
- Business Objective: Continuous Operations
- Risks to the Achievement of the Business Objective:

    Power Failure (which would interrupt continuous operations)

- Internal Controls to Remediate (Reduce) the Risks:

  An Uninterruptible Power Supply (UPS), essentially batteries or a generator to provide electricity to sustain continuous operations in the event of a power failure.

- Tests to Confirm the Suitability and Effectiveness of the Internal Controls:

  - Test of Design:

    Test Criteria: Is the Design suitable given the Business Objectives? Conceptually, yes. UPS's and/or power generators are generally appropriate alternate power sources. They are at least a Good IT Practice, a common practice, if not a 'Best IT Practice'.

  - Test of Continuous Operation:

    Test Criteria: Was the UPS in continuous operation during the audit period? Hopefully, yes.

    Test Criteria: Were there any occasions when the UPS was off or offline? In either case, the UPS would not have been effective if a power outage occurred while the UPS was unavailable, regardless of the reason for the unavailability, which could include maintenance.

  - Test of Effectiveness:

    Test Criteria: Did the UPS operate as intended? Did the UPS kick into action when outside power failed?

    If the power never failed, normal operations did not test the UPS. This means the UPS might have failed, it just was not tested. If nothing adverse happened, the internal control was not tested. This is the problem with negative assurance. In the case of a UPS, test the UPS to confirm that it would have sustained the system during a power outage and the extent of the protection.

    Test Criteria: Were there occasions when the outside power failed, and the UPS sustained operations for the agreed-upon period of time? This is positive assurance, i.e., it operated as intended when needed.

    Test Criteria: Was the power backup periodically tested? Did it perform as designed? Power failures were simulated, and the UPS performed as intended, providing positive assurance.

    Test Criteria: Are the batteries routinely maintained and tested?

    These are preventive tests designed to detect battery degradation. Batteries that are not maintained will eventually fail, defeating their purpose.

UPSs typically have indicators and alerts regarding battery status and life, which could be regularly documented in a log to provide evidence of regular maintenance. IT Auditors could subsequently examine these records to confirm battery maintenance.

A cautionary reminder: Remember the difference between negative and positive assurance. That something did not happen is no assurance that the Internal Control will operate as intended when needed.

This RACM illustrates a **General IT Control**.

Below is a similar RACM illustration for an **Application Control**.

- Business Objective:

    Sell products and services only to *credit worthy Customers* (assuming a B2B relationship).

- Risks to the Achievement of the Business Objective:

    Products and services are only sold to Customers who can pay their obligations in a timely manner. Said in the negative, products and services are not sold to Customers who cannot or will not pay their obligations in a timely manner. The Risks are late payment and non-payment.

- Internal Controls to Remediate (Reduce) Risks:

    A Credit Authorization process that includes the following:

    - Credit Limits,
    - Updating Credit Limits based on purchasing, payment history, other information, and other credit controls.

    For simplicity, this illustration focuses on Credit Limits.

- Tests to Confirm Suitability and Effectiveness of the Internal Controls:

    - Test(s) of Design:

        Test Criteria: Is the Credit Authorization process appropriate given the Enterprise's Business Objectives? Hopefully, yes.

        Test Criteria: Is the use of Credit Limits a recognized good practice? Yes, businesses routinely use credit limits to control their exposure to late payments or non-payments.

    - Test(s) of Continuous Operation:

        Test Criteria: Were Credit Limits continuously enforced?

        Test Criteria: Was Credit Limit enforcement intermittent?

        Text Criteria: Were Credit Limits overridden during the audit period? Were the overrides consistent with Business Objectives (policy)?

- Test(s) of Effectiveness:

Test Criteria: Were Credit Limits enforced for all sales?

Test Criteria: Were Credit Limits enforced for all Customers? Was Credit Limit enforcement applied differently for different Customers? Were these differences within company policy?

Test Criteria: Were any sales authorized contrary to the Credit Limit process? Were the deviations consistent with company policy?

Test Criteria: Ultimately, did the enforcement of Credit Limits decrease late payments or reduce credit-related write-offs? Were the losses significant?

If an Internal Control is determined to be Suitable and Effective, great, but if the Internal Control was determined to be ineffective, what caused the ineffectiveness?

- Was the ineffectiveness related to the design?
- Was the ineffectiveness related to configuration?
- Was the ineffectiveness related to implementation?
- Was the ineffectiveness related to the suspension of Internal Controls in certain circumstances, such as overrides?
- Was the ineffectiveness related to changing environmental or market conditions?
- Was the ineffectiveness attributed to something else?

In essence, was the ineffectiveness the result of:

- Unsatisfactory Design
- Incorrect or inappropriate configuration
- Inadequate Implementation
- Operational Deficiencies
- Environmental Changes
- A combination of Inadequacies
- Or something else

The corollary: Were the deficiencies significant? Were they material? This topic is discussed further in the SOC Reporting chapter.

Even in well-organized businesses, glitches, deviations, occur. Are these glitches once-in-a-while occurrences? Do these deviations exhibit a pattern, such as being ignored for major Customers, colleagues, or family members?

These are the questions that IT Audit must address and the potential information that needs to be included in their analyses and reports.

IT Audit's Conundrum

If the purpose of an Internal Control is to prevent something negative from happening and nothing negative happened, is that because of the presence of an Internal Control or is it because nothing negative happened? If you don't buy a lottery ticket, you can't possibly win, but we routinely buy insurance, which hopefully we do not need and never use. Keep these circumstances in mind to stimulate your thoughts regarding using the absence of a negative to prove a positive.

To be effective, IT Audit must be very clear regarding the following:

- Business Objectives

  State Business Objectives in the positive, avoid stating them in the negative.

  For example, instead of no unplanned outages, state the Business Objective positively, for example, 99.999% (five nine's) uptime, exclusive of planned outages.

  As a colleague is fond of saying,

  > 'It didn't work.' 'If you want a positive statement, okay, it positively didn't work.'

- Risks

  In this context, Risk can be anything that causes unplanned outages.

  Planned outages are expected; the villain is unplanned outages. The assumption is that alternatives are implemented for planned outages, so the attention is on remediating unplanned outages.

- Internal Controls

  In the above case, the Internal Control is a redundant systems such that an outage in one segment of a system does not cause the entire system to shut down.

  Internal Controls can be tested by real failures or by forcing failures to confirm Internal Controls perform as intended.

  For another example, consider banks. The systems that support ATMs are redundant such that a single failure will have little or no effect on the ATMs.

- Tests of Effectiveness

  Effectiveness lies in three dimensions.

  - First, is the Design of the Internal Control suitable and/or appropriate for the situation?
  - Second, does the Internal Control effectively accomplish its purposes?
  - Third, was the Internal Control in effect during the period that is covered by the report?

    On and off does not work. If the insurance lapses, an incident occurs, and coverage is restored, is the insured covered for the incident? The ultimate answer may depend on several factors, but the presumption is the insured is not covered if the insurance was not in effect at the time the incident occurred never mind the fact that the insurance was otherwise in effect.

Auditors need to be clear in their minds that the absence of an event does not prove that an Internal Control operated as intended. For Tests of Effectiveness, the Internal Control must have worked or must be forced to work to provide positive assurance that it will work when needed. Depending upon circumstances, the Internal Control may require maintenance activities, such as battery maintenance or paying insurance premiums when they are due. Provisions to accommodate these circumstances must be part of the Internal Controls.

IT Risks and Increasing Automation

The new normal is ever-increasing amounts of automation, which creates both opportunities and challenges for IT Audit.

Consider the simple case of network monitoring. Years ago, this was challenging. IT asset custodians might have to walk a facility to find and catalog all network components. Finding items in a Data Center was relatively easy; however, finding things in closets, ceilings, walls, and behind other things was more challenging. Today, monitoring software can ping all the assets and identify them down to 'make and model'. In the future, monitoring may even geolocate assets. So, custodians will not have to search for remote devices.

As mentioned elsewhere, switching from physical assets to cloud services drastically changes the equation. Yes, there are still some local assets, such as servers, switches, printers, scanners, desktops, and other local devices, but the 'heavy lifting' is done by the Cloud Service Providers (CSPs). They house servers and allied hardware and software. Hence, businesses are well into a shift away from local physical assets to remote logical assets. An excellent example of the new environment is 'serverless', where servers no longer exist from the Customer's perspective. Customers 'spin up' and decommission servers as needed. They are just services, not physical manifestations from the Customer's perspective. Yes, there are physical assets somewhere tended by technicians and/ or software but they are no longer a concern of the Customer per se.

Two big challenges associated with this switch are reliance and transparency. Businesses are using the computing assets of other entities to accomplish their Business Objectives. This dependence can create problems. For example, an airline is grounded because a service provider's system fails. Everything is in place for the airline to operate flights, except the airline does not know which aircraft were scheduled to be used, where the aircraft are, who will crew the aircraft, who has flight reservations, and in which seats passengers are sitting. Why? Because that information is in a system that is unavailable, i.e., 'down hard'. And yes, that has happened. The airline is dependent on its CSP to operate, and the airline has limited visibility into the actions of the CSP. This is not to say that the airline is necessarily any better off with its own in-house IT assets. The problem is the airline 'doesn't know what it doesn't know' and the airline does not have control. The airline does not know what is happening behind the scenes and has limited or no control over those happenings. As discussed in the chapter on System and Organization Controls Reports (SOC Reports), there are options so things are not necessarily as dire as described above.

A consequence of this switch is that Enterprises that rely on cloud services are reducing their in-house IT staff. With these reductions, the Enterprises are losing their technical knowledge and institutional memory. In extreme cases, businesses may have few in-house IT resources and are forced to rely on other outsourced resources. In a sense, businesses are getting 'dumber' about IT, no insult intended, this is merely a description.

Newer automation includes more intelligence. Consider a simple threshold that triggers an alarm if the threshold is exceeded. Being able to do this on an adaptive basis is more complex. Assuming the threshold is still valid but only comes into play occasionally, a reasonable expectation might be to have the threshold 'kick in' only when something unusual is happening, such as off-peak hours, or where the excessive load remains in effect for a significant period. Up to now, this typically involved human knowledge or investigation and human decisions. In the future, the threshold may be 'smart' enough to be able to adapt to exceptions and only act on situations with a significant impact.

As of this writing, AI has hit the 'daily news'. Everyone is wondering what AI can do for us ... and to us. Both are important questions. In terms of thresholds, AI can consider many more factors before sounding an alarm or maybe the AI will be able to intervene more quickly, more precisely than humans would. For example, implement additional resources without needing to discuss the situation with humans. Hence, AI might evaluate a situation, consider many factors, including external factors, and make a more informed decision and implement that decision without human consultation making the process 'self-healing'.

For IT Audit, increasing automation, especially Intelligent Automation, adds additional levels of abstraction and uncertainty.

- Do we know how the AI reached the decisions it reached, especially if things do not work out as needed?
- Can IT Auditors validate the Data on which the AI was trained and the decisions it makes?
- Can the behavior of the AI be adjusted, if needed? Can the IT Auditors confirm the adjustments and their impact on the AI's behavior?
- Is the AI really intelligent or does the AI just have a larger dataset, a larger set of experiences over a broader set of conditions, than humans have or can remember?

Being able to Audit an AI and its behavior goes beyond the average IT skillset and that of the average IT Auditor. This means IT Audit must adapt as environments change, as complexity increases, as more actors and actions are added to situations. The IT Auditor must have additional knowledge and experience and/ or rely on additional resources to make up for the deficit.

A note in passing, a recent article called attention to additional airplane automation, in particular automated take off and landing, which are more accurate than manual pilots increasing aircraft range and effectiveness.

Addendum: COSO's Five Components and 17 Principles

The foundation for Internal Controls is COSO's Five Components and 17 Principles, which appear below for your convenience.

COSO's Five Components

- Control Environment
- Risk Assessment
- Control Activities
- Information and Communication
- Monitoring Activities

COSO's 17 Principles

Control Environment

1. "The organization demonstrates a commitment to integrity and ethical values.
2. The board of directors demonstrates independence from management and exercises oversight of the development and performance of internal controls.

3. Management establishes, with board oversight, structures, reporting lines, and appropriate authorities and responsibilities in the pursuit of objectives.
4. The organization demonstrates a commitment to attract, develop, and retain competent individuals in alignment with objectives.
5. The organization holds individuals accountable for their internal control responsibilities in this pursuit of objectives."

Risk Assessment

6. "The organization specifies objectives with sufficient clarity to enable the identification and assessment of risks relating to objectives.
7. The organization identifies risks to the achievement of its objectives across the entity and analyzes risks as a basis for determining how the risks should be managed.
8. The organization considers the potential for fraud in assessing risks to the achievement of objectives.
9. The organization identifies and assesses changes that could significantly impact the system of internal control."

Control Activities

10. "The organization selects and develops control activities that contribute to the mitigation of risks to the achievement of objectives to acceptable levels.
11. The organization selects and develops general control activities over technology to support the achievement of objectives.
12. The organization deploys control activities through policies that establish what is expected and procedures that put policies into action."

Information and Communication

13. "The organization obtains or generates and uses relevant, quality information to support the functioning of internal control.
14. The organization internally communicates information, including objectives and responsibilities for internal control, necessary to support the function of internal control.
15. The organization communicates with external parties regarding matters affecting the functioning of internal control."

Monitoring Activities

16. "The organization selects, develops, and performs ongoing and/or separate evaluations to ascertain whether the components of internal control are present and functioning.

17. The organization evaluates and communicates internal control deficiencies in a timely manner to those parties responsible for taking corrective action, including senior management and the board of directors, as appropriate."

— COSO, *Internal Control – Integrated Framework; Framework and Appendices*, 2013, pp. 12–14.

These principles highlight, among other items, the importance of the following:

- Commitment and Accountability
- Clear Business Objectives
- Risk Identification
- Internal Controls that Mitigate the Risks to Achievement of Business Objectives
- General Controls over Technology
- Relevant, Quality Information (i.e., Data)
- Evaluations to determine that Internal Controls are 'present and functioning'.

These are basic principles upon which IT Audit depends.

Chapter 4

Auditing IT Governance

Chapter Contents:

What Constitutes IT Governance?

In its newly published version of ISO/IEC 38500:2024, ISO lists the following principles for IT Governance:

5.3 Value Generation
5.4 Strategy
5.5 Oversight

DOI: 10.4324/9781032689388-4

5.6   Accountability
5.7   Stakeholder Engagement
5.8   Leadership
5.9   Data and Decisions
5.10 Risk Governance
5.11 Social Responsibility
5.12 Viability and Performance Over Time

[Note: the numbering conforms
to ISO 38500:2024.]
—*ISO/IEC 38500 Information
Technology – Governance of IT for the
Organization*, ISO/IEC, 2024-02

By comparison, ISACA's COBIT lists five Information Technology (IT) Governance domains:

EDM01   Ensured Governance Framework Setting and Maintenance
EDM02   Ensured Benefits Delivery
EDM03   Ensured Risk Optimization
EDM04   Ensured Resource Optimization
EDM05   Ensured Stakeholder Engagement

—*COBIT 2019 Framework – Introduction
and Methodology*, ISACA, 2018, p. 21

Elements in common include the following:

- Strategic Alignment
- Value Creation
- Risk Management
- Resource Management
- Performance Management
- Stakeholder Management
- Compliance Management
- Continuous Improvement
- Framework Adoption
- Transparency and Accountability

The first tenet of COBIT is having a Framework, whether it is COBIT or International Standards Organization (ISO) or ITIL is less important. The important thing is having a unified framework. The virtue of frameworks is coverage and integration. Some of the Governance principles listed above may be classified as Management principles rather than Governance principles.

Consider the following summarization of IT Governance:

- Ensure Strategic Alignment. Without alignment, IT's Products and Services are less valuable, maybe even counterproductive.
- Insist on Systemized/Standardized Policies, Procedures, Practices, and Standards.
- Insist on Accountability, Transparency, Conformance, Performance, Compliance, and Stakeholder Engagement.
- Oversight of IT Management, IT Assets, IT Operations, Systems Acquisition and Development, and IT Service Delivery.

Together these mandates ensure Value Creation and Benefit Delivery.

Also, consider IT Governance as the Enterprise's commitment to IT. Lacking this commitment, IT can lose direction, focus, Alignment, and Value.

Enterprise Commitment

The success of IT rests on the following Enterprise commitments:

- An Explicit Commitment to IT.
- Commitment to Supportive Oversight and Direction.
- Commitment to Active Engagement between Corporate Strategic Planning and IT Planning so that IT knows where the Business is going, and the Business knows what IT is planning and doing.
- Commitment to Adequate Operating and Capital Resources, including funding and staffing.

IT is a service component for most Enterprises in the same way that Finance, Sales, Marketing, and Procurement are service aspects of a business. The exception is IT Enterprises. In the case of IT Enterprises, their Technologies are the Enterprises' business; the Enterprises are in the business of Technology. In this case, Technology is more than a service component, it is the raison d'être of the business, its reason for being.

IT Governance in Detail

Alignment

Arguably Alignment is the most important theme. COBIT's Value Creation is the consequence of Alignment between IT and the Enterprise and its mission, vision, values, goals, objectives, and plans. Alignment is an intentional act, not an accident. Alignment ensures that IT's Assets, Products, and Services are consistent with, supportive of, and enable the Enterprise. The last thing an Enterprise should expect is IT working at cross purposes to the organization, which is irrational.

Value Creation

Value creation is the measure of Benefit. Little Value, little Benefit. IT Management must be laser focused on creating Value and Benefit. Otherwise, why have IT?

Frameworks

Having a suitable Framework ensures that IT is asking the right questions, is making the right decisions, is considering all aspects of IT, is aligning with, and supporting the Enterprise of which it is an integral part.

Integration

Integration in the context of IT generally refers to Integrated Systems; here, however, Integration refers to IT being integrated into its host organization. This entails active participation in corporate planning, active participation in corporate management, and active involvement of the Enterprise in IT planning and decision-making.

Integration is the result of, among other things, Alignment, Leadership, Oversight, and Stakeholder Engagement. Integration of IT is a consequence of these aspects of IT Governance, not a happy accident.

When parts of an Enterprise become detached from the Enterprise or from each other, the Enterprise is less effective. IT is most effective when IT is fully integrated into the Enterprise. IT is more likely to be ineffective, to focus on the wrong products and services, and to have inappropriate or inadequate staffing when it is *not integrated* into the Enterprise.

Integration applies both vertically and horizontally. Vertically, IT is integrated into the Enterprise; horizontally, IT supports the Enterprise as a whole.

Stakeholder Engagement

Stakeholder Engagement is active involvement with all elements in the Enterprise and outside the Enterprise that have a 'stake' in IT's Assets, Products, and Services, a 'stake' in IT's success. IT personnel can easily become more focused on technology than on its impact on the Enterprise and the Enterprise's Customers.

Risk Management

From the dawn of computing, IT was aware of things that could go wrong and developed practices to minimize vulnerabilities and reduce the chances of failure to avoid business disruption or to avoid outright embarrassment, the getting-yelled-at syndrome. Ideally, IT embraces Risk Management to enhance its Value and the Value of its Products and Services to the Enterprise.

Accountability and Transparency

Accountability and Transparency go hand in hand. They demand responsibility of IT and openness regarding their actions, activities, and decisions, in the vernacular 'the buck stops here'. Organizations make mistakes; people make mistakes. Focus on getting things right as opposed to punishing wrongdoers. This does not mean mistakes are glossed over. The essential questions are why and how the mistakes occurred, what can be learned from them, and how the Enterprise can improve. This is continuous improvement in action.

Resource Management

Resource Management is another important aspect of IT for at least two reasons:

- First, IT Assets and Resources have long-range implications that are difficult to change, i.e., 'long tails'. Committing to a particular Enterprise Business System is expensive, profound, and not easily changed. The essential characteristic of long-term implications is that they cannot easily be changed. These are decisions with consequences that can be negative, limiting, as well as positive.
- Second, IT Assets and Resources, like other major capital items, are expensive and 'sunk costs'. The preferred outcome is to get value from investments rather than writing them off.

Hence, Resource Management is a critical aspect of both IT Governance and IT Management.

Performance Management

Performance Management is also critical. Both ISO and COBIT include Performance as Principle 5.12 (Viability and Performance Over Time) and MEA01 (Managed Performance and Conformance Monitoring), respectively.

Remember the SMART mnemonic from among the pantheon of models for effective strategic planning. The 'M' stands for Measurable. If something cannot be measured, it cannot be effectively managed, so with IT Governance. IT Governance needs to insist on suitable metrics by which IT can monitor and evaluate its performance.

Compliance

Compliance is an ongoing, constantly changing topic for IT. Compliance is not exclusively a governmental issue; private organizations are involved as well, such as PCI-DSS compliance, but governmental mandates and requirements weigh heavily on Enterprises. Ongoing deliberations regarding privacy, cybersecurity, and Big Tech cannot be ignored. General Data Protection Regulation (GDPR), for example, profoundly changed privacy for Europeans in Europe and abroad as well. Hence, compliance must be on the IT Governance agenda with updates and discussion regarding changes and their impact on IT Policies, Procedures, and Practices.

Oversight

Oversight is the active management of IT, *not at a granular level, not micromanagement*, but the supportive insistence that IT appropriately sustain the Enterprise through the following:

- Compatible IT Assets, Products, and Services
- Appropriate IT Policies, Procedures, and Practices
- Suitable IT Standards to ensure measurable Quality
- Adequate IT Personnel skills and resources sufficient to develop and support effective IT Assets, Products, and Services

Ultimately, IT is most effective when IT is fully integrated with its host Enterprise, with consistent and persistent oversight encouraging IT to find new ways in which IT can support and create Value for the Enterprise. In other words, IT ought to be both supportive and innovative.

Funding

Talk is cheap without an adequate budget to support IT and its assets, products, services, systems, acquisitions, and projects. Everything worth having has a cost, that applies to IT as well. This is not to imply that budget setting is not a negotiation because allocating funds among competing aspects of organizations and their activities is a negotiation. IT should be part of the organization's Operating Budget and Capital Budget planning processes for IT's sake and the Enterprise's sake as well.

Data Governance

5.3 Data Governance is specifically identified in ISO/IEC 38500:2024, in 5.9 Data and Decisions, and in COBIT, APO14 – Managed Data. The discussion of Data Governance is in the Data chapter below.

Leadership, Social Responsibility, and Viability

Leadership, Social Responsibility, Performance, and Viability are a cluster. Leadership is a characteristic of individuals and organizations. It combines corporate culture and forward thinking. The objective is to position the organization for collaboration, growth, and maximizing Value. Social Responsibility is an appropriate objective especially given climate change and questions regarding sustainability. The bottom line with all Governance is Enterprise Viability.

IT Governance versus IT Management

IT Governance oversees IT's Alignment with Enterprise mission, vision, values, goals, objectives, and strategies, while IT Management is responsible for the Policies, Procedures, Practices, and Standards and their execution, which align IT Assets, Resources, Products, and Services with the Enterprise.

IT Governance is responsible and accountable for the big picture, the long-term; IT Management is responsible and accountable for implementing IT Products and Services, which turn the big picture into reality.

IT Governance Policies, Procedures, and Practices

Below are common IT Governance Policies and Procedures:

- Require regular IT Status Reports to keep the Enterprise up to date, addressing the following topics:
  - Accomplishments
  - Challenges
  - Service Delivery Metrics
  - Project Status Summaries
  - Actual to Budget Financial Reporting
  - Future Planning, including Solution/System Acquisition Planning
  - Anything significant to the Achievement of IT's goals and objectives

  The Status Reports may go to the Board of Directors and/or C-Suite officials or the business owner typically monthly to ensure currency and timeliness.

- Have clear Organization Charts that show to whom IT reports and how the IT function is internally organized.

  If the Enterprise relies on Cloud Service Providers (CSPs) and has Outsourced most of its IT functions, the Organization Chart can still exist on a functional basis including Outsourced functions and personnel.

  Ambiguity in an Organization Chart may be a sign of general organizational disfunction. Regardless, IT must at the least have its own Organization Chart to show it is internally organized and how it connects with the Enterprise as a whole.

- Involve IT Management in Corporate Planning, including providing IT Management with timely copies of Enterprise governance and strategy documents, such as plans and meeting minutes.

- Have Service Level Agreements (SLAs) between IT and the Enterprise, as well as with external service providers.

  SLAs are common in outsourcing arrangements. Originally, SLAs focused on performance and 'up time'; however, they can be used beyond their original purposes. For example, SLAs can clarify Enterprise expectations with respect to IT as well as IT's performance metrics, and SLAs can identify IT-related expectations of external parties and their services. What was used originally to identify service delivery promises can be expanded to identify Customer expectations as well providing a mutual understanding of product and service expectations.

- Have and Enforce Acceptable Use Policies (AUPs).

  AUPs spell out acceptable uses, prohibitions, and restrictions. For example, an AUP typically prohibits illegal actions and messaging that brings discredit to the Enterprise. Significant restrictions include wasting Enterprise resources, corrupting data, seeking unauthorized access, 'hacking' Enterprise systems, and so on.

  With respect of IT Auditing, the following are key:

  - Having an AUP,
  - That is consistent with the Enterprise's values and goals, and
  - Enforcing that Policy.

  IT Governance can require an AUP and can oversee its alignment with Enterprise values, goals, and objectives; IT Management is responsible for the contents and enforcement of the AUP.

IT Audit Governance Questions

IT Governance Audit Questions include the following items:

- Do IT Assets, Resources, Products, and Services Align with Enterprise Goals and Objectives?
- Is IT part of corporate planning, especially items that impact IT or that IT can or must support or enable?
- Does IT keep the Enterprise informed of its activities, projects, and priorities?
- Does IT enable business performance and create business value for its organization?
- Does IT reduce business risk? Are IT Risks addressed and remediated?
- How does the Enterprise manage the intersection of business performance and emerging technologies? This is the convergence of things as they are with things as they could be.

IT Audit Governance Challenges

Two big IT Governance Challenges are:

- First, keeping IT inside the Enterprise's strategic planning process.

    This challenge is a two-part challenge: one part is Reactive; the other part is Proactive.

    Reactively, IT must be aware of significant changes in the Enterprise's strategic direction and must adapt to these changes, which may be challenging.

    Proactively, IT being seen as a catalyst, a business partner, and an advisor, i.e., more than merely a service provider.

- Second, IT being part of an Enterprise where ethics and responsibility are minimized or ignored. This is a challenge for the entire Enterprise, not just IT, but the focus here is on IT. How can IT be successful in an Enterprise where ethics and responsibility are ignored? It is difficult.

For IT Audit, these situations can place IT in a precarious position. And IT Audit may have little chance of changing the Enterprise culture.

For IT Governance, ultimately everything comes down to the link between Business Objectives, Strategy and IT.

Chapter 5

Auditing IT Management

Chapter Contents:

Shifting from auditing IT Governance to auditing IT Management.

The Commitment

IT is a service component for most Enterprises. The obvious exception is Enterprises whose Products and Services are technology based. Consider the following case. Are Uber, Lyft and similar businesses, taxi services, or reservation scheduling and routing services? From the Customers' perspective, we pay to be ferried from place to place, not necessarily for reservation, scheduling, and routing services; however, these Enterprises insist they are reservation, scheduling,

DOI: 10.4324/9781032689388-5

and routing services, not taxi services. Regardless of where you land on this issue, are these companies IT companies or non-IT companies, with increasing automation, this distinction may be increasingly difficult to make. Regardless of how you answer this question, technology plays a crucial role in business. Technology is typically a means to an end, not necessarily an end itself.

To be successful, IT depends on the Enterprise's commitment to automation. This commitment can be demonstrated in a variety of ways including:

- Having active IT Governance
- Receiving active Senior Management support
- Having adequate funds for operations and capital projects
- Having adequate personnel to develop and deliver products and services
- And insisting that IT's Assets, Products, and Services align with the Enterprise's Business Objectives and Strategies

Commitment is more than the nod of the head, more than a starvation diet. Ultimately, the success of IT depends on the business' commitment to making IT an integral part of the Enterprise.

IT Management Domains

IT Management domains are broad and encompass all IT Activities, Assets, Products, Services, personnel, standards ... everything. COBIT identifies the following IT Management domains and objectives:

APO	Align, Plan, and Organize
APO01	Managed the I&T Management Framework
APO02	Managed Strategy
APO03	Managed Enterprise Architecture
APO04	Managed Innovation
APO05	Managed Portfolio
APO06	Managed Budget and Costs
APO07	Managed Human Resources
APO08	Managed Relationships
APO09	Managed Service Agreements
APO10	Managed Suppliers
APO11	Managed Quality
APO12	Managed Risk
APO13	Managed Security
APO14	Managed Data Plus
BAI	Build, Acquire, and Implement
DSS	Delivery, Service, and Support
MEA	Monitor, Evaluate, and Assess

BAI, DSS, and MEA will be discussed in detail in their respective chapters.

IT Management Framework (APO01)

Having a Framework provides a holistic view of IT. The Framework does not necessarily have to be COBIT; it could be ITIL or any other suitable Framework that assures that IT Management considers all relevant aspects of IT depending on the Enterprise's needs.

Strategy Management (APO02)

The key to IT Strategy Management is supportive strategic planning and execution.

IT and its operations, like all departments in an Enterprise, must align with the Enterprise values and direction. For this to occur, IT must be privy to the Enterprise's Mission, Vision, Values, Business Objectives, Strategy, Planning, and so on; otherwise, congruence is merely a happy accident. As the saying goes, 'hope is not a strategy'. The essential point is that IT needs to know where the Enterprise is going and how it plans to get there so that IT's goals and objectives, plans, and activities align with, support, and enable the Enterprise to accomplish these Objectives.

The Strategic Risk is that IT will develop and deploy products and services that are at best worthless, and at worst counterproductive. As noted in IT Governance, alignment of IT with its host is critical.

From an IT Audit perspective, the following are good practices to ensure alignment:

- Active participation in the Enterprise's Strategic Assessment and Planning processes.
- Communicating IT's plans to executive leadership.
- Regular communications with stakeholders regarding IT planning and service provision.
- Formal ratification of IT's Strategic and Operational plans as part of the Enterprise's Strategic Planning process.

The point of the first bullet is knowledge. The point of the second and third bullets is congruence. The ideal is that corporate planning and IT planning infuse each other and are complementary and mutually supportive. The last point is the integration of IT's Strategy into the Corporate Strategy.

IT's strategy must include long-term Assets, Products, and Services planning and roadmaps to achieve these plans.

Enterprise Architecture (EA) Management (APO03)

EA is an overarching design for IT Assets, Products, and Services.

The Open Group teaches that the purpose of EA is to optimize business processes, systems, and Data across the business. The outcome of this optimization is "… an integrated environment that is responsive to change and supportive of the delivery of the business strategy". "Furthermore, … achiev[ing] the right balance between business transformation and continuous operational efficiency". [—*The Open Group Standard: TOGAF® Standard – Introduction and Core Concepts*, The Open Group®, 2022, p. 2.]

The Open Group® stresses a systematic, systemic, integrated approach to computer automation that balances business transformation and the support of business operations.

An interesting aspect of EA is that every Enterprise has one. The only question is whether the EA is intentional or accidental. An intentional EA is the result of a design process, such as The Open Group® Architecture Framework (TOGAF) shown in Figure 5.1. An accidental EA is inherited from other decisions, typically the selection and implementation of a major, pervasive application, such as an ERP or a CRM system. The selection of a Business System that uses a specific database management system (DBMS) makes that DBMS a de facto Enterprise standard regardless of whether that DBMS was otherwise used by the Enterprise. If on the other hand, the Enterprise Business System is developed 'in-house', then the Enterprise can design its own database architecture.

One such intentional EA is TOGAF, Figure 5.1.

TOGAF identifies four major inputs for EA.

a. Architecture Vision
b. Business Requirements
c. Information Systems Requirements
d. Technology Requirements

EA begins with the Enterprise's Mission, Vision, and Values followed closely by its business requirements. Consider the advice that Demand drives Sales. Moving that advice into this discussion, Vision and Requirements drive EA, or EA is derived from the Enterprise's Vision and its Requirements. Ultimately, EA is about aligning with, supporting, and enabling the achievement of Enterprise Business Objectives.

While more could be said regarding EA, the reader is directed to The Open Group® for additional information about TOGAF. See https://www.opengroup.org/togaf.

Looking forward with respect to EA, two questions arise:

• How will the EA be applied in future system acquisition and design decisions?

  Having an Architecture and applying the Architecture are different. Unused Architectures can be encountered. And organizations may have Architectures and ignore them when acquiring new technologies.

• How often is the Architecture reviewed and updated?

  Requirement Drift is constant. New technologies spawn new methods. Innovation spawns new approaches. Competitors find new ways of doing things. Flexibility and Ingenuity are required to maintain EAs in the face of business changes. This has to be an intentional action; it does not happen automatically.

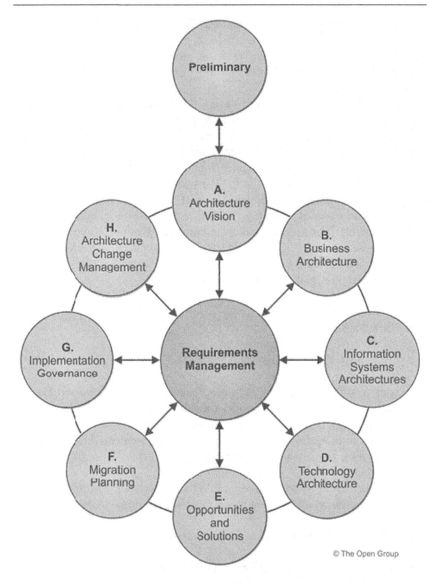

Figure 5.1 The Open Group Architecture Framework (TOGAF). Reproduced with permission of The Open Group®. https://www.opengroup.org/togaf.

From the IT Audit perspective, consider the following:

- Was the Architecture inherited?
  - Was the Architecture inherited? If so, is it suitable for the Enterprise?
  - If the Architecture is not suitable for the Enterprise to achieve its business objectives, the Architecture may need to be reinvented, replaced, or adapted to serve the Enterprise.

- Was the Architecture intentionally designed?

  Does the intentional Architecture include the elements identified in Figure 5.1 plus:

  - Stakeholder Priorities, and
  - Standardization, especially regarding languages, databases, tools, and other fundamental technologies.

- Is the Architecture consistent with the Enterprise's mission, goals, objectives, and plans? Does the Architecture enable the Enterprise to achieve its objectives?
- Is the Architecture maintained? Is it up to date?

  The constant evolution of technology means the Architecture must be updated for changing demands and opportunities.

Finally, is the Enterprise Architecture a foundation and/or a springboard for Innovation?

Financial Management (APO06)

Finances are the inevitable constraint. Few businesses have sufficient funds to do everything that's on their wish lists. Finance is where the ideal meets reality. During the pandemic, IT Enterprises hired profusely; now that the urgency of COVID has subsided, these employers are 'right-sizing' staff, both technical and administrative. Looking at the IT industry over a longer time horizon, staffing swings like a pendulum from hiring to layoffs. Granted, these swings are affected by multiple factors and cycles, but they routinely recur.

IT Financial Management includes the following:

- Expense and Investment Management
- Operating Budgets for routine IT operations
- Capital Budgets (CapEx) for major initiatives and projects

IT must manage its costs and investments. Budgets play an important role as well as prudent purchasing, especially in the realm of long-term contracts, such as Cloud Service contracts and major business systems.

Operating Budgets are constant, whereas Capital Budgets fluctuate around initiatives, projects, and programs. Operating Budgets are the recurring foundation for IT, a constant with potential annual fluctuations. They include expenses such as ...

- Service Subscriptions
- Software Licenses
- Maintenance Requirements

- Replacement Policies
- Personnel, Employees, and Subcontractors
- Supplies, etc.

The keys to both types of budgets are thoughtful preparation and negotiation processes to arrive at mutual agreements.

Budgets are evidence of the Enterprise's commitment to IT. If the funds are inadequate, what does this say about the Enterprise's commitment to IT?

Human Resources (HR)/Human Capital Management(HC) (APO07)

IT's Human Resources or Human Capital contain unique elements, which are not necessarily exclusive to IT, such as

- Recruitment and Hiring of Technical Personnel
- Sustaining and Enhancing Technical Staff
- Providing Appropriate Technical Staff Oversight

Recruiting technical personnel can be difficult. Interviewing is often left to IT and the paperwork to HR. Knowing where to look for candidates and what to expect of candidates can be challenging.

From the IT Audit perspective, the big questions are the following:

- How does IT identify qualified candidates?
- How does IT hire its personnel?
- How are IT personnel managed?
- To what extent does IT use Outsourced personnel? If so, how are Outsourced resources selected and managed?
- How does IT sustain its personnel, training programs, and benefits?
- How does IT oversee its technical resources?

In the context of an IT Audit, these questions involve IT's Personnel Policies, Procedures, Practices, and compliance with these. No single solution fits all situations. The underlying question for IT Auditors is:

- Does IT have the technical expertise it needs to perform the services it agreed to perform?
- Can IT get replacement resources when and as needed in a reasonable timeframe?

As a side note: Artificial Intelligence (AI) is and will continue to have a profound impact on IT, including the amount and type of IT resources a Business Enterprise requires. AI will also have a significant impact on IT careers. Take a simple example: Coding. AI can now quickly respond with code to satisfy a particular set of requirements. A coder can provide the AI with a set of requirements, receive the AI-generated code, evaluate the code, make any revisions that are deemed necessary, and deploy the code in Production much quicker than traditional methods, in minutes or hours rather than days or months. This capability is not limited to trained programmers; Subject Matter Experts (SMEs) can use the same resources to develop applications quickly that satisfy their needs. The problem here is that the development happens outside of IT policies, procedures, practices, and standards.

What is there not to like about this scenario? The code is generated quickly, accurately, suitable as is or with minor tweaks. And the AIs will only get better over time. But this raises a question: Will there be an ongoing need for programmers? If programmers disappear, what happens to their accumulated knowledge? Who will gather the requirements? Who will be able to evaluate the code, especially if the AI makes mistakes? Who will monitor the code to be sure it is performing as needed? The answer to these questions may be the AI. If that is the answer, what happens to programming as a career? By extension, what happens to IT expertise in the Enterprise if the AI handles these processes from beginning to end and other significant IT activities as well? How will AI alter existing career paths and/or create new IT career paths?

A final issue is that you figure out a novel, innovative solution and ask the AI to evaluate your invention and provide feedback. But the AI then knows your invention; it is no longer a secret. Can you tell the AI to forget your invention? AIs are not built to forget; they are built to remember everything they 'see'. Now the AI can apply your invention unbeknownst to you to other problems. What happens to Intellectual Property rights? Will the AI give you credit for your invention and potentially charge future users a fee to use your invention and remit part of that fee back to you? Unlikely, as things stand now. As this book is being written, new AIs are emerging that keep their users Data within a local instance of the AI. The remaining concern becomes leakage. Does the AI leak its Data elsewhere?

For information technologists, there are a host of career questions. For the Enterprise, there are also a host of questions; questions regarding the Enterprise's history, its tribal knowledge and the disappearance of tribal knowledge from the Enterprise. While 'dumbing down' might be the wrong expression, the Enterprise may emerge from this transition with significantly fewer technical skills, knowledge, and resources. If the reduction is significant, one could ask: What will be left of the business? Will the business be contained in a computer? Only time will answer these questions.

Procurement Management (APO10)

Like HR, IT Procurement has distinct requirements, such as:

- Identifying specific products without substitution
- Identifying specific suppliers regardless of price

The Purchasing Department may ask IT to prepare its own Purchase Orders to ensure the specifications are correct and the supplier is appropriate. In this situation, Purchasing becomes relatively perfunctory, delegating sourcing, product selection, and vendor selection to IT.

For IT Audit, the question is:

- What are IT's Procurement Policies, Procedures, and Practices in relation to the Enterprise's normal procurement procedures?

IT may do its own Procurement leaving Purchasing to merely process paperwork on behalf of IT. For IT Audit, how smoothly and accurately does this process work? Does it suit the Enterprise's Business Objectives? Does this practice pose special challenges?

Quality Management (APO11)

How does IT manage Quality? IT, like other Departments in Enterprises, is concerned about the Quality of its Assets, Products, and Services. Typical Quality policies or practices include testing items before they are put into Production, monitoring system performance, measuring IT excellence through a variety of metrics, and so on.

Incident Management and Problem Management can provide a window into Quality issues. These topics will be covered in the chapter on Basic IT Practices.

Regarding the Big Question, 'How does IT manage Quality', consider ITIL's emphasis on Continuous Improvement (5.1.2). Implied in the concept of Continuous Improvement is constant monitoring to improve the Quality of IT workproduct. How does IT ensure Quality and/or Continuous Improvement in the provision of its Products and Services? How is Quality incorporated into IT's Procurement Procedures, into IT's Acquisition Procedures, into IT's Product Development Procedures, and into IT's Service Delivery? As this is being written, Boeing, a symbol of American manufacturing excellence, is suffering from major quality issues, which have significantly eroded Boeing's reputation and finances. A more difficult position than this is hard to imagine.

The ultimate IT Audit question: Is IT's Quality Management suitable and effective for Enterprise Business Objectives?

Relationship Management (APO08, APO09, APO10)

COBIT teaches the idea of managing Relationships, including internal and external relationships. Relationships are spread across three overlapping COBIT Objectives: Relationships (APO08), Service Agreements (APO09), and Vendors, (APO10). Relationships extend beyond supplier relationships to include Relationships within the Enterprise as well as Relationships outside the Enterprise.

As noted elsewhere, Vendors and Service Agreements are related, and Relationships also overlap with Stakeholder Engagement (EDM05).

IT Audit can combine these four COBIT objectives into a single area with the following IT Audit questions:

- How effectively does IT manage its internal Relationships, including Stakeholders?
- How effectively does IT manage its external Relationships, including external Stakeholders?
- Does IT handle Relationships in a manner consistent with and supportive of the Enterprise?

Service Level Agreements (SLAs) present opportunities to go beyond typical performance requirements and clarify essential expectations between parties regarding services, hence, a wider purpose. Enterprises and their constituents have expectations. Relationships is a place to clarify these expectations and build upon them.

Significant aspects, but by no means the only aspects, of internal IT Relationship Management are the IT HelpDesk and IT's user support services. These have a major impact on how IT is perceived by the business.

Risk Management (APO12)

Risk Management is essential. From the beginning of IT, engineers were concerned about failures. Things were more mechanical then, than they are today. Manufacturing techniques were not as precise then as they are today. Together, these factors meant things were likely to break down and failures could be catastrophic. So, engineers started using techniques to reduce the likelihood of damage should a failure occur, i.e., basic Risk Management. Techniques included backing up Data and critical programs and parts so they could be replaced and/or reloaded to get systems back up and operating. It was just what we did to keep things going and to avoid the embarrassment of failure.

Today, especially given businesses' dependence on technology, extensive programs are implemented to identify potential risks and strategies to reduce those risks. Early on this was simply protecting IT assets from significant failures. Today it is more structured involving departments within and outside of IT focusing on Risks, including Risks created by automation.

From the IT Audit perspective, the Big IT Audit Questions include the following:

- How does the Enterprise manage Risk generally?
- How does the Enterprise manage IT Risk specifically?
- How effective are the current controls in remediating the Risks, including Design Risk and Effectiveness Risk?

- Have significant outages, interruptions, or failures, major or minor, occurred during the period being audited?
- How were those outages handled? Were they handled consistent with Enterprise Objectives?
- What lessons were learned from these outages? Could they have been prevented? If so, how? How much did the outages cost the Enterprise, including both financial losses and reputational losses?

Please note that the word failure is not limited to total stoppage or total breakage. Failure also includes the degrading of assets and services.

From its inception, Risk Management was an essential aspect of managing IT although IT might not have recognized it as such then. While its focus has changed, Risk remains a primary concern. RACMs (Risk and Control Matrices) focus on Business Objectives, Risks that interfere with the achievement of the Business Objectives, and Controls intended to reduce Risk ... Risk, Risk, Risk. RACMs are all about managing Risk.

Security Management (APO13)

Security, both physical and cyber, are essential today for every business regardless of size; hence, Cybersecurity is covered below in its own chapter.

Data Management (APO14)

Like Security Management, Data has its own chapter, in which Data Management is discussed.

Software Development Management (BAI)

Software Development Management used to be a major aspect of IT. As Cloud Services and commercial software became dominant, Solution Selection replaced Software Development as the primary approach. This topic also warrants its own chapter.

Project Management (BAI)

Project Management is another area that could have its own chapter; however, as with software development, there are many other resources. Chief among them is the Project Management Institute's (PMI) *A guide to the Project Management Body of Knowledge PMBOK Guide*. PMBOK covers Project Management in detail and is an excellent resource for this domain.

Compliance Management (MEA)

Compliance Management can be considered part of Risk Management. COBIT covers compliance in MEA03. This is another topic with which IT Management and IT Audit must contend. The subject matter content of Compliance Management depends on the specific laws, regulations, and other restrictions to which the Enterprise must comply. To the extent that Compliance involves Cybersecurity and privacy, it is covered in the chapter on Cybersecurity.

Innovation Management (APO04)

In addition to supporting the Enterprise, IT can be an Innovative force within an Enterprise via new technologies and new methods enabled by technology. Alignment is one metric; innovation is another metric. The two work together focusing on Value to the Enterprise.

ITIL stresses Value and Continuous Improvement; COBIT stresses Value and Innovation (APO04). Both frameworks see IT as vital to business success.

With respect to Value creation and Innovation, the IT Audit Big Questions are the following:

- How can IT assist the Enterprise to be more competitive and potentially stand out from its competitors?
- How can IT assist the Enterprise in the creation of novel, innovative Assets, Products, and Services?
- How can IT be a 'game changer' for an Enterprise?

Innovation is consistent with Silicon Valley's ethos of disruption, even disrupting the disruptors.

Clearly, automation has reshaped entire industries, including finance, manufacturing, distribution, and retail, even down to the neighborhood restaurant where servers now place orders in the kitchen via smart devices table-side.

From the IT Audit perspective, the Big Questions are the following:

- How do IT Policies, Procedures, Practices, and Activities promote Innovation?
- Does the Innovation create Value for the Enterprise?
- How is the Innovation valued by and integrated into the Enterprise?

IT Audit Challenges

The Big IT Audit Challenges related to IT Management touch on the effectiveness and efficiency of the IT Department. These can be touchy issues. The range of reception for IT Audit can range from 'don't interfere with IT' to being supportive. The reception is likely to be somewhere in between the extremes, maybe a necessary distraction. IT Management may feel this is an unnecessary intrusion into its domain, or IT Management may welcome the support of like-minded persons, i.e., people concerned about effective and efficient IT products and services.

Remember as an IT Auditor, you can be an 'auditor', an assessor, in the conventional sense of the word, or a consultant or advisor providing knowledge and assistance to IT. Especially today, IT Auditors can be and should be seen as both vigilant and supportive. IT Audit has a wealth of knowledge that can assist IT in the delivery of its Assets, Products, and Services. If IT Audit is involved in the development of Business Objectives, Risks, and Controls, they are no longer independent; however, they can still be objective.

Chapter 6

Auditing IT Infrastructure

Chapter Contents

IT 360° – An IT Model

To put Infrastructure in context, consider the following model. IT 360° is a comprehensive view of Information Technology based on the concept of an IT Stack, as shown in Figures 6.1 and 6.2.

Figure 6.1 looks at technology traditionally as hardware, software, and applications with applications sitting on top of the stack, and hardware and related operating software sitting at the bottom of the stack, and Middleware sitting in between the top and bottom layers. The application layer consists of the applications that businesses rely on. The hardware layer includes the servers, storage, network devices, etc., which support the applications. Middleware includes databases, programming languages, utility software, data analytics tools, data wrangling tools, and so on.

Figure 6.2 expands the model to include the managerial aspects of IT, its Policies, Procedures, Practices, Standards, Methods, Frameworks, Personnel, and so on. With the added managerial parts of IT, Figure 6.2 is the more comprehensive view of IT.

Infrastructure and the Cloud

Traditionally, Enterprises had their own in-house Infrastructure, i.e., Figure 6.1. In this setting, IT was responsible for the design, acquisition, implementation,

DOI: 10.4324/9781032689388-6

Application Software (Business Process)
Middleware (Utilities, Programming languages, Databases, Report Writers)
Infrastructure (Hardware – Operating Systems – Firmware)

Figure 6.1 Simplified Traditional Stack.

Application Software (Business Process)	**Policies** **Procedures** **Practices** **Structures** **Standards** **Methods** **Frameworks** **Personnel**
Middleware (Utilities, Programming languages, Databases, Report Writers)	
Infrastructure (Hardware – Operating Systems – Firmware)	

Figure 6.2 IT 360° Model.

performance, capabilities, and maintenance of the Infrastructure. The Enterprise's applications upon which the Enterprise depended were housed on the Infrastructure and used various Middleware components. IT Audit, in turn, was concerned about the design and effectiveness of the Infrastructure, the Middleware, and the countermeasures implemented to protect the Infrastructure and Middleware and reduce the Risks to the Infrastructure and Middleware that would negatively impact its applications.

Cloud services created a new era. Technology went through a major transition from traditional on-premises computing to cloud computing. 'Cloud First' became the default choice, which simply means when something new is needed, look for it as an Internet service first instead of buying it and putting it in-house. This is not to say that Enterprises do not have in-house infrastructure; only critical pieces of the infrastructure were moved outside the Enterprise.

'Cloud First' shifted the question of Infrastructure away from the traditional model; however, two exceptions exist:

- Residual in-house Infrastructure
- Technology Enterprises that maintain their own Infrastructure and/or the Infrastructure, which is part of their Products or Services

In the first situation, in-house Infrastructure is not completely eliminated but significantly reduced from what it was previously. In this case, the Infrastructure didn't go away, it just moved from the Enterprise to the cloud leaving some pieces behind, a few servers, local storage, network devices, and so on. In the second case, Infrastructure is integral to the Technology Enterprise and hence remains under the Enterprise's control.

From a Customer's perspective, Cloud computing reduced The Stack to a group of Services ... but not completely. As noted above, vestiges of traditional on-premises computing may remain, and in some cases, Enterprises are repatriating some workloads back to their premises for a variety of reasons, often including cost.

The switch to cloud services is significant for Enterprises. It relieves them of having to acquire and manage these physical resources. These functions have not gone away, only their manifestations. They are now services. Because of this change, Enterprises no longer need extensive IT staff to manage physical resources because they have been greatly diminished by cloud services.

Taking this change into account, a contemporary model looks more like Figure 6.3, with a combination of on-premises assets and Software-as-a-Service assets.

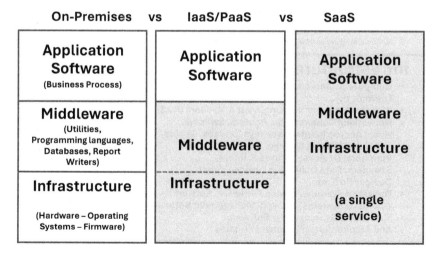

Figure 6.3 Contemporary Infrastructure Models.

Figure 6.3 shows the Customer stack in white and the cloud service portions of the slack in gray. Figure 6.3 teaches a combination of IT assets including On-Premises assets, Infrastructure-as-a-Service assets, Platform-as-a-Service assets, and Software-as-a-Service assets, in which some assets are local while other assets are remote. Today more assets may be remote than local.

In this transition, physical components have not disappeared; they have been **Abstracted**; they have been **Virtualized**. **Abstraction** and **Virtualization** are key terms in the new world, with both positive and negative implications, which will be discussed in subsequent chapters.

This change profoundly impacts IT Audit as well. Even though physical infrastructure has been replaced by virtual cloud services, IT Auditors need to understand and appreciate the physical fundamentals. They have not gone away; they have just gone 'underground'.

Infrastructure in Greater Detail

Regardless of who owns the Infrastructure, it still exists somewhere. It may be in the custody of Cloud Service Providers (CSPs), in the custody of the Enterprise or in some combination of local and remote assets. Figure 6.4 shows traditional Infrastructure in greater detail.

Application Software (Business Process)	
Middleware (Utilities, Programming languages, Databases, Report Writers)	Policies
Infrastructure: • Computers: Servers, Desktops, Workstations, Laptops, etc. • Storage Components – On Server & Network (NAS) • Networking Components: Routers, Switches, Hubs, Access Points, Gateways, Bridges, Cables, including Network Storage, etc. • Peripheral Devices: Such as Printers, Scanners, Data Collection Devices, Smart Devices (IoT), etc. • Operating Systems, Device Firmware, Network Operating Systems, Network Management Software • Firewalls & Cybersecurity Software • And Architecture and Network Design	Procedures Practices Standards Methods Frameworks Personnel

Figure 6.4 Infrastructure Stack.

Basic Infrastructure Components

Infrastructure elements include at least the following:

- Server hardware
- Operating Systems (O/S) and Firmware
- Network Operating Software (NOS) and Network Management Software (NMS)
- Storage Components on Servers and Networks
- Network Components, including Routers, Switches, Hubs, Bridges and Cabling
- Firewalls and Cybersecurity Software to control Internet traffic into and out of the Enterprise
- Desktops, Workstations, Laptops, and embedded controllers
- Peripheral equipment, such as printers, scanners, WiFi access points, phones, and smart devices (Internet of Things (IoT)), such as cameras, thermostats, locks, and so on

This list is illustrative; it is neither exhaustive nor static.

Today, most commercial infrastructure is connected to the Internet via commercial Internet Service Providers (ISPs) using a combination of copper and fiber cables, firewalls, and WiFi access points on the consumer side.

In the 'Cloud First' environment, much of the Infrastructure resides on the CSP's side, while an appropriate amount of Infrastructure remains on the Customer's side. Nothing disappeared. It just got relocated and, in many cases, reduced from physical components to virtual services.

IT Audit – Hardware Considerations

At the hardware level, what could compromise Infrastructure:

- What could compromise the Availability of the Infrastructure?
- What could compromise the Integrity of the Infrastructure?
- What could interfere with the Operation of the Infrastructure?
- What, if anything, makes the Infrastructure unsuitable for the Enterprise?

Regardless of the specifics of the Infrastructure, these and similar questions are relevant for on-premises assets as well as for cloud services. In the latter case, these components remain relevant, and CSPs typically obtain System and Organization Controls Reports (SOC Reports), to confirm their controls because they are relevant to the CSP's Customers. SOC Reports are covered below in their own chapter.

The starting place for an IT Audit is an understanding of the Enterprise's Infrastructure and its components. If a network diagram is available, that is a great place to start. Second would be a list of major components, including make and model, location, and identification numbers. If a network diagram does not exist, constructing one is a good documentation practice. It provides the IT Audit with a basic diagram to evaluate the audit questions posed above.

Detailed questions related to Integrity, Availability, and Suitability include the following:

- Availability: What might interfere with continuous operation? Electrical failures? Overheating? Theft of components? Severing network cables? Tampering? etc.?
- Environmental Hazards: Electrical failure, air conditioning failure, unauthorized physical access, destruction of the space in which the infrastructure sits, etc.
- Mechanical Failure: Device failure, including slowing as well as stopping.
- Sabotage: Intentional actions intended to compromise the Infrastructure.
- Security: Are the components physically and logically secure? Can they be easily taken over by an adversary?

Ultimately, these questions relate to anything that can affect these assets, their use, and/or their behavior.

Basic Countermeasures

Countermeasures are as varied as the challenges.

- Access Control (Physical): Enclosed spaces, locks and keys, security cameras, and appropriate access control privileges.
- Fault Tolerant Systems: Designed to localize the effects of failure so that failures do not affect the larger surrounding environment.

  Redundancy is a frequent method for localizing failures, for example, multiple power supplies, multiple power sources, multiple air conditioning systems, multiple storage devices using Redundant Array of Independent Devices (RAID), and/or replication to spread Data across multiple devices.
- Configuration Management, Patch Management, Incident Management, and Change Management to maintain systems without introducing new vulnerabilities. These are addressed in the IT Good Practices chapter.
- Uninterruptible Power Supplies (UPS) to maintain continuous power.
- Adequate cooling systems to prevent overheating.
- Providing sufficient processing power and bandwidth to maintain normal operations with adequate headroom for fluctuating workloads, where headroom refers to excess capacity.
- Firewalls, Intrusion Prevention and Detection systems (IPS/IDS), Network segmentation, and Demilitarized Zones (DMZs) to reduce the possibility of malicious actions.
- Access Controls and Access Privilege Management to limit logical access to Infrastructure.

The appropriateness of countermeasures depends on the Enterprise's Business Objectives; however, many countermeasures are standard IT operating practices and are present as routine precautions. Remember the admonition that 'bad things happen to good people'. Inevitably something will go wrong.

Obviously, IT does not have unlimited resources; IT competes with other parts of the Enterprise for funding. Hence, sufficient and suitable become overarching criteria.

In terms of types of countermeasures, Preventive Measures are preferred. In second place are automatic failover mechanisms that limit the impact of failures. In third place are automated alerting and messaging with manual follow-up. In the last place, are manual procedures.

Artificial Intelligence (AI) may add a new and significant dimension to countermeasures making them 'smarter' and more reactive as well as proactive. For example, having two or more of anything with automatic failover is great, but having AI identify weaknesses before they manifest themselves and preemptively taking the affected devices or systems out of service would be even better.

Special Cases

Situations that require special attention include the following:

- Mission Critical Systems
- High-Availability Systems

Mission Critical Systems are systems that are critical to the operation of the Enterprise and as such require extraordinary capabilities that allow these systems to operate under adverse conditions and circumstances.

High-Availability Systems are, by definition, designed to be extremely resilient. They are designed to provide a continuous high level of service despite circumstances that might otherwise degrade or halt the service.

In either of these use cases, the control mechanisms need to address both the obvious and the less obvious elements that could adversely affect system performance. The less obvious may be hiding in plain sight or they may be out of sight hiding in walls, ceilings, cabinets, conduits, and so on. The criticality of these systems warrant additional actions and protections beyond standard IT practices.

Reminders

The trend is toward increasing Abstraction, which means that computer users are moving away from physical computing assets into logical environments where services replace physical things. In addition, the automation is continuing to become more intelligent, which means these system will increasingly care for themselves.

One could reasonably expect that Abstraction will, over time, 'dumb' down computer users regarding the technology upon which they depend in the office and at home. For example, you can enjoy a great meal and not know how to cook, you can drive a car and not know how it works or how to repair it. These aspects are left to chefs and mechanics; however, IT Auditors need to be informed regarding these essential elements to effectively audit them and advise their clients.

Chapter 7

Auditing Cloud Services

Chapter Contents:

Introduction – The Evolving IT Landscape

The landscape is evolving from an emphasis on hardware and software to an emphasis on Services, at least from the users' perspectives. 'Cloud First' has become the default acquisition strategy for most businesses. Look first for cloud services; then look for on-premises alternatives if the cloud services do not satisfy the needs.

Hardware and Software have not gone away; they have been hidden behind sophisticated software. This transition means that objects, such as servers and application software, are no longer accessed directly by users. These items have become **ABSTRACTED**, which has led to new terms, such as 'serverless' and 'servers-as-code'. In other words, physical servers are hidden behind layers of software such that to 'spin up a server' is faster, and easier, than ordering food at a fast-food restaurant ... if you understand what is happening behind the scenes.

Keep in mind that this switch is not necessarily an 'all or nothing' switch. Enterprises may migrate some workloads, most workloads, to the cloud and leave some workloads and resources on-premises, resulting in a hybrid or combination architecture. Enterprises are, in some cases, repatriating workloads back to on-premises assets, often to reduce cost.

DOI: 10.4324/9781032689388-7

This transition shifting from physical objects to virtual services is profoundly impacting IT and IT Audit. In hybrid environments, IT Audit concerns include both Cloud Services and on-premises assets.

NIST Cloud Models

Cloud terminology is based on NIST's (National Institute of Standards and Technology) Definition of Cloud Computing. NIST established three cloud models.

- The Five Essential Characteristics Model:

    - On-demand self-service
    - Broad network access
    - Resource pooling
    - Rapid elasticity
    - Measured service

NLST
National Institute of
Standards and Technology
U.S. Department of Commerce

Special Publication 800-145

The NIST Definition of Cloud Computing

Recommendations of the National Institute of Standards and Technology

Peter Mell
Timothy Grance

Figure 7.1 NIST Cloud Definition.

- The Three Services Model:

  - Infrastructure as a Service (IaaS)
  - Platform as a Service (PaaS)
  - Software as a Service (SaaS)

- The Four Deployment Models:

  - Public Cloud
  - Private Cloud
  - Community Cloud
  - Hybrid Cloud

https://nvlpubs.nist.gov/nistpubs/Legacy/SP/
nistspecialpublication800-145.pdf

Readers can easily download a copy of this paper from https://csrc.nist.gov/pubs/sp/800/145/final.

NIST's Cloud Service Model

- Infrastructure-as-a-Service

  IaaS converts physical assets, such as servers, into services. In the case of Infrastructure-as-a-Service, the Infrastructure, which is described in the preceding chapter, becomes services. Instead of buying servers and storage, the customer 'spins' up virtual servers via a Cloud Service Provider's (CSP's) console. The person configuring the service must understand the attributes of the server that are needed to serve the requirements.

  Critical to IaaS is Resource Pooling and Rapid Elasticity, two of the five Essential Characteristics of cloud services. Resource Pooling allows CSPs to pool, or cluster, servers and storage, and provision them on demand in tranches (to borrow an expression from finance). In addition to provisioning, the as-a-service method can easily scale by quickly increasing the size of resources in a pool. Expanding and contracting the size and cost of the service is easy; however, the CSP may not reduce the cost of the service as fast as it reduces the service.

  CSPs behave like utilities where customers pay for the utility based on their usage be it electricity, water, gas, trash, or in this case cloud services.

- Platform-as-a-Service

  PaaS is like IaaS with additional capabilities that extend beyond basic servers, storage, and networking. The additional capabilities can include databases, data analytics tools, data migration tools, and a host of other technical services.

  In terms of IT Audit, the comments related to IaaS apply equally to PaaS with a larger range of items.

- Software-as-a-Service

  SaaS is an Application sitting on top of an Infrastructure using various Platform technologies, such as databases. With Software-as-a-Service, customers get Applications on Infrastructure that includes various Platform services. All three layers are managed by the CSP. Hence, the customer is subscribing to a cloud application service and leaving the Infrastructure and Platform issues to the service provider.

NIST's Cloud Deployment Models

- Public Cloud vs. Private Cloud

  Generally, customers deal with a Public Cloud Service. Why? Because it is less expensive than Private Cloud Services. The exception would be an Enterprise that deals with extremely confidential data or has 'deep pockets' and is fine with the additional cost.

  Regarding Cloud Services in general, they were initially introduced to the public as a less expensive alternative to on-premises assets. Over time, the invoices from CSPs have piled up and some Enterprises moved some workloads back on-premises to reduce costs. Whether repatriation is a trend, or a blip, remains to be seen. Enterprises with substantial cloud services receive substantial invoices and may reconsider their alternatives.

  Public Cloud is less expensive because the service providers pool resources and sell fractional pieces to their customers offering 'economies of scale'. Hence, the cost of the Infrastructure including its operations, maintenance, and technical resources is spread across a broad customer base. The adage 'cheaper by the dozen' epitomizes this cost reduction.

  An important characteristic of Public Cloud is Co-tenancy, which means customers rely on the service providers to keep their processes and data separate, at least logically, from other customers using the same underlying resources. If the customer is not okay with co-tenancy, Private Cloud is an alternative.

- Hybrid Cloud – Hybrid

  Hybrid is an interesting term. While NIST defined Hybrid Cloud as 'a composition of two or more distinct cloud infrastructure', there is no reason why customers could not combine on-premises resources with cloud resources. In this context, Hybrid has a broader meaning than NIST originally intended. For example, a customer may copy its Data to on-premises assets, which brings us to 'Hybrid' without the word 'cloud' attached to it.

  Ultimately, Enterprises rely on a combination of multiple cloud services and on-premises assets. Given these factors, Hybrid, without the word cloud attached, is more realistic.

NIST's Essential Characteristics

The Essential Characteristic model lists the traits of cloud services; they include on-demand, self-service, broad network access, resource pooling, rapid elasticity, and measured service.

Cloud services are readily available on-demand. Customers establish and maintain their cloud services using consoles to adjust the type and quantity of services received. Because of Resource Pooling, the services can be easily expanded and contracted as needed even if the financial model favors increasing services over decreasing them. Resource Pooling allows the cost of expensive assets to be spread across multiple customers reducing the per unit cost, at least theoretically. Finally, customers only pay for the services they use in the quantity they use them.

The big characteristic that NIST does not include is the Enterprise's dependence on its CSPs, or said differently, customers are 'using someone else's stuff'. Dependence is not new. Companies are dependent upon their suppliers, but the degree of dependence customers have on their CSPs is 'stickier', tighter, and more difficult to live without than traditional customer-supplier relationships.

If an Enterprise depends on cloud services to operate, the absence of that service may stop the Enterprise's business activities. The example used in this book is that of an airline that operates its flight and crew scheduling and reservation systems on cloud infrastructure. If the cloud infrastructure fails, the airline is grounded. Yes, this could also happen if the airline maintained its own infrastructure. This same argument could be applied to every Enterprise automated system; yes, bad things do happen; however, Enterprises have more control over their own assets than they do over assets managed by others. A variety of countermeasures at different cost points exist, but the nature of the dependence is tighter and the Enterprise's visibility into the service provider is limited; hence, the Risks are different.

From an IT Audit perspective, the dependence of Enterprises on their CSPs should be closely evaluated in terms of Risks to the Enterprise and suitable controls adopted to limit damage to the Enterprise in the case of service failures.

Cloud Service Concepts Outside the NIST Models

Beyond the items identified in the NIST models, there are other terms and concepts, which are essential for businesses to understand.

- Autoscaling

  Autoscaling means system resources expand and contract automatically as needed based on usage and rules. With autoscaling, these services do not need to be manually expanded or contracted; it happens automatically.

- Availability Zones (AZs)

  AZs are distinct locations within Regions where resources are housed, i.e., data centers. AZs and Regions provide geographic distribution of services, which can isolate system failures, such as the destruction of a data center or a grid power failure.

- Compute Instance

  A cloud Compute Instance is a virtual server. Amazon Web Services (AWS) calls them Elastic Compute Cloud (EC2). Microsoft calls them VMs (Virtual Machines). Google Cloud calls them Compute Engines, different words to refer to the same thing, a virtual computer.

- 'Co-Tenancy'

  Co-Tenancy, as mentioned earlier, is about customers' sharing resources. If this is unacceptable, a Private Cloud may be a better choice; however, it is more expensive.

- High Availability Architecture

  High Availability Architecture, which is not limited to CSPs, involves the design and implementation of multiple components that operate in conjunction with each other to ensure uninterrupted service, i.e., high availability. Depending on the environment, High Availability can include redundant applications, redundant infrastructure, and data redundancy. The objective is to guarantee constant availability by eliminating all single points of failure.

- Load Balancing

  Load Balancing is a method to balance traffic among different resources to improve or sustain performance. It is also not unique to cloud platforms; it can be done with on-premises resources as well; however, CSPs routinely provide Load Balancing.

- Replication

  Replication is also not unique to cloud platforms. Replication is a method of distributing data across redundant infrastructure. This is typically done to improve reliability, availability, and fault-tolerance.

- 'Shared Responsibility'

  'Shared Responsibility' is a critical concept for cloud providers and customers alike. 'Shared Responsibility' delineates the responsibilities of the CSP and the responsibilities of the customer. It recognizes that success is shared mutually. Shared Responsibility says that the Provider will do what it can to ensure safe, reliable services but the Provider's countermeasures can be defeated by unintentional acts as well as intentional acts of customers.

The CSP is generally responsible for the integrity of the infrastructure, hardware, software, networking, and facilities that provide the cloud services, while the customer is responsible for its use of the services and its Data.

The Customer's responsibilities are a function of the services the customer selects. In general, customers are responsible for at least configuration, Data, and Identity and Access Management (IAM). Figure 7.2 compares on-premises, IaaS, PaaS, and SaaS in terms of Shared Responsibility. Moving from left to right, responsibilities shift from the customer to shared responsibilities, to responsibilities that are solely those of the provider.

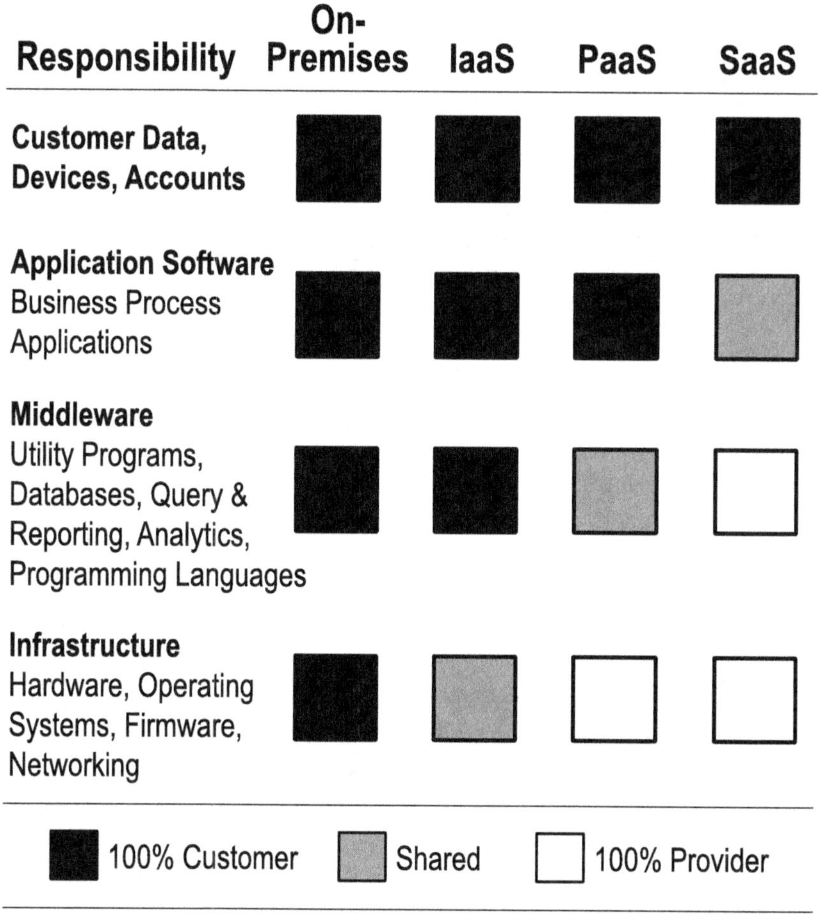

Responsibility	On-Premises	IaaS	PaaS	SaaS
Customer Data, Devices, Accounts	100% Customer	100% Customer	100% Customer	100% Customer
Application Software Business Process Applications	100% Customer	100% Customer	100% Customer	Shared
Middleware Utility Programs, Databases, Query & Reporting, Analytics, Programming Languages	100% Customer	100% Customer	Shared	100% Provider
Infrastructure Hardware, Operating Systems, Firmware, Networking	100% Customer	Shared	100% Provider	100% Provider

■ 100% Customer   ▨ Shared   □ 100% Provider

Figure 7.2 Shared Responsibilities.

AWS, for example, specifically identifies the following 'Shared Controls':

- "Patch Management – AWS is responsible for patching and fixing flaws within the infrastructure, but customers are responsible for patching their guest OS and applications.
- Configuration Management – AWS maintains the configuration of its infrastructure devices, but a customer is responsible for configuring their own guest operating systems, databases, and applications.
- Awareness & Training – AWS trains AWS employees, but a customer must train their own employees."
  —https://aws.amazon.com/compliance/shared-responsibility-model/

Microsoft differentiates responsibilities as follows

- Microsoft responsibilities
- Customer responsibilities
- Shared responsibilities where the focus for the physical aspects of the Infrastructure shifts from the customers to Microsoft.

Microsoft includes the following statement:
"Regardless of the type of deployment, the following responsibilities are always retained by you [the customer]:

- Data
- Endpoints
- Account
- Access management"
  —https://azure.microsoft.com/mediahandler/files/resourcefiles/
  shared-responsibility-for-cloud-computing/Shared%20
  Responsibility%20for%20Cloud%20Computing-2019-10-25.pdf

Every CSP has its own version of 'Shared Responsibility', which varies by CSP and type of services.

- Service Level Agreements (SLAs)

  SLAs are commonplace today. COBIT has a specific Objective or domain for SLAs called APO09 Managed Service Agreements.

  SLAs began as agreements, as contracts, that dealt with performance, quality, and availability. They included, among other aspects, Up Time, Mean Time Between Failures (MTBF), Mean Time to Repair or Recovery (MTTR), and so on.
  The essential characteristic of SLAs is an agreement between the Service Provider and the Customer. SLAs can be adapted for different services and

may be subject to negotiations with different customers requiring different characteristics that extend beyond quality and service timeliness. SLAs are an opportunity for customers to identify their expectations of their suppliers.

- System and Organization Control (SOC) Reports

SOC Reports "are designed to help service organizations that provide services to other entities, build trust and confidence in the service performed and controls related to the service through a report by an independent CPA." [—AICPA]

SOC Reports come in multiple formats, including

- SOC 1 – SOC for Service Organization: ICFR (Internal Controls for Financial Reporting)
- SOC 2 – SOC for Service Organization: Trust Services Criteria
- SOC 3 – SOC for Service Organization: Trust Services Criteria for General Use Report

SOC Reports are also discussed in detail in its own chapter below.

- Serverless Computing

Serverless Computing is a byproduct of the cloud model. Serverless computing merely means the CSP provisions and manages servers. One may see the terms Server-as-Code, Infrastructure-as-Code, and Configuration-as-Code. These terms highlight items that we traditionally considered physical elements which now exist in code that can be run whenever, wherever needed to generate servers, a particular infrastructure, or a particular configuration. This is the **Abstraction** of physical assets, as previously mentioned.

- Virtualization

Virtualization is an essential technology for CSPs. IBM provides several definitions and descriptions of Virtualization including:

Virtualization enables the hardware resources of a single computer—processors, memory, storage and more—to be divided into multiple virtual computers, called virtual machines (VMs).

Virtualization uses software [a hypervisor] to create an abstraction layer over computer hardware that allows the hardware ... to be divided into multiple virtual computers, commonly called virtual machines (VMs). Each VM runs its own operating system (OS) and behaves like an independent computer, even though it is running on just a portion of the actual underlying computer hardware.

... virtualization enables more efficient utilization of physical computer hardware ...

Today, virtualization is a standard practice in enterprise IT architecture. It is also the technology that drives cloud computing economics. Virtualization enables cloud providers to serve users with their existing physical computer hardware; it enables cloud users to purchase only the computing resources they need when they need it, and to scale those resources cost-effectively as their workloads grow.

—https://www.ibm.com/topics/virtualization

The mechanism that creates the abstraction layer is a hypervisor. Hypervisors allow CSPs to create virtual servers 'on-the-fly' as needed. The virtual servers are created from a cluster that spans multiple resources. The cluster is a unit under a single IP address, from which virtual servers, virtual storage, and virtual network (VNet) resources can be provisioned. Note, that a major benefit of clustering is fault tolerance. If a component in the cluster fails, the workload can be shifted to other components within the cluster without affecting the cluster as a whole.

AWS explains Virtualization as follows:

Virtualization is technology that you can use to create virtual representations of servers, storage, networks, and other physical machines. Virtual software mimics the functions of physical hardware to run multiple virtual machines simultaneously on a single physical machine. Businesses use virtualization to use their hardware resources efficiently and get greater returns from their investment. It also powers cloud computing services that help organizations manage infrastructure more efficiently.

By using virtualization, you can interact with any hardware resource with greater flexibility. Physical servers consume electricity, take up storage space, and need maintenance. You are often limited by physical proximity and network design if you want to access them. Virtualization removes all these limitations by abstracting physical hardware functionality into software. You can manage, maintain, and use your hardware infrastructure like an application on the web.

—https://aws.amazon.com/what-is/virtualization/

From a CSP's perspective, Clustering and Virtualization are key to efficient hardware utilization. Clustering provides flexibility, scalability, availability, performance, and fault tolerance at a reduced cost by spreading costs across multiple clients.

- Virtual Private Cloud (VPC)

VPCs are 'logically' isolated resources. Google Cloud calls these resources VPC. Microsoft's Azure calls them VNet.

Private Virtual Cloud can be either 'physically' or 'logically' isolated resources. They may or may not involve co-tenancy.

Abstraction

The term Abstraction derives from mathematics.

> **Abstraction** in mathematics is the process of extracting the underlying structures, patterns or properties of a mathematical concept, **removing any dependence on real world objects** with which it might originally have been connected, and generalizing it so that it has wider applications or matching among other abstract descriptions of equivalent phenomena. [Bold type added by author for emphasis.]
>
> —https://en.wikipedia.org/wiki/Abstraction_(mathematics)

In Computer Science, abstraction is defined as "the process of removing or generalizing physical, spatial, or temporal details or attributes ..." [—https://en.wikipedia.org/wiki/Abstraction_(computer_science)]

In the current context, Abstraction refers to replacing physical things, such as computers, servers, storage, etc., with logical virtual copies. In the process, customers lose contact with the physical elements. Their needs are satisfied by virtual resources. The characteristics are the same, at least from the customer's perspective; however, customers are completely removed from the physical layer. Customers provision assets, such as servers, storage, and networking services via a console. At some point, customers no longer care about physical infrastructure because they are isolated from it, but customers need to remember the basic requirements of servers to adequately provision them using the CSP's console.

The Challenges

First and foremost, the customer is relying on a third party for critical aspects of its operations, for its Data, and for its financial records. The third party has its own business objectives, which may, or may not, align with its customers' business objectives. Alignment, as previously mentioned, is critical not only inside an Enterprise but also between an Enterprise and its suppliers.

Second, a major challenge for businesses is maintaining expertise. While 'Self-service' is part of the NIST's Essential Characteristics, to adequately exercise 'self-service', customers need to have sufficient in-house or outsourced expertise to know how to appropriately use 'self-service'. If most, if not all, of the IT expertise disappears when customers move their workloads to the cloud, customers can lose the knowledge of how to configure and maintain adequate cloud services. This loss is more difficult when it involves IaaS and PaaS than it is when the services are SaaS. In the case of SaaS, customers are interacting with applications instead of raw computing resources insulating them from the raw computing resources.

Third, the customer must recognize the nature of the 'shared responsibilities' and have sufficient expertise to adequately handle 'shared responsibilities'.

This boils down to two aspects:

- Dependence on a third party for critical operational systems
- Potential lack of IT expertise to appropriately utilize 'self-service' and to adequately fulfill 'shared responsibilities.'

Both circumstances can be serious problems for customers, especially for smaller businesses that adopt cloud resources to decrease their internal IT workload.

IT Audit Considerations

IT Audit Considerations include at least the following:

- What cloud services and resources are the Enterprise using?
- Do the CSPs have SOC Reports for the services and resources the Enterprise is using?
- Do the SOC Reports contain items that are challenging for Enterprise management?
- Does the Enterprise have access to appropriate in-house or outsourced expertise to manage its supplier relationships, including fulfilling its 'shared responsibilities'?
- What IT assets, resources, and services remain in the Enterprise?
- Does the Enterprise have access to sufficient expertise to appropriately manage its on-premises IT assets and resources?

Potential Internal Controls

Potential Internal Controls include at least the following:

- First and foremost, obtaining SOC reports and examining their contents for potential Risks to the Enterprise and limitations on the CSP's services.
- Second, having an accurate, up-to-date inventory of the services, assets, and resources used by the Enterprise. This includes contracts, SLAs, 'Shared Responsibility' documents, and other relevant documents related to the services, assets, and resources provided by CSPs and the customer's obligations related to these services.
- Formal arrangements that include either in-house staff and/or outsourced resources that enable the Enterprise to effectively use and manage the CSP's resources.
- Incident Management 'tickets' for all CSP-related issues, questions, challenges, and problems properly tagged for review and potential Problem Management resolution, if the incidents have implications beyond the 'one off'.

The challenge for IT Audit is to confirm the following:

- That the services, assets, and resources are relevant and consistent with the Enterprise's Business Objectives, strategy, and current and future plans.
- That the Enterprise has access to sufficient resources to manage the services, assets, and resources received from the CSP and its relationship with the CSP. Outsourcing does not absolve the Enterprise of its responsibilities to itself and its utilization of outsourced services and resources.

Reminders

The overall trend is toward increasing reliance on cloud resources, which *Abstract* what were previously physical assets and processes. *Abstraction* may lead to less in-house IT expertise and make adequate oversight more difficult, a 'perfect storm'.

Chapter 8

Enterprise Business Systems (EBS)

Chapter Contents:

Introduction to Enterprise Business Systems (EBS)

Enterprise Business Systems (EBS) are essential for business operations. These systems run businesses large and small. They enable online retailers to process many orders. They enable manufacturing companies to control their operations. They enable distributors and retailers to keep track of their inventories. They enable banks to keep track of their customers' deposits and withdrawals.

These systems are large, general in nature, and designed to handle a broad range of clients. Their goal is to automate core business processes. Once installed and in operation, companies rely on these systems to satisfy their Business Objectives. These Enterprises and their systems become intertwined and inseparable.

Try to imagine Amazon without its mammoth order processing capability. Or try to imagine an airline without its systems to handle passenger reservations, aircraft scheduling, and crew scheduling. Or try to imagine a bank without its banking systems. These systems are closely linked with the operations they support. When these systems fail, business operations stop.

These systems can be developed or purchased. Since the 1980s, purchasing or subscribing has been the predominant theme. The sellers of these systems

DOI: 10.4324/9781032689388-8

include, in alphabetical order, Deltek, Epicor, IFS, Infor, Microsoft, Oracle, Net-Suite, Sage, SalesForce, SAP, SYSPRO, and Workday to name but a few.

These systems may be referred to as:

- Enterprise Resource Planning systems (ERP)
- Customer Relationship Management systems (CRM)
- Material Requirements Planning systems (MRP)
- Master Production Scheduling systems (MPS) and Advanced Production Scheduling (APS)
- Inventory Management systems (IMS)
- Computer-aided Manufacturing systems (CAM)
- Supply Chain Management systems (SCM)
- Product Lifecycle Management systems (PLM)

Major Themes of Enterprise Business Systems (EBS)

System Design

These systems are designed to operate basic business processes, such as procurement, sales, inventory management, manufacturing, accounting, and so on. Their traditional 'sweet spot' was discrete manufacturing; however, today, these behemoths have spread beyond their initial design points. Who would have guessed that the Hollywood Studios would embrace a German manufacturing system, SAP, as their ERP system?

Other EBS are designed for specific applications, such as inventory control, production scheduling, Data collection, time entry, CRM, Field Service Management (FSM), routing and delivery, product development, payroll, human resources/human capital, online web sales, point of sale, and so on.

Over the years, ERP has grown horizontally, adding new features and functions, and vertically adding more special use cases to support the broadest customer base possible. This is not to say that some ERP systems are not specialized and grew by adding more special use cases as opposed to more applications. Many of these systems date back to the 1980s and 1990s, which means they have stood the test of time both in terms of dependability and a robust set of features and functions.

From the IT Audit perspective, these systems are critical because they control business behavior. They are also critical because they generate, contain, and use the business' Data for their operations. Ultimately this Data is the foundation for the Enterprise's operations, accounting, financial reporting and strategic planning.

Acquisition

As mentioned above, these systems can be purchased or custom-developed. In the early days of computing, much of this type of software was custom-developed, but over time, the tide changed to the selection and implementation of Commercial-Off-The-Shelf (COTS) systems. In special situations, Enterprises may elect to self-develop applications, but the commercially available alternatives captured the market.

Regardless of whether the systems are custom developed or purchased or leased, IT Auditors need to be familiar with Software Development Life Cycle (SDLC) methodologies and the selection and implementation of commercial packaged software. The larger the Enterprise the more likely the business is to have multiple packages with components that were specifically developed for them, i.e., customized.

Selection and Implementation

While the Selection and Implementation of Enterprise Business Software will be covered in detail in the chapter on IT Acquisition Policies and Procedures, an element to keep in mind at this point is the long-term effects of system selection, and their 'long-tails'. These systems are not easily replaced. Hence, poor selection decisions in this area can impact Enterprises for decades to come. It is hard to understate the importance of 'getting it suitable' given the complexity of these systems.

From an IT Audit perspective, the Enterprise should have processes for Selecting, Developing, and Implementing new business applications. The good news is that 'COTS' systems have decades of experience and maturity. They are feature and function-rich. They have many customers, and many implementations. Over time the inevitable errors were eliminated, and functionality expanded. Functionality has expanded to the point where if the system 'out of the box' is not quite 'right' the system can be configured to work appropriately.

The primary driver of system selection is business requirements.

- What is needed?
- What is wanted?
- What is expected?
- What limitations restrict choice?

Together these factors form the basis for an appropriate selection.

'Requirements drift' is normal, especially in hypercompetitive markets where businesses are constantly looking for an edge over the competition. This means over time requirements may change, may 'drift'. This can affect the selection, this can affect implementation, and almost certainly will affect future maintenance, nothing is forever.

A major implementation activity is configuration. Configuration determines how systems behave, and how they operate. Getting configurations correct before putting systems into Production is prudent. If some requirements are missed, re-configuration or re-design, in the case of companies that develop their own applications, will hopefully fix these issues.

Another issue during selection and implementation is 'bending'. Will the system bend to the business, or will the business bend to the system? Bending the system to the business, especially if this involves customization, can have future repercussions. So, thought, effort, and clarity are important in implementing new systems. As a practical matter, both may occur. The system may bend to the business and the business may also bend to the system, a meeting in the middle.

IT Auditors need to be able to confirm that system selection and implementation or development is managed according to the Enterprise's IT policies, procedures, and standards established for these activities.

Application Controls

From the IT Audit perspective, the two most significant aspects of EBS are the dependability of business process automation and the internal controls, which are built into the automation to control system behavior. COSO refers to these controls as 'Application Controls'. They regulate system behavior. They determine what is permitted and what is not permitted. They determine how exceptions will be handled.

For example, consider three-way matching and credit limit checking. In the case of three-way matching, vendor invoices are only paid if the Purchase Order, the Receiver, and the Invoice reconcile. If not, the controls determine how the inequality will be handled, whether the matching portions are paid and/or the inequalities are referred for special handling. In the case of credit limit checking, Sales Orders are processed only when sufficient commercial credit is available. Orders that exceed available credit are referred for special handling. In the first case, the Enterprise is prevented from paying invoices that do not reconcile with their Purchase Orders and Receivers. In the second case, the Enterprise is prevented from selling goods and services to customers without available commercial credit. Both are preventive mechanisms.

IT Auditors need to understand these internal controls and their purposes and be able to confirm their effectiveness.

EBS from Three Perspectives

EBS can be viewed from several different perspectives:

* Business Entities
* Business Processes
* Configurability

Entities are the subjects of actions, in this case, the subjects of business processes. For example, Customers purchase Products from Suppliers. In this example, the entities are the Customers, the Suppliers, and the Products. Typical Entities include Customers, Suppliers, Products, Employees, Locations, Currencies, Units of Measure, literally every object involved in Business Processes.

Business Process is the 'sweet spot' for ERP/EBS software. These processes are the Enterprise's engines for income, costs, and activities. They control how processes occur from initiation to completion, step by step. These processes may be described in terms of workflows. The process may go from beginning to end in a matter of minutes or take days or months or longer to complete depending upon the process. Typical business processes include Buying, Selling, Making, and Stocking of Products and Services, and many more. These are the transactions that are summarized in the business' Financial Statements, especially the Income Statement.

The Internal Controls related to Entities and Processes ensure the integrity of the Enterprise's processes and Data. They keep the Enterprise on track, operating according to its goals and objectives.

Configurability is crucial because it determines how processes occur and how entities are established and maintained. These systems allow for variation, many variations. For example, inadequate commercial credit can be handled in a variety of ways including asking for a payment to decrease outstanding debt, or increasing the credit limit either temporarily or permanently, or shipping the order Collect on Delivery (COD), or some other mechanism. In addition, these alternatives can be applied differently to different customers, different customer classes, and different products and services. This is merely a short list to illustrate system flexibility.

Configurations ...

- Enable systems to be tailored to specific operational needs and requirements.
- Provide flexibility to adjust these systems as needs and requirements change over time, i.e., requirements drift.

EBS are massive pieces of business application software with a myriad of alternatives built into the software to make EBS comprehensive, flexible, and competitive. Configurability allows Enterprises to choose among the alternatives provided enabling the system's behavior to be adjusted to accommodate current and future requirements.

Given the sheer size of these systems, these systems include thousands of potential configurations with which customers must contend. This is one reason why these systems are difficult, expensive, and time-consuming to implement.

Another aspect of configuration is misconfiguration, which may or may not be obvious when the system goes into 'Production'. If misconfigurations show up after the system is in Production, often through Incident Management, hopefully, re-configuration will resolve these situations, but not always. In this case, IT Auditors need to know if the re-configuration was successful without creating new problems.

IT Audit Considerations

From the IT Audit perspective, the importance of EBS cannot be understated. These systems contain the business transactions. This is 'where the action is'.

While General IT Controls focus on the integrity of the environment on which the systems operate, Application Internal Controls address business process integrity and Data integrity.

Big IT Audit Questions for EBS include at least the following:

- Are the EBS configured according to Enterprise Business Objectives? (Alignment)
- Are the Internal Controls that are built into the application software implemented suitably, and effectively in terms of Enterprise Business Objectives? (Application Controls)
- Do gaps exist between needs and requirements and system functionality? (Gap Analysis)
- Are changes to EBS configurations managed to ensure continuing conformance with Enterprise Business Objectives? (Change Management, Monitoring, and Conformance)
- Do significant business processes occur outside of Enterprise Business Software? If so, what internal controls ensure process integrity and Data integrity for these processes? (Integrity)
- Are the Entities in the EBS established and maintained consistent with Enterprise Business Objectives? (Alignment)
- Under what circumstances are Entities established and maintained outside the application controls of the Enterprise Business Software, if any? (Integrity)
- Do EBS processed transactions occur in accordance with Enterprise Business Goals and Objectives? (Alignment)
- Under what circumstances is transaction processing overridden or processed partially or completely outside the application controls of the Enterprise Business Software? (Exception Processing)
- Are the application controls effective? Do they work as required? (Effectiveness)
- Were the application controls in effect continuously throughout the audit period? (In Effect)

IT Audit Challenges

The biggest challenge regarding Enterprise Business Software (EBS) is understanding its Internal Controls. These controls are inherent in these systems whether the systems are leased, purchased, or custom-developed. Each configuration represents an Application Control either directly or indirectly, which means these systems, which span multiple business processes, potentially have thousands of Internal Controls.

The next biggest challenge in EBS is appropriately implementing the systems to properly handle normal operations and typical variations. One place where complexity is obvious to casual users is the information provided by online retailers regarding their products and services. Today these platforms provide descriptions, images, videos, instructions, specifications, cross-selling, up-selling, and various service options, such as establishing recurring orders for consumables. That is a lot of information to enable users to determine the appropriateness of their purchases in contrast to bricks-and-mortar retail, where users can physically browse the objects they are considering.

Generally, the sheer size and complexity of these systems make them extremely complex. They require sophisticated IT Auditors to understand the Business processes, Business Objectives, and Constraints, and determine the appropriateness of the designs to satisfy these needs and requirements and their ultimate effectiveness.

Business Automation Trends

The biggest trend is increasing amounts of automation. This is occurring along different dimensions.

- First, EBS continue to add features and functions in response to customer requests and changing business conditions. For example, a major change occurred when these systems switched from flat file structures to databases making the Data independent of the application and accessible outside the application. Another major change was designing these systems to operate continuously, with no time to shut them down for batch processing.
- Second, manual processes and procedures traditionally handled outside of EBSs are increasingly being automated by either bringing the processes into the EBS or implementing Robotic Process Automation (RPA). The objective is simply to automate every business process possible including processes that would otherwise be manual processes.
- Third, business process software is becoming more intelligent.

Over the years, MRP became increasingly sophisticated as Enterprises manage their inventories for distribution and manufacturing. The evidence of this transition is easy to see on a comparative basis. Compare today's Item Master files with those of ERP systems decades ago. The increased number of Item Master features and functions is evident even in small manufacturing systems. In one small system, over 30 separate Data entry screens relate to the Item Master. In terms of magnitude, with 10–20 or more Data elements per screen, that is 300–500 or more Data elements related to Items, to those not involved in manufacturing this number of Data elements may be incomprehensible.

- Fourth, Artificial Intelligence (AI) is becoming part of EBS.

  Processes are becoming more intelligent, and their Data is becoming more accessible. AI can automatically survey an Enterprise's entire dataset and suggest changes that are not otherwise obvious. To the extent, the AI has access to Data beyond the Enterprise; it can compare the Enterprise to the market in general and potentially to specific competitors and advise the Enterprise what and when to make products.

  To the extent that today's marketplace could be described as hypercompetitive, AI stands to make the marketplace even more hypercompetitive as businesses are able to compare their operations with their competitors in realtime. In this case, you have your AI and I have my AI, and the two AI are focused on outsmarting each other. Where does this end?

- Fifth, AI is becoming a tool for IT Audit as well. IT Auditors are already using AI to draft IT Audit programs and to evaluate controls. These uses will only increase over time and will increase the sophistication of IT Audit.

The increasing role of automation makes the job of IT Auditing more complex and demands more sophisticated IT Auditors. When AI becomes omnipresent, IT Auditors will also need the skills and tools to evaluate the AIs in terms of their design, the appropriateness of their analysis and recommendations, and their alignment with Enterprise Business Objectives.

Chapter 9

Auditing Data

Chapter Contents:

Introduction

In the era of Artificial Intelligence (AI), Data Analytics, Data Science, Evidence-based Decisions, and Enterprise Business Information Suites, **the importance and value of Data is impossible to understate**. Data is the currency

DOI: 10.4324/9781032689388-9

of the 21st century. Data is business' life blood. Data enables businesses to operate. Data records business operations. Data both facilitates business processes and records business transactions. Data is, as such, a significant byproduct of business processes. Data is an inherent part of business.

Data Governance

Data Governance is a subset of IT Governance, which is a subset of Corporate Governance. To understand the scope of Data Governance, consider the following definitions, which include different topics emphasizing different aspects of Data Governance.

The Data Governance Institute defines Data Governance as:

> a system of decision rights and accountabilities for information-related processes, executed according to agreed-upon models which describe who can take what actions with what information, and when, under what circumstances, using what methods.
>
> —https://datagovernance.com/governance-and-decision-making/

The Data Management Association (DAMA) defines Data Governance as:

> Data Governance provides direction and oversight for data management by establishing a system of decision rights over data that accounts for the needs of the enterprise.
>
> —*DAMA-DMBOK2*, 2nd edition, DAMA, 2017, p. 45

> Data Governance (DG) is the exercise of authority and control (planning, monitoring, and enforcement) over the management of data assets.
>
> —*DAMA-DMBOK2*, 2nd edition, DAMA, 2017, p. 67

DAMA identifies eight domains related to Data Governance:

- Data Strategy
- Data Policy
- Data Standards and Quality
- Data Oversight
- Data Compliance
- Data Issue Management
- Data Management Projects
- Data Asset Valuation

> —*DAMA-DMBOK2*, 2nd edition, DAMA, 2017, p. 68

The following quote nicely summarizes Data Governance.

> ... planning, oversight, and control over management of data and the use of data and data-related sources.
> – https://www.cio.com/article/202183/what-is-data-governance-a-best-practices-framework-for-managing-data-assets.html, citing DAMA

The Government Accountability Office (GAO) provides a government perspective of Data Governance:

> Data governance is the framework or structure for ensuring that an agency's data assets are transparent, accessible, and of sufficient quality to support its mission, improve the efficiency and effectiveness of agency operations, and provide useful information to the public.
> —GAO highlights, *Data Governance: Agencies Made Progress in Establishing Governance, but Need to Address Key Milestones*, GAO, December 2020, p. 1

Gartner provides yet another viewpoint listing Seven Key Foundations for Data Governance:

- Data Trust
- Data Transparency and Ethics
- Data Risk and Security
- Data Education and Training
- Collaboration and Culture regarding Data
- Data Accountability and Decision Rights
- Data Value and Outcomes
  —https://www.gartner.com/smarterwithgartner/7-key-foundations-for-modern-data-and-analytics-governance

To summarize, Data Governance is the system of policies, procedures, practices, standards, and formalities that affect Data. Data Governance is part of IT Governance, which is a part of Corporate Governance making Data Governance ultimately part of Corporate Governance.

Data Governance is the insistence by the Enterprise that the Enterprise's Data meet the following criteria:

- Data is suitable to operate the Business.
- Data accurately represents business operations and activities.
- Data is suitable for analytical purposes and for evidence-based decisions.

Enterprise Data comes from two sources:

- Data may be captured or generated by businesses' internal operations.
- Data may be acquired by businesses from external third parties, such as Data Brokers.

Internal Data, which is under the control of the Business, ought to be of appropriate Quality. If it is not, shame on the Business. Poor Quality Data leads one to wonder about that Business' commitment to IT and to its Data.

When Data is acquired from third parties, there is no guarantee; there may be assurances, but every download can contain surprises. Hence, Businesses are obligated to do what they must do to bring the external Data into conformity with their Businesses' Data Quality standards.

From an IT Audit standpoint, Data Quality policies, procedures, practices, and standards are essential to Data Governance, to Businesses, and a critical area for IT Audit.

Data-Related Concepts

Every domain has its own terminology. Data is no exception. IT Auditors should be familiar with the following terms and definitions:

Data Literacy is fluency and knowledge of Data. It includes the ability to explore Data, to understand Data, to analyze Data, and ultimately to communicate about Data. It also includes the ability to use Data to understand reality. The latter idea was popularized in the COVID pandemic phrase: 'What does the Data say?'

Data Compliance refers to external Data requirements, such as Data security, privacy, and confidentiality. Data Compliance typically involves regulations by governmental and non-governmental entities, for example, Health Insurance Portability and Accountability Act (HIPAA) from the U.S. Department of Health and Human Services and PCI-DSS from the Payment Card Industry Security Standards Council®.

Data Council, or a similarly named body, is responsible for overseeing all aspects of Data in an Enterprise. The Data Council is an Enterprise's Data oversight body.

High-Quality Data sets the gold standard for Data, namely Data that is Accurate, Correct, Consistent, Reliable, Timely, Valid, and in effect 'Fit for its Intended Purpose'. [—Thomas C. Redman, *Data Driven: The Field Guide*, Boston: Digital Press, 2001, page 73.]

Data Access Policies are critical to Data protection. These policies grant and restrict access to Data and its storage facilities.

Data Architecture is the plan, the design, for Data. It identifies at least the various components of Data, their interrelationships, their various storage facilities, and their potential uses.

Data Models are the schemes that identify Data and their interrelationships, and their various storage facilities. Databases are typically based on these Models.

Single Source of Truth (SSOT) is a philosophy and practice for aggregating Data into a central repository so that everyone in a Business sees and bases their decisions on the same Data. The opposite is decision-makers who have their own private stashes of Data that support their viewpoints. When it comes time to making decisions, having multiple versions of truth makes decision-making difficult.

Data Strategy is the Enterprise's Plans and Strategy with respect to Data.

Strategic decision-making emphasizes evidence-based decisions, especially strategic decisions that have long-range implications.

Stakeholder Alignment, in this context, focuses on Data consistent with the needs and requests of Enterprise stakeholders be they senior executives, managers, users, or others.

Data Management Frameworks

Data Management Frameworks are not as well-known as IT Frameworks; however, the DAMA's *DAMA-DMBOK2, Data Management Association-Data Management Body of Knowledge*, (recently revised) is widely recognized within the Data Management and Data Wrangling communities. *DAMA-DMBOK2* is an important resource for IT Audit.

Consider the following definitions and models from DAMA and the EDM Council.

DAMA defines Data Management as:

> ... the development, execution, and supervision of plans, policies, programs, and practices that deliver, control, protect, and enhance the value of data and information assets throughout their lifecycles.
>
> —*DAMA-DMBOK2*, 2nd edition, DAMA, 2017, p. 17

The EDM Council has several different Data Management Models, including Data Management Capability Assessment Model (DCAM) and Cloud Data Management Capabilities (CDMC).

The EDM Council's DCAM teaches:

1. Data Strategy & Business Case
2. Data Management Program & Funding
3. Business & Data Architecture
4. Data & Technology Architecture
5. Data Quality Management
6. Data Governance
7. Data Control Environment
8. Analytics Management

—https://edmcouncil.org/frameworks/dcam/

The EDM Council's CDMC teaches:

1. Data Control Compliance
2. Cataloguing & Classification
3. Accessibility & Usage

4. Protection & Privacy
5. Data Lifecycle
6. Data & Technical Architecture

And the CDMC also teaches:

1. Data Compliance
2. Data Catalog Field Ownership
3. Authoritative Data Sources and Provision Points
4. Data Sovereignty and Cross-Border Movement
5. Cataloguing
6. Classification
7. Entitlements and Access for Sensitive Data
8. Data Consumption Purpose
9. Appropriate Security Controls
10. Data Protection Impact Assessment
11. Data Retention, Archiving, and Purging
12. Data Quality Measurement
13. Cost Metrics
14. Data Lineage

—https://edmcouncil.org/frameworks/cdmc/

DAMA uses a wheel metaphor to identify the following aspects of Data Management (Figure 9.1):

- Data architecture
- Data modeling and design
- Data storage and operations
- Data security
- Data integration and interoperability
- Documents and content
- Reference and master data
- Data warehousing and business intelligence (BI)
- Metadata
- Data quality

The point is not to overwhelm but to illustrate different viewpoints regarding Data and its Management.

At the risk of oversimplification, consider the following short list:

- Data Administration and Governance, including Data Management
- Data Architecture, Design, and Modeling, including Metadata, Data cataloging, and Data classification
- Data Quality and Data Integrity characteristics and controls

Figure 9.1 DAMA Data Governance Wheel. Reproduced with Permission of DAMA. *DAMA-DMBOK2*, 2nd edition, DAMA, 2017, p. 36.

- Data Access Controls
- Data Ownership, Custody, and Use, including accountability, data analysis, and evidence-based decision-making

Data Management

Data Management is the administrative aspects of Data, being under the general oversight of Data Governance. Data Administration includes the Enterprise's policies, procedures, practices, and standards that apply to Data and their enforcement.
Consider the following general Data Management domains.

Data Architecture, Data Design, Data Modeling Domain

Every business has a Design for its Data. The design may be intentional or accidental, explicit or implicit. An intentional design is typically explicit, the result of a software development project or a specific IT Audit. However, given the pervasiveness of commercial business software today, the more likely scenario, at least for non-technology companies, is an accidental implicit design. The Design is both accidental and implicit in the sense that the Design was derived from the commercial software, for example, the determination of a specific data storage methodology. Implementing the software meant implementing the Data Design implicit in the application software.

A third alternative is multiple Data Designs by virtue of a combination of different systems each with its own Data architecture. This alternative is the most demanding for IT.

Typically, a Data Architecture is expressed in a Data Model, which is a combination of diagrams and narrative. The basic contents of the model include:

- Enumeration of the Datasets and their Data Elements
- Interrelationships among the Datasets and their Data Elements
- Business Rules associated with the Datasets and their Data Elements
- Data Storage methods
- Sources and Uses of the Data operationally, analytically, and for reporting

Given the importance of Data Models and Data Modeling, this topic is covered in its own chapter.

Regardless of their origins, the Data Designs and Models are key to IT Auditing whether the Audit is a general IT Audit or a Data-specific Audit.

The Models provide a comprehensive window into the Enterprise's Business Data, its generation, its storage, and its uses inside and outside the systems that generate the Data.

Data Storage and Databases Domain

As with Data Architectures, Data Storage and Databases may be the result of deliberate software development processes or the consequences of business systems selections. Regardless of the origins of the Data Storage methods and tools, the topic of storage comes into play when Data is imported into or exported out of their host systems, or business Data is viewed directly in their repositories.

Inside business systems, Applications Controls manage the Data including its Quality and Integrity. While the Data is sufficient for systems operations, that does not necessarily mean that Data will be useful for other purposes outside the systems without some effort, which could compromise Data Quality and Data Integrity.

Data Availability and Data Access Controls Domain

Data Availability and Access Controls are interrelated. Data is Available to users and for uses depending on Access Rights. Access Rights enforce specific privileges, which can be broad or narrow. Typically, they are based on the principle of 'Least Privilege' and Segregation of Incompatible Duties (SOD). They include the functions that generate, collect, store, and use Data.

Data Availability includes Data that is exported from its host systems for uses outside these systems.

IT Audit questions related to Data Availability and Data Access include:

- How is Data Availability controlled inside of its host Applications and Systems?
- How is Data Availability controlled and used outside of its host Applications and Systems?
- Is Data exported? By whom? By what processes? For what purposes?
- Is Data imported? By whom? By what processes? For what purposes?
- What limitations are imposed on Data outside of their hosts?

Two Primary Data Uses Cases

Discussions regarding Data often evolve around two basic interrelated Use Cases.

The first Use Case deals with the question of *Source*, from where did the Data come?

- Is Data generated, collected, and processed by Enterprise Business Systems, or
- Is Data acquired from third parties outside of the Enterprise?

The second Use Case deals with *Usability*, how is the Data used?

- Does the Data perform suitably in the Enterprise Business Systems?
- Does the Data perform suitably outside the Enterprise's Business Systems for other uses?

In the case of internal Data, the assumption is that the Data performs suitably in the business systems within which it lives. If not, fix the systems. If the Data originates outside the Enterprise, its quality and usefulness could be an open question with no fixed answer, sometimes okay and sometimes not okay.

In the Usability Use Case, while the Data performs suitably in the Enterprise Systems where it lives, this is no guarantee it is 'fit for other purposes'. The Data may be incomplete or misleading for other purposes and therefore not 'fit for other purposes'. It all depends. Data wrangling may be required to organize and enhance the Data to make it useful outside of their host systems. For example, Theatre Box Office Data is sufficient for distributing the box office receipts, but box office Data is insufficient for film scheduling, where genera, franchise, stars, ratings, producers, studios, and so on play important roles in determining which films to show when and where.

Data Quality and Integrity Domain

Data Quality and Integrity are major concerns for businesses and IT Audit. Is the Data suitable for operations? Is the Data suitable for decision-making? Data Quality and Integrity include at least the following elements:

- Accuracy
- Correctness
- Appropriateness
- Cleanliness
- Completeness
- Consistency
- Dependability and Reliability
- Trustworthiness
- Validity and Verifiability
- Adequately Protected
- Managed, Assessed, Evaluated, and Documented

For a more detailed discussion of these qualities, see the discussion below in the section on Auditing Data. Also, keep in mind the expression Garbage In Garbage Out (GIGO), which used to be a common expression. Today that idea might be rephrased as Garbage In Bad Decisions Out.The key to good decision is 'good' Data.

Quality and Integrity are arguably the most important aspects of Data. Lacking this characteristic, operations lack integrity, analyses can be inaccurate, and decisions can be incorrect. The negative implications are too numerous to name. An open question with AI is the effect of 'poor' or misleading Data on the AI. How does the AI handle compromised Data? Does the AI recognize the Data is compromised? Remember AI is based on the Data it 'sees', the Data on which it was trained.

The point of Data Wrangling is to make the Data more useable by repositioning it, by cleaning it, by enhancing it, by organizing it and re-organizing it, by analyzing it; all of this without diminishing the Quality, the Integrity, or the Value of the Data.

Data Challenges

Master Data Management (MDM)

MDM addresses standardization and consistency across an Enterprise. Master Data is Reference Data that is used to identify entities and processes. An example is a Customer and their Orders where the Customer deals with different parts of the Enterprise, which are independent of each other. In this scenario, Customers may have different identifiers, IDs, in different parts of the Enterprise.

Gartner defines Master Data as follows:

Master data management (MDM) is a technology-enabled discipline in which business and IT work together to ensure the uniformity, accuracy, stewardship, semantic consistency and accountability of the enterprise's official shared master data assets. Master data is the consistent and uniform set of identifiers and extended attributes that describes the core entities of the enterprise including customers, prospects, citizens, suppliers, sites, hierarchies and chart of accounts.

—https://www.gartner.com/en/information-technology/glossary/
master-data-management-mdm, August 2023

Informatica offers an alternate definition:

Master data management (MDM) involves creating a single master record for each person, place, or thing in a business, from across internal and external data sources and applications. This information has been de-duplicated, reconciled and enriched, becoming a consistent, reliable source. Once created, this master data serves as a trusted view of business-critical data that can be managed and shared across the business to promote accurate reporting, reduce data errors, remove redundancy, and help workers make better-informed business decisions.

—https://www.informatica.com/resources/articles/
what-is-master-data-management.html, August 2023

IT Audit questions related to Master Data and MDM include:

- Are entities and processes identified consistently across the Enterprise?
- Do identical entities and processes have the same or different identifiers in different systems?
- If the identifiers are different in different systems, how are these differences managed?
- When Data is obtained from external sources and imported into Enterprise Data Storage, are the identifiers consistent with or different than the Enterprise's identifiers? If different, how are these differences managed?

Note: GUIDs (Globally Unique Identifiers) are a great help. The primary problem is whether they exist. VIN (Vehicle Identification Numbers), UPC (Universal Product Codes), GTIN (Global Trade Item Numbers), postal codes, telephone area codes, and MAC (Media Access Control) numbers are examples of GUIDs. GUIDs are often used in a limited context, for example, GUID means unique within a specific system, such as state or province vehicle license plates.

Standardization and Consistency

Standardization can be a challenge for multi-entity businesses as noted above, especially when the entities operate autonomously. Getting Enterprise agreement and compliance can be challenging. This challenge extends to imported Data as well. External Data will be in whatever forms and formats it is and the entity importing the Data may have different standards or no standards at all. Take a simple example, dates can be expressed in a variety of formats with and without timestamps. Consider a 24-hour clock versus a 12-hour clock. Naming conventions can also easily vary, including how entities, processes, and files are named.

The easiest approach is for a Business to have consistency standards and enforce them. If this is not possible, then conversion and cross-reference methods may be employed.

Relevant IT Audit questions include:

- Does the Enterprise have Data Consistency Standards?
- Are these Standards enforced?
- How does the Enterprise deal with differences, especially differences involving master data such as entity, process, and file identifiers?
- Do the differences compromise or limit the value of the Data?

Relative to the last question, Value may depend on how the Data is used or can be used.

Auditing Data

Data may be Audited as part of a general IT Audit or as a specific Data Audit. Either way, major IT Audit questions relating to Data include:

- Is Data Governance present and active? Does the Enterprise effectively comply with its Data Governance requirements? Are they adequate?
- Is Enterprise Data suitable for operations, analysis, decision-making, and other uses?
- Do Data Architecture/Models/Structures exist? Are they appropriate and suitably documented?
- Is Data Quality suitable for Enterprise purposes?
- Is external Data adequately reviewed and cleaned to ensure Data Quality and Data Integrity?
- Is Confidential, Sensitive, and Personally Identifiable Information (PII) suitably catalogued and protected especially from unauthorized access and use?
- Is the Data Accurate? Valid? Relevant?
- Is the Data Usable? Under what conditions?
- What processes ensure Accuracy and Usability?
- What happens to Data that does not meet these requirements?

Specific Data Qualities that IT Audit should consider when evaluating Data and its Usability include at least the following:

Accuracy

If the Data comes from Enterprise systems, one expects the Data to be accurate. If not, why not? To what degree is Data inaccurate? Is the Data accurate for business purposes, for operational purposes, for decision-making purposes? The Data may be sufficient for operations but not sufficient for decision-making.

If the Data comes from outside of the Enterprise, it may be accurate or inaccurate depending upon its source, and the accuracy may fluctuate from one import to another. Either way, the Business is obligated to do whatever is needed to bring the Data into compliance with Business standards. Lacking that ability, the Data may be quarantined or deleted. The least desirable outcome is corrupting good Data.

Correctness

Correctness is like accuracy but different. Accuracy deals with precision, whereas correctness deals with truthfulness. In an extreme case, Data may be accurate but not truthful. Accuracy generally deals with measurement while Correctness is being free of errors, mistakes, faults, or misleading.

Thinking ahead to decision-making, is the Data in question misleading or misrepresentative because it is incorrect, inaccurate, or incomplete?

Completeness

Completeness comes in degrees, as with accuracy. The Data may be complete for one purpose but not for another.

Why the difference between operations and decision-making? Because decision-making demands on the Data may be more strenuous, more extensive, than operational demands. Often Data is enhanced to support decision-making. A simple example, obtaining Data that resides outside of the Business' systems regarding a Business' competition to provide a broader, more complete basis for decisions.

Consistency

Consistency can be along several different dimensions. Recall MDM, which is one criterion. Other criteria include Data Format, Data Attributes, time stamps, and so on.

An interesting Data Consistency problem involves anomaly detection. In this use case, Data is inspected for unusual or unexpected situations, including the absence of something that is normally present or the unexpected presence of something that is normally absent, or outside of normal ranges. If the Data is in a SQL database, which is often the case with business data, searching for missing or null values is straightforward; however, a blank value does not indicate whether a value actually exists or not. Orphan records are another anomaly. Another perspective on Consistency is General Consistency across an entire Enterprise as opposed to Application Consistency, which is limited to a specific Application.

Standardization is one way to enforce consistency.

Relevant

Relevance deals with use, purpose, and appropriateness. Does the Data address the topic or question at hand? Is the Data relevant to the questions being raised, to the decisions being made?

Timely

Is the Data timely?

Data and Time include several use cases.

- Is the Data up to date?
- Is the Data complete within a specific date range?

    Accounting has the concept of 'cutoff'. Cutoff asks when a transaction should be recognized. The basic questions are: When are transactions recognized? When do they occur? When are they recorded? When are they effective?

- Does the Quality or Usefulness of Data decline over time?

    Is the Data no longer relevant? Has the Data deteriorated? Does the Data lose predictiveness over time?

- Does Data change over time?

    Does the Data become more complete with the passage of time, such as Sales Order processing which may extend over days, weeks, or even months between order receipt and item shipment?

Validity

Validity and Verifiability are closely associated. Can the Validity of the Data be Verified? Validity implies standards, and criteria; Verifiability measures the Data's conformance with those standards.

Suitable for Intended Purpose

All Data Quality characteristics may be summed up with T. C. Redman's phrase 'fit for intended uses'. [—Thomas C Redman, *Data Driven: The Field Guide*, Boston: Digital Press, 2001, p. 73.]

The notion of 'fitness' pulls together all characteristics of Data Quality based on how the Data will be used as opposed to certain intrinsic qualities. Similar terms are 'appropriate use' and 'suitable use'. Applying the appropriateness and suitability criteria to the use of Data focuses attention on how Data is used. This means working backward from use to determine quality, appropriateness, and suitability.

Data Protection

Is the Data adequately protected? Is the Data adequately protected in terms of conformance with business policies and standards and is the Data adequately protected in terms of compliance with external regulations?

In summary, Data is the 'fuel' that powers the 21st Century business.For IT Audit guidance, the objective is to advise and assist the Enterprise in the generation, maintenance, and use of Data. For IT Audit assessment, the objective is to confirm that Data meets the needs of the Enterprise.

Chapter 10

Auditing IT Resource Acquisition

Chapter Contents:

Introduction to IT Acquisition

IT Acquisition may be referred to as IT Resource Acquisition, IT Solution Acquisition, or Technology Acquisition. The emphasis is shifting from buying 'bits and pieces' to buying solutions. Even the concept of buying is morphing from buying to subscribing, leasing, or renting resources, especially cloud-based resources. Hardware, Software, Systems, and Services are being bundled into single Solutions; hence, the widespread use of the word Solutions.

However, IT Acquisition is not limited to purchasing or subscribing to items; it also includes developing hardware or software. Hence, Software Development Life Cycle (SDLC) methodologies are included in this domain.

IT Acquisition includes both capital items and operating items. The Acquisition of IT Resources or Solutions is more significant than one might think because their consequences live long into the future. Enterprises may use these resources for decades to come. They become the Enterprises' Architectures.

IT Acquisition also includes the Selection and the Implementation of these items. Hence, this topic is broad.

DOI: 10.4324/9781032689388-10

Historically, IT resources including computer hardware and software were acquired by assembling, building, and/or developing these items. Today, Solution Acquisition is the more likely situation for several reasons:

- First, resources are often obtained as a package, such as an Enterprise Business System (EBS). The package can include application software, a database(s), other subsystems such as data capture or time-keeping systems and even hardware components.

  Non-technology companies are more likely to acquire Solutions rather than acquiring hardware and software and assembling systems. Technology companies, on the other hand, are more likely to develop their own systems because they are their products and services; however, even Technology companies may use commercial business systems in their back offices instead of developing their own backoffice systems.

- Second, 'Cloud First' is now the default strategy for most Enterprises.

  On-premises assets are diminishing in the face of a primary emphasis on Cloud Services. However, even in a 'Cloud First' environment, traditional assets remain on-premises such as local hardware, local software, and local systems.

- Regardless of cloud services or on-premises, the focus began shifting away from individual components to integrated solutions since the nineteen eighties.

The 'Cloud First' strategy emphasizes services over assets where the cloud services are subscribed, leased, or rented instead of being outright purchases.

Whether Products or Services, do not underestimate the 'long shadow', the 'long tail', that Solution Acquisition casts. The Acquisition may establish an Enterprise Architecture (EA), it may re-enforce an existing EA, or it may disregard an existing EA and EA practices. Resource Acquisition can adhere to existing standards and practices or it can create technical diversity, a nicer way of saying technical sprawl, which creates increasing demands on IT having to support multiple diverse tools, platforms, architectures, and capabilities. From an IT Management standpoint, the fewer the number of platforms and standards that IT must maintain, the easier support and maintenance are. However, this is ultimately a balancing act between stable legacy resources and new, innovative alternatives that benefit the Enterprise.

IT Acquisition includes at least the following items:

- Acquisition of applications, systems, and components
- Acquisition of hardware, including servers, storage, desktops, laptops, and networking gear

- Acquisition of software, including operating systems and application software
- Development of custom applications and systems

Keep in mind that this list may be different for Technology companies that develop their own unique products and services. They use employees or contract engineers to analyze, develop, test and implement their products and services. They typically have significantly more technical resources than non-technology companies have. They may also rely on Open-Source products including providing in-house support for them.

The COBIT Framework

COBIT covers Acquisition in its Build, Acquire, and Implement (BAI) Domain. BAI focuses on significant projects and programs, including Requirements Definition, Selection and Implementation of Resources, Change Management, Asset Management, Knowledge Management, and Project Management. BAI also includes Solution Development, and Management of Availability, Capacity, and Configuration. This is a broad set of related topics.

Routine IT procurement is covered in varying degrees in multiple COBIT Objectives in the Align, Plan, and Organize (APO) domain, in the Deliver Support and Service (DSS) domain as well as in BAI.

Requirements

Everything is based on Needs and Requirements.

In the same way, that demand drives sales, Business Needs, and Requirements drive Resource/Solution Acquisition be it purchasing, leasing, subscribing, or developing solutions. Whether by design or accident, Requirements are the first Objective in COBIT's BAI domain. This position reflects the significance of Requirements. As Lewis Carroll said, "if you do not know where you want to go, it doesn't matter which path you take". [—Lewis Carroll, *Adventures in Wonderland*.] Or in slightly different words, if you do not know what you want, you will not get what you need. Everything stems from Requirements.

Requirements may be an assessment or evaluation at a relatively high level, more of a rough cut than a detailed list of Requirements. A high-level assessment may be used to determine feasibility and project scope. A complete Requirements Definition requires thorough investigation and understanding of the Enterprise's entities, processes, desired results, needs, requirements, wants, and wishes. If the stakes are high enough, a Proof of Concept may even be required to confirm whether a proposed solution will satisfy the Requirements. In the aerospace industry, for example, 'fly off's are common, i.e., the competitors are asked to build prototypes and demonstrate them against each other, which makes sense given the costs involved.

Requirements are discovered, identified, defined, and/or explored. They may be tangible; they may be intangible. They may be easy to describe; they may elude an easy description. Requirements may be conceptual, theoretical, physical, and/or practical. Requirements may reflect current operations, products, and services. They may also reflect desired future states that are not completely understood, hence, the often-used distinction between 'current state' and 'future state'.

A constant question regarding Requirements is the degree of detail. Technically, this may be done in levels where Level 0 is the most conceptual, the most summarized, the most abstract, and Levels 1, 2, 3, etc., go into successive levels of detail with the last level containing the greatest amount of detail. This process can be described as hierarchical decomposition or granulation. The objective is a process that produces high-level summaries and varying degrees of detail as needed.

Requirements may be packaged in a Business Requirements Document (BRD). The organization of the BRD can be project specific. Its 'artifacts' generally include diagrams, narratives, illustrations, user stories, and samples, such as sample screens, sample reports, and sample documents. The narrative portion is generally a structured outline as opposed to freeform text. Typical diagrams include flowcharts, decision diagrams, entity relationship diagrams (ERDs), wireframes for screens and reports, and copies of existing materials, such as screens and reports that need to be replicated.

In an Agile environment, the project may be broken down into sub-topics, stories, and use cases, which focus on anticipated outcomes with a different, quicker cadence than the older traditional phased Waterfall method.

Acquisition Methodologies

Two development methodologies are common today:

- The Traditional Structured Methodology, often referred to as the Waterfall SDLC, and
- The Agile methodology, which may be described more accurately as an approach rather than a methodology.

  Agile's originators were looking for ways to improve what had become a burdensome step-by-step document-intensive process that was not necessarily flexible and did not necessarily work well with input, feedback, and user participation.

The traditional SDLC methodology included multiple phases or stages:

- An Initial Planning phase
- An Analysis phase
- A Design phase

- A Construction phase, including testing
- An Implementation phase, including deployment in Production
- A post-implementation support and evaluation phase

Different experts may break the SDLC up differently with fewer phases or with more phases. In the end, it is a stepwise process in which the next step does not start until the previous step is completed and agreed to be complete. The traditional SDLC mirrors typical construction projects, where architects, engineers, and designers design a structure down to the smallest details before construction begins. And the construction proceeds in phases according to the design beginning with a foundation and ending with a completed building ready for occupancy. Hence, the traditional methodology is not an irrational approach.

Agile is less focused on trying to completely understand and analyze a situation and then design, construct, test, and implement a solution based on that understanding.

To learn more about Agile, consider the following resources:

- The Agile Alliance at https://www.agilealliance.org/
- The Project Management Institute (PMI) at https://www.pmi.org/
- The *Agile Practice Guide*, 2017, which was a joint project of the Agile Alliance and PMI

Among other resources, read Agile 101, the Agile Manifesto, and the 12 Principles Behind the Manifesto. These are available from the Agile Alliance.

SCRUM is arguably the best-known implementation of Agile. Basic information about SCRUM is available at https://www.scrumalliance.org/.

The Waterfall is Predictive, whereas the Agile approach is Adaptive. Regardless of the specific method, these approaches apply to non-software development projects, such as selecting and implementing cloud applications, as well as software development projects.

Acquisition Paradigms

Historically, there were two acquisition paradigms, build or buy. Now at least three different alternatives exist, each with distinct elements:

- Build
- Buy
- Subscribe, Lease, or Rent

Building is the traditional paradigm. It was the only choice in the early days of computing. Hardware was bought, but most applications were custom-developed. Initially, building systems, especially applications, were the 'only game in town'. Soon commercial products became available, which were traditionally purchased, but no Software-as-a-Service (SaaS) yet.

For more than two decades, Subscription/Rental/Lease, whichever term you prefer, has become the paradigm of choice for many Enterprises and vendors as well. The advent of NetSuite and Inacct, two ERP systems, at the end of the 20th-century, ushered in commercial subscription EBSs. Today, many vendors of EBSs have moved to the subscription model. As this trend continues, buying these systems will decrease further. Buying may become limited to minor on-premises items.

Having grown up in a Build/Buy world, the demise of purchased systems is hard to imagine. Commercial application subscriptions have attractive advantages for vendors over selling systems, especially more predictable revenue streams, which appeal to Wall Street. For customers, there are advantages as well, most notably spreading the cost over time as opposed to large upfront payments; however, over the long haul, subscription costs may exceed upfront costs.

Common Procurement Mechanism

A common procurement mechanism is a Request for Proposals (RFP) or something less formal such as a Request for Quotations (RFQs) depending on the situation. The objectives of an RFP are to specify what is being sought, to solicit input and proposals from vendors, to establish a formal response procedure, and to provide a timeline. The procurement process may include formal interviews and demonstrations. RFPs tend to lend themselves to larger or mission-critical acquisitions, which tend to be project or program oriented, while RFQs tend to be supply and/or replacement oriented or precursors to large projects.

Another common procurement method is 'refresh cycles'. Refresh cycles focus on hardware. The purpose of Refresh Cycles is to continually modernize Infrastructure. Everything has a shelf life. Hardware is constantly being upgraded with new features and functions, which forces the Operating Systems to upgrade to keep up with the new features and functions. Hence, the references to the Intel Microsoft duopoly. They nudge each other forward.

Acquisition Good Practices

Consider the following Good Acquisition Practices:

- Having established policies, procedures, practices, and standards for IT Acquisitions.
- Acquiring products and services consistent with established Architectures and Standards minimizing the number of different platforms IT must support.
- Identifying carefully and thoroughly the Enterprise's requirements and selecting products and services consistent with those requirements.

- Limiting acquisitions to vetted, approved vendors.
- Routinely assessing new technologies and their potential value to the Enterprise.
- Having an Operating Budget for routine expenses, such as computers, desktop software, small applications, support services, personnel, and supplies.
- Adopting Refresh Cycle Practices.

  - Having a Refresh Cycle Acquisition Plan shifts businesses from 'break-fix' to planned replacement. Simple examples include replacing desktops every three or four years, and replacing servers every five, six, or seven years. This means, on average, the Enterprise is replacing a third or a quarter of its desktops every year.
  - Including exceptions for new technology, for new operating software and for situations in which new systems trigger needs for new hardware and software.

Other acquisition practices include the following:

- Enterprises may delay their acquisition and implementation of new technology to let the 'early adopters' identify unanticipated problems.
- Having an IT storeroom with extra equipment to replace items that frequently need to be replaced, such as desktops, laptops, and mobile devices.
- Remember extra hardware sitting in a storeroom only gets older. Rotate the extra equipment into service before it 'expires'.
- As with other technical acquisitions, IT should work closely with the Purchasing Function to source IT goods and services.
- Adopting a Vendor Partnership stance.

  - Treat Vendors as partners as opposed to transactional suppliers.
  - Evaluate Vendors based on their Advisory and Support services in addition to traditional criteria, such as price and availability.

The overarching goal for IT is a coherent, effective, efficient operating environment.

Acquisition Challenges

Major challenges to Resource Acquisition include the following:

- Knowing in advance what is needed
- Communicating with stakeholders regarding needs
- Identifying and articulating the terms associated with acquisitions
- Meshing new methods with existing methods
- Understanding new processes and their eccentricities
- Understanding the interaction of existing architectures, standards, and practices with new technologies and resources

- Accepting and embracing new processes and methods, new ways of doing things
- Working in a constantly changing reality

When talking about IT investments, a lot is said about Return On Investment (ROI), Total Cost of Ownership (TOC), and similar schemes that associate cost and benefit, the practical side of IT expenses. In addition to these criteria, there is an argument for 'Business Essential'. The Business Essential argument focuses on the need to acquire and implement something to be competitive, to remain competitive, and to compete effectively in hypercompetitive markets. In other situations, these acquisitions might be described as 'table-stakes', i.e., required to be in the game. Business Essential doesn't necessarily replace ROI or TOC, but ultimately decisions may be made based on something being essential to remain viable in the marketplace.

IT Audit Considerations

From the IT Audit standpoint, the two basic considerations are:

- Adopting a Resource or Solution Acquisition methodology
- Using that methodology

As impossible as it sounds, Enterprises may have Resource Acquisition procedures and methods and not follow them. This happens.

From an Audit perspective, IT Auditors need to be sure the Enterprise has a methodology, that the methodology is suitable, and that the methodology is used. Its use can be in degrees from none to fully used for all Acquisitions.

IT Audit questions include the following:

- Does the Enterprise have a Resource Acquisition methodology?
- Is the Resource Acquisition methodology suitable for the Enterprises?
- Does the Enterprise use that methodology?
- Under what circumstances is that methodology not used?
- Are Requirements defined in sufficient detail for realistic decisions?
- How is the application of the methodology, its adherence, and deviations documented?
- What is the process and criteria for launching Acquisition projects?
- How is Acquisition progress monitored, evaluated, and adjusted, especially during development, configuration, and implementation?
- How are Acquisitions ultimately integrated into the Enterprise? This may require outside Change Management expertise and techniques.
- How does the Enterprise identify new Technologies and determine their potential value to the Enterprise?

IT Auditor Considerations

Do IT Auditors need to be experienced IT professionals? No, but IT Auditors do need to be familiar with Enterprise Acquisition Methodologies and their artifacts and have sufficient experience to determine the methodology's suitability and compliance with the methodology. Since the advent of the Agile approach to development, IT Auditors need to be familiar with both highly structured, sequential methods and an Agile iterative approach, for at least three different reasons.

- Acquisition projects may involve elements of both approaches.
- Different Acquisition projects may require different methods.
- The best approach may be a combination of traditional and Agile techniques as opposed to adherence to one method.

From the Enterprise's standpoint, the goal is a suitable outcome be it a selection, or a development, or an implementation. Unfortunately, IT implementations are well-known for being less than fully successful, dare one say 'failures'. The reasons for failure are multiple. They include a lack of realistic planning, lack of executive project commitment and support, lack of an attentive focused implementation, lack of willingness to accept optimum solutions, lack of effective change management, and so on.

Resource Acquisition projects are excellent Opportunities for IT Audit assistance, where the Auditor's role is to assist as opposed to evaluate.

Ultimately, the purpose of an Acquisition Methodology is to increase the likelihood and the amount of success. Hurray!

Chapter 11

Auditing Basic IT Practices

Chapter Contents:

Introduction

From the beginning of computing, there was recognition that things break and that despite our best intentions, things can go wrong. These realizations gave birth to basic standard good practices such as back up and testing. Over time this collection expanded. The 11 listed Good Practices are illustrative, not necessarily exhaustive. Over time this collection will be impacted by new technologies, such as Artificial Intelligence.

The first eight of these Basic IT Practices have a single theme, **Change**. They include Change in general and Changes in specific situations. The interesting aspect of Change is its ability to break the unbroken. Change can fix things, Change can enhance things, Change can extend things … and … Changes can break things that previously worked. Unfortunately, many of us have experienced the breaking of the unbroken. Continuity and Fault Tolerance are closely related; Border Security has become a cybersecurity necessity; and Testing has been a perpetual IT Practice, test to find to find errors, and test to confirm behaviors.

DOI: 10.4324/9781032689388-11

Each of these Good Practices can be an IT Audit concern, especially if the audit is a general IT Audit, as opposed to a specific investigation.

Change Management

Change Management is a broad-reaching Basic IT Good Practice. This discussion begins with general considerations regarding Changes and then moves into specific types of Changes, such as patches, updates, configurations, incidents, and so on.

Regarding Changes in general, 'The only thing that doesn't change is change itself' or 'change is the only constant'. Change is a given for businesses and for IT. IT's job is to manage Change rather than having Change be the author of chaos, which puts IT in damage control mode.

Changes involve altering or modifying existing hardware or software, adding additional assets, and removing existing assets; hence,

- Changes can fix or repair existing problems and improve situations.
- Changes can fail to fix existing problems, which means they persist.
- Changes can introduce new problems that did not previously exist.
- Changes can exacerbate existing problems.
- Changes can be incremental in the sense of partially fixing or partially breaking things.

    As with other situations, Change is not necessarily binary, not on or off. Outcomes can partially remediate or partially degrade existing assets and processes.

In other words, Changes can fix, improve, or exacerbate existing situations. Changes can fix the broken or break the unbroken.

Change Management's purpose is to control the process of Changing IT assets, products, services, and systems.

The first step in Formal Change Management is having a tool, a mechanism, typically a Logging or Ticketing system in which Changes are tracked. This topic will be discussed in detail under Incident Management.

The second step is having a formal process that includes the following:

- Identifying Changes before they are implemented.

    - Changes can be individual changes, such as new patches, upgrades, or be part of a larger project, such as a system development or a system implementation.
    - Individual changes are typically identified as a patch, an upgrade, an enhancement, or in connection with an incident or problem.
    - System Development Life Cycles (SDLCs) typically include Change Management procedures making them part of the methodology. In this case, Changes are evaluated in terms of the project or as distinct items.

- Registering Changes in a 'Logging' or 'Ticketing' system before they are implemented.

  - Classifying Changes by type, such as Patch, Update, Enhancement, or Repair.
  - Classifying Changes as Hardware, Software, or System related.

  Patches are typically vendor supplied. They may fix something, they may change something, and they may add something.

  Updates and Upgrades typically change existing functionality and/or add new functionality.

  Enhancements generally add new features or functions.

  Repairs fix things that were previously identified as incidents or problems.

- Evaluating the Change. Does it ...

  - Fix something that is broken?
  - Change existing features or functions?
  - Add new features or functions?
  - Involve a combination of fixing, changing, and adding?

- Testing the Changes before they are implemented.

  - A variety of approaches are available for Testing Changes.

    In terms of IT Auditing, the essential element is identifying and executing appropriate test procedures, including documenting Changes and test results.

  - The outcome of the testing could include the following:

    - Confirmation that the Changes did what they were supposed to do, i.e., they were consistent with their specifications.

    - Confirmation that the Changes did not make unplanned, unanticipated changes.

    - Confirmation that the Changes did not adversely affect existing systems.

      This is the tricky part, knowing that Changes reached beyond their intended effects.

  Realizing that nothing is perfect, the following practices are common:

  - Deploying the Changes in a Test Environment using robust datasets to fully evaluate Changes before deploying them in Production.
  - Identifying procedures by which the Changes can be removed quickly with the least damage to process and Data if adverse impacts are subsequently detected.

- Formally Reviewing and Approving Changes after Testing prior to Deployment.
- Deploying Changes in Production, and recording the systems affected by the Changes and the date and time the deployment occurred.
- Subsequently reviewing the Changes to confirm appropriate behavior.

Each of these steps should be clearly documented in a Change Management System.

In smaller businesses, the documentation may be manual. In larger Enterprises, a formal Change Management System may be present that automatically tracks Changes and documents them.

The worst scenarios for Change Management are implementing Changes that subsequently 'break' or negatively affect existing functions and systems, especially if the breakage is not immediately determined.

Configuration Management

Configuration Management is part of Enterprise System Implementation and part of Change Management.

In terms of sequence, when Enterprise systems are initially implemented, a major implementation task is **configuration**. In large systems, such as Enterprise Resource Planning (ERP) systems, configurations easily number in the thousands. ERP systems became massive both horizontally by providing many features and functions and vertically by providing many ways of executing these features and functions. Hence, configuring the different features and functions and determining how these features and functions will interact with each other is a major implementation task. After systems Go Live, errors may be discovered that trace back to previous configuration mistakes. This is not uncommon.

All Configuration decisions made during the implementation process need to be documented, if for no other reason than to understand why the system is behaving the way it is, and how to correct incorrect Configurations. Remember each Configuration is a decision, is a Change, that can subsequently come back to haunt a system; hence, Configuration Management is an essential aspect of SDLC methodologies as well as a standalone practice.

Once a system is Configured and placed in Production, Changes to Configurations may be required to correct or expand the features and function. This is Change Management.

Consider this approach: 'A Golden Image'. Golden Images are copies of systems that are determined to be working as designed, as implemented, and as intended. Anything that 'changes' a Golden Image falls under the umbrella of Change Management. This includes Changes in Configurations, and possibly the creation of new 'Golden Images', which in turn, introduces the concept of Version Control which is discussed below.

Patch Management

Patch Management is a specific domain within Change Management. Patches are developed by hardware, software, and system developers to update their products. Patches are issued for a variety of reasons:

- To fix a software or firmware defect
- To fix a security defect
- To change existing functionality
- To add additional functionality

Patches may be:

- Automatically downloaded, installed, and implemented by the system without customer interaction.
- Patches may be available for download from the supplier's website at the customer's discretion.
- The deployment may be a multiple-step process, where downloading and installing are separate steps. This allows customers to download patches and install them at their discretion.

In the case of a manual process, customers retrieve Patches and subsequently install them. Because the process is a two-step process, customers can decide what to do to confirm the efficacy of Patches before implementing them in Production.

Two variations to this process exist. As noted by the first bullet above, the process may be completely automatic. The positive, the customer does not have to do anything; the negative, the customer does nothing. In a negative situation, customers are forced to contact their suppliers to obtain assistance. This typically takes time, which means the customer must limp along with erroneous behavior.

The other major variation is using software, such as Microsoft's Windows Server Update Services (WSUS), to manage the deployment of updates across the Enterprise. WSUS is a simple example. There are more sophisticated patch managers that control patching across different platforms and applications.

From the IT Audit perspective, the big questions are:

- Does the Enterprise have Patch Management Policies, Procedures, Practices, Standards, and Tools?
- Are these Procedures and Tools used consistently?
- Are the Patch Management Policies, Procedures, Practices, Standards, and Tools suitable for the Enterprise?
- What are the Enterprise's objectives regarding continuity and disruptions?

Patches for Operating systems, Patches for Security, and Patches for Applications are not necessarily the same.

Security patches are typically implemented as quickly as possible to reduce potential cybersecurity risks, especially zero-day vulnerabilities, which are discussed in the Cybersecurity chapter.

On the other hand, the Enterprise may be less interested in Application patches if the underlying application is customized. Applying these patches can open 'a can of worms'. Since the Enterprise is dependent on the applications to operate, the Enterprise may be slow to evaluate and install application patches. The problem with this hesitancy is that the Enterprise Application can quickly become out-of-date, further complicating the installation of subsequent patches and updates.

Operating System Patches may fall somewhere in between, important but not necessarily urgent.

From the IT Audit perspective, the following questions are relevant:

- What are the Enterprise's Patch Management policies and procedures?
- Are different types of Patches treated differently?
- What are the Enterprise's Patch Testing policies and procedures?
- How are Patch Testing and Installation documented?
- Are these policies and procedures suitable for the Enterprise?
- Are systems or applications falling behind because Patches have been delayed?

Update/Upgrade Management

Updates and Upgrades may be distributed as Patches or as formal Updates or Upgrades. They tend to be more extensive than Patches. They typically add features/functions or expand existing features/functions. They may also repair items.

As with Patches, unintentional negative impacts can occur. Depending upon the extent of the changes, users may need to be trained on the changes to existing features/functions and on new items before they are implemented. If the systems have not been customized, the Updates/Upgrades should be straightforward. Problems arise when the Updates/Upgrades affect customizations that have been made to systems.

An **exception** to Patch and Update/Upgrade Management is Cloud Services. Patching, Updating, and Upgrading are handled by the Cloud Service Providers (CSPs) 'out of sight' of the Enterprise. Occasionally, customers experience problems related to Patch, Updates, and Upgrades made by CSPs. Ideally, CSPs notify their customers of Changes before they occur, but often they do not. Some CSPs take pride in their ability to constantly improve their systems, which is great until something breaks.

Incident Management, Service Request Management, and Problem Management

Incident Management, Service Request Management, and Problem Management are interrelated. Because Incidents and Service Requests may be symptoms of underlying problems, incidents may need to be referred to Problem Management for further investigation and resolution because they recur.

Incident Management and **Service Request Management** can be viewed from two perspectives:

- From the perspective of something is broken, which is often called 'break fix'
- From a Service perspective where something is being requested but nothing is broken

  For example, users may request assistance finding things, setting things up, backing things up, using hardware, using software, etc.

In the first case, something is broken and needs to be fixed; in the second case, there is a request for service with no indication anything is broken. The contrast is the difference between my keyboard is not working, the keys are sticking, and how do I find a lost file or retrieve Data from a database.

Incident Management can be the entrée to Problem Management. For example, sticking with the humble keyboard, which is worn out or had too many cups of coffee spilled on it, Problem Management looks at the underlying problem. In the case of keyboard problems, Problem Management might focus on refresh cycles, in other words, how often should keyboards be replaced to keep users productive, and/or users should be discouraged, or prohibited, from having cups of coffee in proximity to their keyboards.

A more complex situation could be processing errors in an application or Data errors in a database. In either of these situations, the issue is first reported via Incident Management or a Service Request and is subsequently referred to Problem Management because the resolution is more than a quick fix.

Going back to the initial situations, only after an evaluation is the situation determined to be more complicated. In terms of process, the three steps are as follows:

Step 1: Receive a Service Request
Step 2: That Requires a Fix
Step 3: That is subsequently determined to be an underlying Problem

Hence: Service Request → Incident Management → Problem Management

These Requests can be handled by a Service Desk or Service Facility. Today this service can be a web-based application or an email address, such as support@enterprise.com or helpdesk@enterprise.com. In the first case, users create their own Service/Incident/Problem tickets. In the second case, users request service or report an incident, and their requests are entered into a tracking system.

The process for handling Service Requests might be the following:

1. Create a Service Ticket
2. Confirm the Receipt of the Service Request
3. Evaluate the Service Request
4. Prioritize and Assign the Service Request to a Service Provider
5. Investigate the Service Request
6. Resolve the Service Request
7. Escalate the Service Request from Incident to Problem, if needed
8. Confirm Resolution
9. Close the Service Ticket

Consider these steps in detail.

1. Create a Service Ticket.
   Critical parts of the Service Request are the following:

   - Nature and Specifics of the Request
   - Requester
   - Request Date
   - Urgency and/or Priority,

     For example, does the issue involve a service or device that is completely broken, is 'down hard', or is the issue a nuisance or inconvenience?

2. Confirm the Receipt of the Request.

   Provide a Ticket Number and Acknowledgement to the Requester confirming the Request.

3. Evaluate the Service Request to determine what is affected and the extent of the issues.

4. Based on the Evaluation,

   a. Classify the Service Request with respect to the products and services involved
   b. Determine Severity/Importance/Priority of the Request
   c. Assign the Request to a Service Provider

This step may be referred to as **Triage**. Think of the initial screening that occurs when patients arrive at Emergency Rooms.

After the evaluation, the Requester is informed of the priority that was assigned to the Request, to whom the Request was assigned, and an initial response regarding resolution and timing.

5   Investigate the Request.

This is a formal investigation of the request. Depending upon the complexity of the investigation, the response may be a quick fix such as a reset, or it may be transferred to subject matter experts for resolution, or it may be 'escalated' to advanced technical resources.

6   Resolve the Request.

The Request may be something that first line service providers can handle. If so, the Request is resolved. If more intensive investigation or highly technical knowledge and skill is required, the Request may be 'escalated'.

7   Escalate the Request.

8   Confirm Resolution.

When the Request is resolved, send a confirmation to the requester.

A common fault in Incident Management is failing to notify the Requester of the outcome and failing to get confirmation from the Requester that the Request was resolved.

9   Close the Service Ticket.

Closing the Service Ticket could be as simple as changing its Status from Open to Closed; however, the closing process may consider the ticket from a historical standpoint. Maybe the situation is a symptom of more complex issues. If so, the Closing process may include Escalation of the Service Ticket to Problem Management even though the initial Request was resolved ... at least temporarily.

Key to Incident and Service Request Management is maintaining at least the following Data:

- Description of Incident or Services Requested
- Requester Name and Contact information
- Request Category
- Request Priority
- Request Status
- Assigned Personnel
- Findings
- Remediation or Support provided
- Date and Time the Request was submitted
- Date and Time the Request was Resolved or Completed
- Date and Time the Requester acknowledged the successful resolution
- If escalated, Date and Time the Request was Escalated

Typically, the biggest challenge for Service Request Management is prematurely closing Service Request Tickets because Technicians believe the Requests were resolved. One way to reduce this problem is to require the Requester to acknowledge the resolution before the ticket is closed and closing the ticket only after a specific time limit if no response is received from the Requester.

Escalating typically means Incidents are not necessarily isolated events but symptoms of underlying recurring problems, which may require extensive effort.

Problem Management

Problem Management delves into causes. Incidents are the symptoms; Problems are the underlying defects that need to be resolved to prevent recurrence. Underlying issues can easily lead to the escalation of a Problem from Incident Management to a SDLC project, in which case the problem goes through a full analysis, design, repair, and test process prior to implementation.

Version Control

Version Control is another aspect of Change Management. Version Control may be discussed in the context of objects or documents. Version Control allows the objects or documents to be sequenced by Version Number from oldest to newest.

As a part of Change Management, Version Control keeps track of Changes to assets, processes, and items over time. Ideally, this Data is maintained in a database that can be searched for patterns and trends and allowed Changes to be sequenced.

When Problems arise and users need to restore previous versions of systems or functions, this repository provides a necessary history. Version Control is the history of systems. It documents the changes that occurred over time as well as provides the basis for restoring previous versions.

Backup Practices

Backup Practices are another Standard IT Practice. It may be among the oldest practices still actively used. Backing up systems and Data began with mechanical devices, paper tape, punch cards, magnetic tape, and hard drives, which were subject to failure one way or another. The best remediation was to make copies of the systems and Data so if the media failed at least the system or Data was not lost.

However, transferring Data from one mechanical device to another does not completely protect the Data. Backup mechanisms could fail as well as the primary storage facility, so better to make multiple copies, and test them to ensure the backups work to avoid the embarrassment or disgrace of losing a system or Data or compromising Data ... one might even lose their job because of lost or compromised Data.

Fault Tolerance

Fault Tolerance is another protective mechanism. The essential objective of Fault Tolerance is to design and operate systems in a manner such that they continue to operate when parts of the system fail. These are like parallel streams in a river where processing can shift from one stream to another stream unnoticed by users.

Fault Tolerance is usually accomplished by having redundant devices or systems in place either operating in parallel, like branches in a stream, or designed to 'failover', which means one device takes over when another device fails. RAID, a Redundant Array of Independent (used to be Inexpensive) Drives, is an example of parallel behavior whereby copies of Data are written across multiple hard drives such that if one drive fails the Data remains intact. Multiple power supplies are an example of 'failover'. If one power supply fails, another power supply automatically kicks into action to prevent a power interruption. Fault tolerance can even extend to personnel. In this case, multiple engineers or technicians have the same information and skill such that one of them can step in whenever needed and the organization is not dependent on a single person, on a 'single point of failure'.

Multiple parallel assets not only provide Fault Tolerance, but they also provide additional performance. In the case of multiple streams in a river, the river can carry more water. So not only do the multiple streams provide alternate paths, but they also provide additional bandwidth. In IT, this is Replication. Databases, for example, have their Data Replicated across multiple instances to provide both Data protection and increased performance. The Replication can extend beyond physical boundaries across multiple Data Centers in different locations such that even in an extreme case if a Data Center is unavailable, the Data contained in the Data Center is readily available from other locations. In addition, databases can be designed to be broken up into chunks situated in different locations, which is referred to as 'sharding'.

Alternate Processes, while not necessarily a fault tolerance method, provide alternative mechanisms to accomplish specific outcomes. Manufacturers, for example, may have multiple factories that manufacture the same items. Retailers have multiple 'brick and mortar' stores to better serve their customers. Cities have multiple fire stations to decrease response time. Cellphone companies have multiple cell towers to provide coverage and improve call quality. Accordingly, businesses may have alternate procedures for the same circumstances.

Testing

Testing is another protective mechanism that dates to the early days of IT and is not limited to IT. From the beginning of software development, software testing was and remains a standard procedure. A programmer who does not test their work is either very lucky or unemployed (said with a wink). Quality Control engineers test to confirm that things and processes comply with their specifications. Accountants test to confirm their calculations. Engineers test to confirm their work.

Border Security – Firewalls

Firewalls are another standard protective mechanism serving the same purpose as physical doors. They control traffic into and out of networks. As with other Standard IT Practices, Firewalls and similar mechanisms are Standard Operating Practices; the lack of which would be a severe deficiency. Firewalls are discussed in detail in the Cybersecurity chapter.

IT Audit Considerations

These IT practices are designed to enable organizations to continue operations even when destructive forces are at work. They are Internal Controls designed and operated to ensure business operations and to avoid IT embarrassment.

In auditing parlance, Internal Controls only provide **reasonable assurance**, not absolute assurance, or in street language, 'bad things do happen to good people'. This is the nature of things. These Standard IT Practices are in place to reduce the Risk of bad things harming Enterprises, their operations, and their Data.

To provide reasonable assurance, Enterprises must …

- Clearly define their Business Objectives
- Recognize the Risks to the achievement of those Business Objectives
- Identify appropriate Internal Controls, and appropriate countermeasures, to reduce these Risks, such as these Standard IT Practices

IT Audit Considerations regarding these and other Standard IT Practices include:

- Does the Enterprise have Change Management Policies, Procedures, Practices, and Standards?
- Are these Policies, Procedures, Practices, and Standards consistent with the Enterprise's needs, requirements, and objectives? (Alignment)
- Are these Policies, Procedures, Practices, and Standards effective? Do they adequately address the Risks? (Effectiveness)
- Are these Policies, Procedures, Practices, and Standards continuously in effect? Are they ever disregarded? If so, under what circumstances? (In Effect)

Because these practices are Standard IT Practices, IT Auditors can enlist the assistance of IT technicians to assist in the assessment of the appropriateness and effectiveness of these controls Internal Controls and/or assist in their analysis, design, and implementation.

Chapter 12

Auditing IT Service Management

Chapter Contents:

Introduction of Service Management

IT is a service department, especially for non-technology businesses. In technology businesses, however, the service delivery component is in addition to the Enterprise's technology business activities. In the case of Tech companies, IT services can be wide ranging from providing technical support to software development to cybersecurity vigilance to supporting technology projects.

COBIT's Service domain, Deliver, Service, and Support (DSS), includes six Objectives:

DSS01 – Managed Operations
DSS02 – Managed Service Incidents and Requests

DOI: 10.4324/9781032689388-12

DSS03 – Managed Problems
DSS04 – Managed Continuity
DSS05 – Managed Security Services
DSS06 – Managed Business Process Controls

ITIL, IT Service Management (ITSM), is primarily about service delivery. ITIL contains many of COBIT's topics. While originally developed to serve the needs of the United Kingdom, it was subsequently developed into a comprehensive framework for Service Management appropriate for any Enterprise regardless of its business activities. Chapter 19 provides a side-by-side comparison of ITIL and COBIT based on topics. At least from the perspective of topics, the two frameworks overlap; however, each framework has distinct elements. In the United States, IT Auditors are more likely to encounter COBIT than ITIL; but regardless of which framework an Enterprise uses, knowing both frameworks is a plus.

Basic IT Service Delivery Practices

IT Operations

IT Operations are both singular and all encompassing. In a narrow definition, IT Operations are the service aspects of IT. In a broad definition, IT Operations encompasses the entirety of IT's activities. In this broader definition, IT Operations is the sum of routine operational activities and other activities that do not necessarily fit neatly into a narrow definition, which is why ITIL includes all aspects of IT, not just activities directly related to IT Operations.

The list below includes basic IT Operations topics, several of which were previously covered in Basic IT Practices

Availability Management

A major concern for IT is that its products and services are always **available when needed**. 'When needed' used to be regular business hours; however, the world is increasing 'constantly on'. While traveling abroad, I discovered that I could get something to eat anytime of the night or day, but I could not get gasoline late at night. In the United States, I can get gasoline 24 hours a day but not something to eat late at night, different cultures, different value systems. Increasingly, we can purchase things online anytime of the day or night, any day of the week. This is the new normal.

Consider ATMs. They allow us to withdraw cash and make deposits anytime of the day. Consider International businesses. While they may be available for only limited periods in individual time zones, over a 24-hour period, their systems are in constant use. These situations demand IT products and services that are available around the clock with no interruptions even during holidays. The consequence: IT is, or will become, the service that never sleeps. IT empowers the 24-hour-a-day world.

Therefore, systems are designed specifically to enable 24-hour Availability.

Capacity and Performance Management

Closely allied with Availability are Capacity and Performance Management. To be constantly available, systems need greater capacity and constant performance monitoring to adjust to varying workloads. In the past, the monitoring was manual; today automatic monitoring is the norm, which means deploying performance management software to automatically balance workloads and scale resources up and down as needed.

Traditionally, capacity looked for utilization under a threshold, say 60% or 70% or 80%, depending upon workload fluctuations. The idea is to balance capacity and cost. If additional capacity were free, excess capacity would not be a concern, but cost is reality.

Cost is one realm where cloud services shine. In a cloud service environment, Customers can quickly scale up to meet increased demand. Customers can also scale down, but the reduction may not be reflected in the bills as quickly. In a cloud services environment, scaling is easy. In an on-premises environment, scaling involves excess resources, excess in the sense that they are only used periodically, only during times of high demand. During routine demand, these resources are unneeded, but they were purchased and implemented to provide 'headroom'.

Availability, Capacity, and Performance are interrelated. Availability is not an On/Off proposition. Availability becomes unacceptable as performance declines. Hence, Availability sits on a continuum between satisfactory and unsatisfactory performance, becoming less satisfactory as performance degrades.

Change Management

As noted above, Change is a given for IT; Change is a central theme for IT Service Delivery. IT's objective is to manage Change rather than being managed by Change, rather than reacting to Change.

ITSM requires control over Changes to avoid disruptions caused by Changes. The worst scenarios for Service Management are implementing Changes that subsequently 'break' or degrade existing systems and services.

The best IT Change Management result is continuous Operations without interruptions caused by Changes.

Incident Management and Service Request Management – Service Desk

Incident Management and Service Requests, as discussed above, are essential parts of ITSM. IT is evaluated in terms of responsiveness and effectiveness.

Responsiveness includes how quickly IT responds to initial requests and how quickly requests are resolved. Effectiveness is measured by resolution. Were the issues resolved? Were the resolutions appropriate given their severity?

A common weakness in this area is prematurely closing Service Tickets. The best remedy is obtaining positive confirmation that the incident has been resolved to the satisfaction of users.

Monitoring and Event Management

Monitoring and Event Management are central to managing systems today. The good news is that there are a variety of applications that do this and that they are becoming more intelligent. They are capable of monitoring server performance, storage performance, network performance, device performance, application performance, providing downtime alerts, and more. These are the 'eyes and ears' of IT. They allow IT to stay ahead of issues. They alert IT to issues as soon as they occur to enable IT to maintain performance, integrity, and availability.

Log files are the raw Data of Monitoring and Event Management software. They allow the events leading up to failures to be examined to determine potential causes.

Artificial Intelligence (AI) may significantly improve and expand these services to be more responsive and *more anticipatory*.

Problem Management

Problem Management, another Basic IT Good Practice, is also essential to IT Service Delivery. From the IT Service Delivery perspective, identifying and resolving underlying issues eliminates repetitive incidents, allows IT to focus on new issues.

Service Catalogue Management

Service Catalogue Management is an ITIL specific topic and something additional to consider. IT Service Catalogues list service activities and explore the need for new or improved services, which is consistent with Continuous Improvement and Capability Maturity Models (CMM).

Service Configuration Management

ITIL considers Configuration Management as a service delivery activity; COBIT considers Configuration Management as part of its Build, Acquire, Implement (BAI). As part of BAI, COBIT's focus is on Configuration Management during system implementation. However, after Configurations are implemented, Configurations may need to be revised for a variety of reasons; hence, Configuration Management is also a Service Delivery function. In this capacity, IT is responsible for maintaining Configurations and documenting all Configuration changes.

Business Continuity Management

Historically, Business Continuity meant backing up business Data and the means to process that Data. Over time, that capability expanded to include being able to respond to the destruction of IT assets and services. This shifted the question from how to restore the systems and Data to how to reconstruct systems from scratch, which is Disaster Recovery. Business Continuity is the next step in the evolution of protecting assets and getting them back into service. Business Continuity shifted the discussion a step further to how to maintain **Availability despite failures and disruptions**. This is particularly the case for systems requiring continuous operation.

This shift in emphasis can be illustrated as:

Backup/Restore → Disaster Recovery → Business Continuity

Depending on a business' resources and needs, Business Continuity can involve all three of these approaches. Ultimately, the business needs to be able to function at certain levels of activity for sustained periods of time regardless of what happens to its assets and capabilities.

From an IT Audit perspective, there is no single scheme, 'no one-size that fits all'. Business Continuity will reflect the Enterprise's Business Objectives and its Business Constraints, one of which is cost.

Big IT Audit Questions regarding Business Continuity include the following:

- Is Backup and Recovery sufficient?
- Is Disaster Recovery sufficient?
- Does the Enterprise require 24-hour operations?
- Does the Enterprise require a combination of Backup/Recovery, Disaster Recovery, and Continuous 24-hour a day Operation?
- How do business constraints affect these needs and requirements?
- Is the Business Continuity provided to the Enterprise suitable?

Looking at Business Continuity for Cloud Service Providers (CSPs), it is difficult to imagine CSPs that have not designed their architectures and resources such that when failures occur other resources automatically step-in and assume the workload of the failed components and/or systems. For their Customers, CSPs offer an uninterrupted service ... although sometimes the uninterruptible is interrupted. This raises the question: What do CSP Customers do when the uninterruptible service is interrupted? Because failures do occur. Customers may need to develop contingency plans as well as, insisting that CSPs do everything possible to avoid service disruptions because they in turn disrupt their Customers' operations and services.

Service Level Management

Service Level Management and Service Level Agreements (SLAs) were also previously discussed. Service Delivery needs to know the Service Levels promised to users and ensure they are met. These Service Levels typically include Availability, Performance, Capacity, and the features/functions required by the users, including both what was contracted and what was promised.

Monitoring and Event Management are essential tools for determining whether what was contracted or promised is delivered. Remember, the feelings and impressions of users and stakeholders count. If a system is slow, for example, users notice the slowness and usually comment on it, especially if the slowness affects their effectiveness.

Security and Cybersecurity Services

Security and Cybersecurity, while always significant, have become even more significant given the potential damage adversaries can inflict on Enterprises. Adversaries today are typically well resourced, well skilled, and perform their malicious activities with competency. What else would one expect of a business or a government? And they typically perform their activities beyond the reach of the Enterprises they attack. Hence, Cybersecurity is a critical aspect of IT. Given the 'stakes' in this area, a separate chapter specifically discusses Cybersecurity.

Other IT Service Delivery Practices

IT has an abundance of Basic Service Delivery Practices. The list below is only a partial list with new technologies supplementing and replacing older technologies.

- Designing and deploying Fault Tolerant environments and systems to avoid and/or minimize disruption.
- Implementing Monitoring Systems to detect negative behaviors, errors, and anomalies and alerting appropriate IT resources of adverse or potentially adverse events.
- Maintaining robust Incident Management, Service Request Management, and Problem Management procedures and resources to maintain Service and to resolve requests and disruptions promptly and when necessary to escalate them for more intensive investigation and resolution.

- Given Enterprise Objectives, maintaining robust System Back Up and Restore processes, and/or Disaster Recovery procedures, and/or Business Continuity systems and procedures appropriate to the Enterprise and the resources available for these services. Typically, the biggest constraint is cost.

The ultimate benchmarks are service levels and business continuity that are consistent with the Enterprise and its constraints.

IT Audit Considerations

IT Audit Considerations include at least the following:

- An explicit understanding of the Services the Enterprise requires, and the Services IT provides.
- What constitutes appropriate, satisfactory, and suitable IT Services?
- Which of these Services are cloud based, which are on-premises, which services are provided by employees, which are provided by outsourced resources?
- What are the metrics for appropriateness, satisfaction, and suitability?
- Are the Enterprise's investments in IT commensurate with the resources and services that the Enterprise requires? To what extent are IT Services constrained by funding, by resources, and/or by staffing?

The perpetual balancing is needs versus costs.

IT Audit Challenges

By way of an endnote, Services are inherently less tangible than physical assets, such as Infrastructure items. Their physicality is easier to comprehend and manage. Services are less tangible; however, metrics can be chosen, typically related to time, and monitored. Hence, IT does not have to be dependent on users to tell them when their systems' performance is unacceptable. Monitoring software handles this task and provides advance notice, so the Enterprise is not dependent on users telling the Enterprise that its services are unsatisfactory. This software monitors workloads and proactively adjusts systems to avoid slowness and failures. This is an area where AI may provide significant improvements.

Chapter 13

Auditing IT Assurance, Compliance, and Improvement

Chapter Contents:

General Assurance Procedures

General Auditing IT Assurance, Compliance, and Improvement procedures include:

- Monitoring
- Self-Assessments and Self-Awareness
- Independent Assessments

Monitoring

COBIT describes Monitoring as Engaging "… with stakeholders … to define the objectives, scope and method for measuring business solution and service delivery and contribution to enterprise objectives". [– *COBIT 2019; Governance and Management Objectives* , p. 273.] Monitoring is more than oversight. It includes establishing and tracking metrics related to performance, conformance, compliance, and assurance. Monitoring is collecting and analyzing this data and ensuring timely remedial actions.

DOI: 10.4324/9781032689388-13

Self-Assessments and Self-awareness

The self-assessment and self-awareness focus on Internal Controls, achievement of Enterprise Business Objectives, and effectiveness of Internal Controls. COBIT describes this as an evidence-based process. Risk and Control Matrices (RACMs) are an approach for evaluating the appropriateness and effectiveness of Internal Controls. They provide documentary evidence regarding the completeness and effectiveness of management's Internal Controls. Any deficiencies identified in this process require attention by management and remedial procedures to ensure the controls continue to be suitable and effective. Remedial actions may require root cause analysis and/or reconsideration of the Risks to the achievement of Business Objectives.

Independent Assessments

In addition to Self-Assessments and Self-Awareness, Enterprises may contract with appropriate third parties, such as CPA firms, Outsourced Internal Audit firms, and/or Cybersecurity firms for Independent Assistance and Assessments. Their work can be done in conjunction with IT Audit and/or Internal Audit. The objective is to get unbiased, independent, objective feedback regarding Performance, Conformance, Compliance, Assurance, and Improvement.

Performance Monitoring

COBIT combines Performance and Conformance Monitoring into a single domain. For IT Audit purposes, let's arbitrarily separate them.

Performance is a primary measure of IT Products and Services. If you oversee IT, the last thing you want to hear is 'the system is slow today'. Sometimes the reasons are obvious, other times they are not.

One thing IT can do is establish a robust monitoring program, which can include:

- IT Infrastructure – Inventory (hardware and software), Health, Performance, Availability, Logging, and Event Monitoring
- Server Utilization – Processor Utilization and Memory Utilization Monitoring
- Storage Capacity Monitoring
- Network Management – Volume, Speed, Bandwidth, Configuration Changes, Bottleneck Analysis, by device or network segment
- Monitoring Firewall Activity – Monitoring, Logging, and Threat Detection Monitoring
- Endpoint Lockdown
- Monitoring Uptime
- Monitoring Website Performance

- Tracking User Activity, including Geolocation and Job Site Tracking, Keystroke Logging, and Video Recording, being sensitive to both users and potential insider threats. Note: This is controversial.
- Monitoring Business Processes and complex business process systems
- Online Metrics, Reports, Automated Notification
- Comprehensive reporting including Availability and Service Level Agreement (SLA) compliance
- Monitoring Cloud Services

One vendor describes its monitoring tools as a 'Full-stack Observability Platform'. The basic idea is that the tool covers the entire infrastructure observing all its activities.

Sub-genres of Performance Monitoring include:

- Application Performance Monitoring (APM)
- Availability or System Monitoring
- Network Monitoring and Management
- Remote Monitoring and Management (RMM)
- Security Information and Event Monitoring (SIEM)
- Web Performance Monitoring

A myriad of tools and vendors exist in this marketplace. When selecting tools, look for inventorying capabilities, including make and model and location, real-time monitoring, real-time alerting, and remote control. These tools can not only monitor activity but also record states and events. Since these log files can grow to a significant size, they are pruned regularly to keep them in check.

IT Audit Considerations

IT Audit Considerations include:

- Does the Enterprise have suitable Monitoring and Management Policies, Procedures, Practices, Standards, and Tools?
- Are these Policies, Procedures, Practices, Standards, and Tools consistent with the Enterprise's needs, requirements, and Business Objectives?
- Are these Policies, Procedures, Practices, Standards, and Tools effective?
- Are these Policies, Procedures, Practices, Standards, and Tools continuously in effect? Are they ever disregarded? If so, under what circumstances?

Conformance Monitoring

For purposes of clarification, while COBIT combines Performance Monitoring and Conformance Monitoring, though similar, they are slightly different.

Performance deals with the operational performance of IT products, systems, and services while Conformance deals with conformance with the Enterprise's goals, objectives, strategies, and requirements.

In this sense, Conformance Monitoring looks beyond sheer Performance to the degree to which IT's Assets, Products, Systems, and Services satisfy the needs of the Enterprise.

An Adequate System of Internal Controls

'An Adequate System of Internal Controls' became law for Securities and Exchange Commission (SEC) Registrants with the passage of the Sarbanes-Oxley Act (SOX) in 2002. This is not to say that an Adequate System of Internal Controls was not critical before SOX, but SOX made An Adequate System of Internal Controls a legal requirement for entities registered with the SEC. An Adequate System of Internal Controls is enshrined by the American Institute of Certified Public Accountants (AICPA) in AU-C 315 and AU-C 330 making this a requirement for all financial audits regardless of whether the Enterprise is registered with the SEC.

COBIT reinforces this requirement in Monitor, Evaluate, and Assess (MEA02). The basic idea here is that an Adequate System of Internal Controls is not static but continually monitors and evaluates Internal Controls to ensure they are, and they remain adequate, suitable, and effective.

Having an Adequate System of Internal Controls includes:

- Having a clearly defined catalog of 'material' Internal Controls. RACMs are one but not the only approach to such a list of Internal Controls.
- Monitoring the effectiveness of General IT Internal Controls.
- Monitoring the effectiveness of Business Process Controls, i.e., Application Controls.
- Performing Internal Control Self-assessments.
- Identifying and remediating Internal Control Deviations and Deficiencies, including their root causes.

Consistent with this approach is the use of Monitoring software to ensure that Internal Controls are doing what they are supposed to do especially as environments inevitably change over time. The Monitoring software must keep up with the advances in the systems and Data that they are monitoring.

IT Audit Considerations

From the perspective of IT Audit, the keys are continuously monitoring and evaluating the system of Internal Controls to identify control deviations, deficiencies, and ineffectiveness, and remediating these items.

Compliance Management

Compliance Management involves compliance with external laws, regulations, and requirements. These may be general commercial requirements or specific legal requirements, such as privacy regulations, PCI-DSS requirements, or import/export regulations. The nature and extent of Compliance Management reflects the external regulations and requirements that affect the auditee.

The beginning point is knowing which laws and regulations apply to the Enterprise. Obvious ones include PCI-DSS if the Enterprise accepts credit cards and SOX if the Enterprise is registered with the SEC. If the Enterprise is in the Defense Industry, ITAR (International Traffic in Arms Regulations) may apply. If the Enterprise is in healthcare, Health Insurance Portability and Accountability Act (HIPAA) probably applies. These are obvious. Less obvious are laws and regulations from other jurisdictions that have local implications, such as GDPR (General Data Protection Regulations) which affect citizens of the European Union (EU) and European Economic Area (EEA) countries regardless of their location.

Compliance Management begins with the Enterprise having identified the applicable laws, regulations, and other external requirements with which it must comply. The Enterprise must review and adjust its Policies, Procedures, Practices, and Standards to ensure compliance. If gaps are identified, the Enterprise must address these gaps and remediate them in a timely manner. Obtaining assurance of compliance may involve the use of external parties for assistance and assessment.

IT Audit Considerations

IT Audit Considerations include:

- Does the Enterprise have suitable Compliance Management Policies, Procedures, Practices, and Standards?
- Are these Policies, Procedures, Practices, and Standards consistent with the legal and regulatory environment which applies to the Enterprise?
- Are these Policies, Procedures, Practices, and Standards effective?
- Are these Policies, Procedures, Practices, and Standards continuously in effect? Are they ever disregarded? If so, under what circumstances?

Assurance Management

COBIT breaks Assurance Management down into nine areas:

1. Ensuring that Assurance Providers are independent and qualified
2. Planning Assurance Initiatives from a Risk-based perspective

3. Defining the Objectives of Assurance Initiatives with the concurrence of stakeholders
4. Defining the Scope of Assurance Initiatives
5. Defining the Work Program for Assurance Initiatives
6. Executing Assurance Initiatives focusing on design effectiveness and cost-effectiveness
7. Executing Assurance Initiatives focusing on operating effectiveness
8. Documenting the Findings of Assurance Initiatives including the impact of weak internal controls.
9. Following up on Assurance Initiative Recommendations

Items 3–8 are a basic work plan for Assurance projects. Using a Risk-based approach and using independent assurance providers, and ensuring the recommendations are adopted and implemented are bookends for assurance initiative projects.

Chapter 14

Auditing Cybersecurity

Chapter Contents:

Introduction

Cybersecurity has emerged as a critical business issue regardless of business size, market segment, or location. No business is immune to cybersecurity challenges. Hence, cybersecurity is a major IT Audit topic and a service opportunity for IT Auditors, Cybersecurity experts, and IT experts. The purpose of this chapter is to lay a basic foundation for IT Auditing of Cybersecurity, entire books are written on this topic and curriculums have been designed to cover this topic.

Basic Cybersecurity terminology includes the following words. Keep their distinctions in mind.

- **Vulnerabilities** are weaknesses that can be taken advantage of.
- **Threats** are malicious acts that exploit, or take advantage of cybersecurity vulnerabilities.
- **Exploits** are actions that take advantage of vulnerabilities for the benefit of attackers.

DOI: 10.4324/9781032689388-14

These terms recur frequently.

The Cybersecurity & Infrastructure Security Agency of the U.S. Government (CISA) listed over 1180 'known exploited vulnerabilities' (KEV) in mid-2024. For an updated list, go to: https://www.cisa.gov/known-exploited-vulnerabilities-catalog. The CISA explains the purpose of the catalog as follows:

> For the benefit of the cybersecurity community and network defenders—and to help every organization better manage vulnerabilities and keep pace with threat activity—CISA maintains the authoritative source of vulnerabilities that have been exploited in the wild. Organizations should use the KEV catalog as an input to their vulnerability management prioritization framework.
>
> – https://www.cisa.gov/known-exploited-vulnerabilities-catalog

For purposes of this discussion, cybersecurity can be approached from two perspectives:

- **Unauthorized access to** and/or use of **business assets**, especially resulting in interruption, degradation, or compromise of these assets.
- **Unauthorized access to** and/or use of **business data**, especially 'sensitive data'.

Unauthorized use of business assets ranges from inappropriate use of business assets, such as for personal use or crypto mining, to significant interruptions or diminished capability, such as interfering with a power grid. Unauthorized use of business data includes the unauthorized viewing of data, the unauthorized copying of data, unauthorized changes to data, and/or unauthorized damaging or deleting data.

The challenging aspect of cybersecurity is the unbalanced nature of the playing field. Today, the playing field favors the adversaries, which makes cybersecurity so daunting. Several factors are at work:

- First, adversaries today tend to be well resourced whether they are criminal organizations in the business of cybercrime or nation-states that use cyber exploits for political or military purposes.
- Second, these actors are generally outside of the judicial reach of the entities they target.

    These actors set up shop in places that are hostile to or at least outside the judicial reach of their targets. Even if the adversaries are identified, they are in places where extradition and/or prosecution is not possible; hence, they are free to carry on their activities with little concern about apprehension.

Adversaries are in the business of cyber mischief, cybercrime. Their business model is making money, gaining intelligence, or causing disruption via cyber-attacks. These factors place an enormous burden on Enterprises to provide adequate cybersecurity defenses and, in the worst case, remediation.

Cybersecurity Resources

On the positive side, Cybersecurity resources are readily available. Businesses do not have to figure out Cybersecurity from scratch. Established standards and protocols exist.

- ISO 27001 – https://www.iso.org/standard/27001
- NIST Cybersecurity Framework – https://www.nist.gov/cyberframework
- Center for Internet Security (CIS) – https://www.cisecurity.org/controls
- The CIA Triad is another common approach to Cybersecurity focusing on Confidentiality, Integrity, and Availability. The CIA Triad is not a framework per se, but is an easy-to-understand approach to Cybersecurity.

While this list of resources may change over time, Enterprises have no excuse for not knowing what to do because mature Cybersecurity resources are readily available. IT Audit also has access to these resources making them important tools for IT Audit as well.

NIST Cybersecurity Framework (CSF) 2.0 (Figure 14.1)

NIST considers Cybersecurity in five dimensions:

- Identify
- Protect
- Detect
- Respond
- Recover

The Identify dimension teaches being aware of

- Vulnerabilities
- Exploits

The basic elements of cybersecurity are vulnerabilities and exploits. These are the weaknesses in businesses and the methods attackers use to exploit these weaknesses.

They could be roughly divided into two major categories:

- Technology Related Vulnerabilities
- Human Related Vulnerabilities

Technology Vulnerabilities

The solution for technology vulnerabilities is removing them. This generally involves installing patches or replacing technology to remove the vulnerabilities.

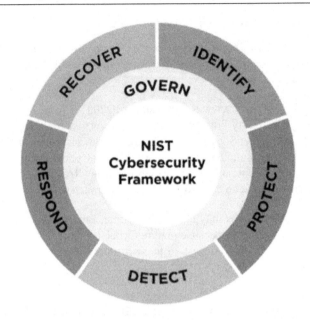

Figure 14.1 NIST Cybersecurity Framework. https://www.nist.gov/itl/small businesscyber/ planning-guides/nist-cybersecurity-framework

'Zero-day' vulnerabilities are unique because they already exist, but their existence is unknown. The vulnerability becomes known when it is discovered and/or exploited. Because the vulnerability already exists, there is no time in which to respond, hence, 'zero-day'. The best remedy for zero-day vulnerabilities is to install security patches as soon as they are released.

Human vulnerabilities

Human Vulnerabilities are the mistakes that we humans make unintentionally, maybe intentionally, opening doors for attackers. The most common of these is phishing whether by email, or telephone, or by saying we won something, or we are in danger, or we will be embarrassed. The message is designed to motivate us to open the door to the attacker. To be sure, there are attacks that do not involve fooling humans, but human exploit attacks are common and difficult for businesses to prevent. Because the requests are plausible and urgent, we may rush to comply.

A simple example: A business management firm received an urgent telephone call supposedly from a television production client that the crew had not been paid and were ready to walk off the set. The caller instructed the firm to immediately wire money to a bank account so the crew could be paid. Only after the money was sent did the firm find out that it was a scam. The anatomy of the scam was to panic employees into doing something that seemed legitimate but was not. A recent Washington Post article by Michelle Singletary was titled, "Put your smugness away. You are not too clever to be conned". These attacks are frequent. They are successful, even among intelligent sophisticated people. [– Michelle Singletary, "Put your smugness away. You are not too clever to be conned", *The Washinton Post*, February 21, 2024.]

Cybersecurity Vulnerabilities

The Cybersecurity landscape constantly changes. Tomorrow's list will inevitably include new items, but many vulnerabilities will continue to exist.

Reviewing the CISA's KEV in March of 2024, the vulnerabilities included 177 references to 'inject' and 752 references to 'code' out of a total of 1,083 vulnerabilities. This means 86% of these vulnerabilities allow attackers to control hardware and/or software by injecting malicious code or executing malicious code. The recommended action for 914 of these vulnerabilities was to 'apply updates'. About 219 of these vulnerabilities were associated with ransomware. The KEV referred to authenticate and authentication 283 times (26%), which means access controls could be defeated in approximately a quarter of these vulnerabilities. Remote Code Execution (RCE) is another favorite exploit. These numbers are provided for illustrative purposes. Different sources may classify these vulnerabilities differently and the list is constantly growing.

In terms of remediation, CISA suggests the following:

One of the most effective best practices to mitigate many vulnerabilities is to update software versions once patches are available and as soon as is practicable. If this is not possible, consider applying temporary workarounds or other mitigations, if provided by the vendor. If an organization is unable to update all software shortly after a patch is released, prioritize implementing patches for CVEs that are already known to be exploited or that would be accessible to the largest number of potential attackers (such as internet-facing systems). This advisory highlights vulnerabilities that should be considered as part of the prioritization process. To further assist remediation, **automatic software updates should be enabled whenever possible**. [Bold type added by author for emphasis.]
    – https://www.cisa.gov/news-events/cybersecurity-advisories/aa21-209a

Cybersecurity Issues

Consider the following common cybersecurity issues:

* Configuration Errors

    Misconfiguration of hardware or software can open the door to intruders. This is not a hardware or software vulnerability per se; it is an implementation failure. It can be as simple as failing to change default passwords, failing to patch systems, exposing sensitive information, and continuing to use vulnerable, outdated components, such as an ancient PC.

- Cybercrime

  Cybercrime is a business, like other businesses, except it involves malicious theft or interference. Ultimately, Cybercriminals are looking for ways to make money or interfere with the activities of others. They are motivated, skilled, and persistent. Do not underestimate them. They are as competent as any other trained person doing their job, only for malicious purposes.

- Cybersecurity Actors

  Insider Threats are the classic cases of angry, aggrieved employees or ex-employees who want to disrupt a current or former employer. In the early days of computing, this vulnerability was common. It still exists but is overshadowed by outsider attacks.

  Outsider Threats are malicious actions by cybercriminals and nations whose focuses are making money, disrupting normal activity, and gaining control, with slightly different motivations than disgruntled employees and ex-employees who want their employees to feel pain.

- Nation-State-Sponsored Attacks

  State-sponsored Actors are potentially the most troubling because they have access to 'deep pockets' and resources and they are protected. Their attacks are not limited to national targets, they focus on any entities they perceive as threats or as useful. Their attacks are an ideal way of obtaining information about other nations or influencing foreign nations and being able to deny culpability. Putting 'boots-on-the-ground' is obvious; hacking a foreign nation's infrastructure or industry is more difficult to attribute to the aggressor.

  As this book is being written, Russia is at war with Ukraine. This war has brought cyberwarfare to the front. There is now an abbreviation for cyberwarfare (CW). Unmanned drones and missiles are being used by both sides. Technology is being used to guide drones and missiles to their intended targets without having to acknowledge from whom the drones and missiles came (although that may be obvious) and being able to do this from a distance makes retaliation more difficult.

  Misinformation is also an essential aspect of cyberwarfare as both sides try to gain intelligence, deceive their adversaries, and gain control.

- Social Engineering

  Social Engineering is the application of sociological and psychological principles to deceive people. Social Engineering compromises people taking advantage of them by tricking them into performing certain actions, such as downloading malicious software, or giving out their credentials. Social Engineering fine-tunes these attacks to make them irresistible.

  It is one thing to get an email that tells you that you won a lottery you did not enter but it is another thing to get an email that goes into details regarding an inheritance and asks you to merely confirm a couple of pieces of information, maybe only a bank account number. The attacker may already know where your accounts are, which adds apparent credibility to their requests.

  As noted above, we are never too clever to avoid being scammed. Michelle wrote she "... wasn't prepared for how that criminal would use my hysteria to quash my common sense". [– Michelle Singletary, "Put your smugness away. You are not too clever to be conned", *The Washington Post*, February 21, 2024.] Social Engineering is designing irresistible pleas.

- Phishing and Ransomware

  Phishing and Ransomware often go together. Phishing, a form of Social Engineering, asks employees to download software, open an attachment, or click on a link which leads to ransomware that encrypts everything it can access. Subsequently, the attackers ask for a ransom. As noted above, 20% of the 'known exploited vulnerabilities' (KEV) identified by CISA were associated with ransomware.

  Phishing is not limited to emails and ransoms. It can occur via telephone and urge receiving parties to wire money to an account to avoid government actions, such as deportation, tax collection, or other harsh measures. Only recently, the author received a telephone call regarding a relative that was supposedly being booked at a police station. The caller offered to connect the author to a lawyer who would explain the situation and how to post bail for the relative.

- Third-Party Risk – Supply Chain Attacks

  Several recent attacks have raised the question of Third-party Risk. Recall the SolarWinds attack where the adversary entered businesses through a SolarWinds update. Also recall the Target Department Store attack where the adversary entered Target via Target's Heating, Ventilation, and Air Conditioning (HVAC) vendor.

Suppliers may have lax controls that allow their systems to be compromised so that when Suppliers connect their systems with their customers' systems, malware spreads across the connection.

Another avenue is Outsourced services. The Outsource may have compromised systems and may bring the malware into the Enterprise by virtue of the Outsource arrangement such as providing Administrative user services. This type of exploit recently hit the frontpages with exploding pagers and walkie talkies in Lebanon.

Cybersecurity Good Practices

The good news: multiple cybersecurity good practices exist. To list them all would involve another book so the list below cherry-picks good practices.

- Cybersecurity Plan

   Adopt and maintain a Cybersecurity Plan. A business may have considered a formal Cybersecurity Plan optional in the past but no longer. Cybersecurity incidents are no longer 'if' but 'when' the business will be subjected to an attack and will be compromised.

   Prudent assessment and planning assume that sooner or later a Cybersecurity incident will occur and prepares the business for that eventuality.

   A Cybersecurity Plan contains preventive, detective, and corrective actions. Businesses lacking a cybersecurity plan do not have to start from zero; the frameworks identified above provide a starting point that can be tailored to a business's specific objectives, situations, and constraints. In terms of urgency, a colleague pointed out that businesses do not necessarily survive a significant cyber incident. In other words, your business could be on the line.

- Border/Boundary Security and Intrusion Prevention

   Border or Boundary Security includes both physical and logical countermeasures, everything from having locks on doors (and windows) to having firewalls to control traffic into, out of, and around an Enterprise.

   Firewalls and Intrusion Detection and Prevention software are the most common devices between the Internet and a network or an individual computer. Their purpose is to prevent intruders and malware from invading a business and to prevent unauthorized exfiltration of data.

- Breach Management

   Breach Management assumes that the business will be compromised at some point. Notification requirements vary by jurisdiction and by marketplace. Enterprises need to know the requirements and be able to comply appropriately satisfying notification requirements and timing requirements. This requires a plan ready for that eventuality.

- Cybersecurity Insurance

  Cybersecurity Insurance is a necessity. Hopefully, it will continue to be available at an affordable price in the future as the number and cost of cyber claims increase.

  A side benefit of cybersecurity insurance is the insurer's assessment of the applicant's cyber readiness, including the adequacy and implementation of cybersecurity prevention, containment, remediation, and notification measures.

- Encryption

  Encryption involves converting text into an unintelligible combination of characters such that the only way to make sense of the combination is to decrypt it, which requires the encryption key. A good practice is to encrypt sensitive or confidential data so that if it is compromised, the hacker is unable to use the data. This is a basic requirement for healthcare data thanks to Health Insurance Portability and Accountability Act (HIPAA).

- Endpoint Security

  Endpoint security protects endpoints such as desktops, laptops, network devices, and other devices. It includes anti-virus endpoint software but is not limited to anti-virus software. Basically, it includes any cybersecurity software installed on a device to prevent and/or detect the presence of malware, malicious activity, and nuisance-ware.

  Spam is not necessarily malware. Spam is at least 'nuisance-ware'. It is inconvenient; it wastes resources. It may contain malware, but it is often just an annoyance, a time waster.

- Identity and Authorization Management (IAM)

  Authentication and Authorization are the two prongs of access control. Authentication identifies the identity of people and/or groups of people. Authorization determines what that person or group of people can do, where they can go, what privileges they have.

  IAM is a basic backbone of security, i.e., limiting access to authenticated users and controlling their access according to the privileges they are entitled to by virtue of their responsibilities.

  A corollary to IAM is the concept of 'Least Privilege', which is another way of saying users are only allowed to go and to do things that are specifically related to their responsibilities, nothing more, just the bare minimum.

  A second corollary is high-privilege accounts, such as system administrators. Because high-privilege accounts have the digital equivalent of a master key, these accounts require special attention and limitations. For example, persons with high-privilege accounts may have two accounts: a normal account for non-administrative uses and a separate high privilege account, which is reserved for activities that require administrative access. For non-superuser access, these parties are required to use their normal access accounts.

- Password Management

  Conventional wisdom is complex passwords that are regularly updated. This is a critical element in IAM, but it does have unintended consequences, such as causing users to write down their passwords because they are complex, and because they change frequently. Password vaults simplify this situation while Passkeys envision a 'password-less' future. For more information on Passkeys, see the FIDO Alliance.

  The FIDO Alliance is changing the nature of authentication with open standards for phishing-resistant sign-ins with passkeys that are more secure than passwords and SMS OTPs, simpler for consumers and employees to use, and easier for service providers to deploy and manage. The Alliance also provides standards for secure device onboarding to ensure the security and efficiency of connected devices operating in cloud and IoT environments.

  – https://fidoalliance.org

  Multi-Factor Authentication (MFA) adds an extra layer of confirmation to passwords by requiring additional verification, such as possession of a device linked with the account and biometric markers like fingerprints or facial images.

  Devices often come with administrative passwords, which can typically be discovered by a simple Google search. Consequently, whenever new devices are put into Production, change the default password and put the new administrative password under lock-and-key.

- Network Security (Firewalls, Segmentation)

  Network Security typically includes:

    – Firewalls to filter traffic into and out of a business
    – Network segmentation to limit access to different network segments
    – Using programmable network devices to control traffic within an Enterprise

  The underlying premise is that peoples' access is limited in the same way that submaster keys limit physical access within buildings.

- Segmentation

    Segmentation is an architectural design element. To understand seg-mentation, consider a large multi-floor commercial office building. The inside of the building is separated from the outside by a 'skin', the walls. To access the building, people need keys. Once inside the build-ing, their access is limited to certain parts of the building, such as dif-ferent floors or wings. Within a floor, access may be further limited to a suite of offices, and within the suite, further limited to specific offices.

    Segmentation is the logical equivalent of building compartmentaliza-tion. Network segmentation limits peoples' access into and around a network.

- Patch Management

    Patch Management involves at least two elements.

    First, patches need to be evaluated to confirm that the patch does what it is intended to do without undesirable side effects, such as breaking existing resources. In other words, avoid fixing one thing and breaking another.

    Second, patches are developed for multiple reasons, including imple-menting new functionality, changing existing functionality, fixing defects, and patching security vulnerabilities.

    Security patches generally need to be applied immediately because the issues they address may already exist, like seeing an open door, that should be closed, and closing it. Non-security patches may wait for a while before they are installed, and in some limited cases, non-security application patches may never be installed because that portion of the application is never used.

    The point is having policies and procedures that govern patch manage-ment including decisions regarding when and how to handle patches, which was previously covered under Change Management.

- Virtual Private Network (VPN)

    VPNs are used to ensure connection integrity whenever employees, suppliers, customers, or guests connect from outside the Enterprise with Enterprise systems. VPNs encrypt the portion of the connection that is over public communication links to prevent others from 'listen-ing in', which is referred to as 'the man in the middle'.

- Zero-Day Protection

    Zero-Day vulnerabilities are vulnerabilities that exist in computing resources that have not yet been identified. The vulnerabilities exist, but their existence is unknown until they are discovered. When hackers become aware of these vulnerabilities, they can take advantage of them before countermeasures can be developed and deployed.

Consequently, security patches are implemented as quickly as possible to remediate zero-day vulnerabilities.

- Training

    Many problems are easy to fix, such as infrastructure-related vulnerabilities; however, human mistakes, especially when people are rushed, overworked or stressed, are more difficult to address.

    The idea behind cybersecurity training is knowledge and awareness. While this is not perfect, it alerts users to typical cybersecurity risks and their roles in minimizing these risks. Training is like teaching people not to leave doors unlocked. In the case of zero-trust, not to be confused with zero-day, requests are confirmed before being acted on, links are checked before they are clicked, dubious websites are avoided, and so on.

- Vulnerability Assessments and Penetration Testing

    Implement regular vulnerability assessments and penetration testing to identify and mitigate potential security weaknesses.

- Configuration Management

    Ensure systems, devices, and applications are securely configured. If there is a default password, change it.

- Cloud Services

    Cloud Services are Shared Services. In other words, Cybersecurity is a 'shared responsibility', shared between Cloud Services Providers (CSPs) and their customers. Cybersecurity is not exclusively the responsibility of CSPs; customers must do their share to prevent cyber compromises.

- Application Security

    Ensure that your Applications are appropriately configured, operating securely, and residing on secure Infrastructure.

- Regular Backups

    Regular backups regularly tested are a critical corrective tool.

- SEIM

    Security Information and Event Management (SEIM) tools provide real-time analysis and alerting.

- Software Development

    If the Enterprise develops its own software, include security in the development process (AppSecDevOps).

- Decommissioning and Disposal

    Ensure that equipment is securely wiped or destroyed to prevent data recovery when it is retired.

- Monitor the Cybersecurity Landscape

    Keep up to date with the latest cybersecurity developments, threats, and best practices. Continuously adapt and strengthen your security posture. Your adversaries never sleep.

Auditing Cybersecurity

Auditing Cybersecurity requires a basic understanding of Cybersecurity. The actual implementation of various techniques and technologies can be delegated to engineers.

The role of IT Auditors, at a minimum, is reviewing the Enterprise's Cybersecurity Plans, Policies, Procedures, Practices, Standards, Tools, and Guidelines to confirm their efficacy and effectiveness.

Basic Cybersecurity auditing questions include at least the following:

- Does the Enterprise utilize an established Cybersecurity Framework?
- Does the Enterprise have written Cybersecurity Plans, Policies, Procedures, Practices, and Standards?
- Does the Enterprise actively maintain its plans, policies, procedures, practices, and standards?
- Are they suitable given the Enterprise's goals and objectives?
- Are they effective?
- Are they continuously in effect? Under what circumstances might they be suspended?
- Does the Enterprise have a Cybersecurity Training program, which all employees are required to attend at least annually?

Cybersecurity Audit Challenges

Cybersecurity today is a serious 'playground' for nefarious activities by well-funded organizations. These organizations, be they for-profit or for national gain, are constantly looking for ways to make money and/or disrupt the operations of their targets. This is not a 'gentleman's' sport; it is serious business by hostile actors engaged in money-making activities and/or seriously disrupting their targets. The challenge is keeping up with their activities. While most organizations cannot compete economically, they need to at least implement basic countermeasures including keeping their employees alert to the activities of 'bad actors'.

Privacy

Privacy is an interesting concept but not an 'inalienable right'. Being a private person with private information is to some extent a modern concept. People from day one had their secrets, but they lived in communities where they depended upon each other, and where they knew a lot about each other. Fast forward to urban communities where we know less and less about our neighbors and where we cherish our privacy. In this setting, Privacy becomes a major issue.

Two major problems with protecting Privacy:

- Privacy is dependent on statutes. It is a statutory right. Privacy does not exist in the absence of statutes. Encroaching on privacy may be intrusive or unethical, but not necessarily illegal.
- The Privacy we seek to protect funds businesses.

    Consider the free services we get from various Internet Service providers. Who pays the bills of these providers? From where does that money come? Answer: Our Data, our Private Data. We allow businesses to use our Private Data to fund their operations. This is the proverbial 'Deal with the Devil'.

Historically, people traded or sold goods and services to each other. We knew what we had to sell; we knew what others had to sell. For its survival, the community was closely intertwined with a lot of interdependence. Today, this relationship is transactional. There is some interdependence and some preferences, but sales and purchases are merely transactions. In this environment, the more suppliers know about their customers, the better off suppliers are, and maybe even the customers as well.

Our transactions are recorded as they occur, they are digitized, and the digits are passed from party to party. For example, our transaction information is passed from a seller to a fiscal intermediary, to other Third Parties. These 'digits' have a life of their own. They can be aggregated by suppliers and analyzed to determine customer preferences and habits. The 'digits' can be bought and sold in secondary markets outside of the customers' knowledge. In both situations, Data becomes essential revenue streams for businesses that collect this Data.

Lacking legal restrictions and requirements, no wonder Privacy is rapidly overrun.

As the NIST Figure 14.2 shows, Privacy and Cybersecurity overlap.

The big complication is the 'free services' we carve. We depend upon Google to answer our daily questions, to obtain information, which is fine, except none of us pay for this service. It is 'free', supposedly. The Big Questions:

- What Data is collected? Answer: Potentially every element of every interaction.
- What limitations are there on this data collection? Answer: Potentially very little.

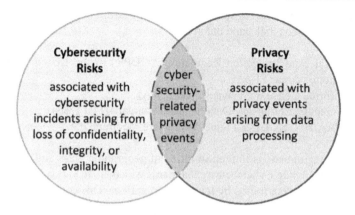

Figure 14.2 NIST Privacy Framework. *NIST Privacy Framework: A Tool for Improving Privacy through Enterprise Risk Management*, Version 1.0, NIST, p. 3.

Are we okay with everybody knowing everything about ourselves and being able to use that information to their advantage and potentially to our disadvantage?

The next crucial factor is the distinction between Personally Identifiable Information (PII) and information that is not Non-PII. Both are collected, stored, analyzed, and sold. The U.S. Department of Labor (DOL) defines PII as follows:

> Personal Identifiable Information (PII) is defined as: Any representation of information that permits the identity of an individual to whom the information applies to be reasonably inferred by either direct or indirect means. Further, PII is defined as information: (i) that directly identifies an individual (e.g., name, address, social security number or other identifying number or code, telephone number, email address, etc.) or (ii) by which an agency intends to identify specific individuals in conjunction with other data elements, i.e., indirect identification. (These data elements may include a combination of gender, race, birth date, geographic indicator, and other descriptors). Additionally, information permitting the physical or online contacting of a specific individual is the same as personally identifiable information. This information can be maintained in either paper, electronic or other media.
>
> – https://www.dol.gov/general/ppii, March 2024

This distinction becomes important because much of the information that is bought and sold is not necessarily PII. It is information about our activities, our habits, and our preferences with and without being specifically linked with us.

In the United States, the federal government has been hesitant to step in to regulate this area. Yes, there are regulations, but the European Union (EU) has been much more aggressive in this area than the United States. Separately, we can wonder why.

While there are many regulations, there is a dearth of regulations regarding Privacy. Regulations that stand out are:

- General Data Protection Regulations (GDPR) of the EU and European Economic Area (EEA)
- California Consumer Privacy Act (CCPA)
- Payment Card Industry Data Security Standard (PCI DSS)
- HIPAA/HiTech, United States healthcare requirements

Each set of regulations is limited to different geographic areas and/or different marketplaces. Unlike Cybersecurity Standards which are to varying degrees universal, Privacy is determined by location and market. This could change, but at least for now, this is the case.

From the IT Audit perspective, given these limitations, Privacy involves the following dimensions:

- Does the Enterprise have Privacy Policies?
- Are these Policies consistent with the Enterprise's values?
- Are the Enterprise's activities consistent with these Policies?
- Is the Enterprise subject to external Privacy requirements by virtue of venue, statute, or membership?

While transparency may be preferred, there is little that insists on transparency. Hence, transparency ultimately depends on Enterprises and their values, especially related to the sales of customer and business partner Data.

What is lacking in the Privacy arena is Data Rights, which give people the right to manage their own Data. GDPR gives the citizens of the EU those rights to manage their Data. The rights belong to them regardless of where they are, which means if they are outside of the EU, they still have those rights. They did not forfeit them when they left the EU. This allows Europeans to manage their Data on The Internet and while traveling, and businesses are obligated to comply with their users' wishes.

Ultimate Cybersecurity Challenge

As if all of this is not enough, consider the following: The Ultimate Cybersecurity Challenge, at least of this decade, maybe Artificial Intelligence (AI).

- Will attackers be able to use AI to create malware and attack targets?
- Will AI make the targeting more effective, more irresistible, and more demanding?
- Will AI be more effective in stealing Data?

- Will AI be more effective in distributing fake information? Already, AI can create sounds and images purportedly of reality which are nearly impossible to verify.
- Will AI be more effective in taking over remote devices and using them for malicious purposes?
- Will AI be more effective at disrupting operations, especially of critical infrastructure?
- Will AIs be able to infect each other causing malicious activity?
- Will developers of AI take the time to ensure none of these outcomes can occur, especially in the current rush to market Generative AI?
- Will Privacy and Cybersecurity boil down to a war between competing AIs?

We have already seen the adoption and adaption of AI to war. One can only imagine the effects of AI on future wars, including robots fighting robots. This raises the question of what AI ought to be able to do and what ought to be 'out of bounds' with unalterable protections to prevent unacceptable uses.

Chapter 15

Conducting IT Audits

Chapter Contents:

Introduction

Conversations about IT Audits involve the intersection of

- Professional Standards, and
- Practice Opportunities.

IT Auditors can function:

- As Auditors
- As Consultants, Advisors, or Assistants

While this distinction was always the case, the CPA Evolution Initiative, which went into effect in January 2024, recognized a new third discipline for Certified

DOI: 10.4324/9781032689388-15

Public Accountants (CPAs), Information Systems and Controls (ISC). While the third discipline is new, *it is also long overdue.* CPAs have been actively involved in computerized records since the beginning of computer applications. IT Auditing fits neatly into this newly identified discipline. It is a practice opportunity for CPAs and non-CPAs as well.

Professional Standards impose certain restrictions. Consider the following. Auditors, of whatever type, are expected to be fair, impartial, neutral, nonpartisan, free of bias, and free of conflicts of interest. This characteristic is referred to as Objectivity. Auditors are expected to be Objective, to see things impartially without bias. This expectation includes both CPAs and non-CPAs, such as Internal Auditors and IT Professionals.

However, the Professional Standards for financial auditors, especially CPAs, take this requirement one step further. They require CPAs to be Independent in addition to being Objective. Independence means CPAs cannot audit or issue opinions on work in which they were previously involved or with which they were or are related. Independence means no connections with the entities being audited.

Below are five overlapping practice use cases. They illustrate these distinctions.

1. First, and foremost, are IT Audits being performed in *conjunction with a Financial Audit.*

   The primary objective of the IT Audit in this use case is confirming the Suitability and/or Adequacy of the Auditee's System of Internal Controls.

   The IT Auditor may be part of the Financial Audit team or a resource working in conjunction with the financial auditors. If the auditee is registered with the SEC, the audit would occur under the Public Company Accounting Oversight Board's (PCAOB) audit rules. If the auditee is not SEC registered, then the AICPA's Auditing Standards Board's (ASB) rules apply.

2. The second use case is an IT Audit *not associated with a Financial Audit.*

   This is like the first use case, but in this use case, the IT Audit has no direct connection with a financial audit and could be performed by any suitable IT Audit practitioner.

3. The third use case is an IT Audit performed for the purpose of generating a System and Organization Controls Report (*SOC Report*).

   This use case is limited to CPAs and is performed according to the AICPA's SOC requirements, which are covered in the next chapter. This practice area has grown significantly and continues to grow.

4. The fourth use case is an IT Audit for a *special purpose* or project.

   This may focus on a specific application, or service, or on business process improvement, or be in the context of Cybersecurity assurance, or for some other reason. It also could be performed by any skilled practitioner.

5. The fifth use case is *IT assistance*, which may include both assistance and assessment.

This could be done in conjunction with a specific project, initiative, or as a routine activity. It can be performed by Internal Auditors or by experienced IT professionals. It does not require a CPA license. This may, however, require some re-tooling or special training for accounting practitioners.

This may be the largest practice area for IT Audit professionals where assistance is required to assure management and/or ownership that automation is performing as intended with appropriate safeguards consistent with the entity's Business Objectives.

All five cases require **Objectivity**. Clearly, the first and third use cases also require **Independence**. The second, fourth, and fifth use cases may or may not require **Independence** depending on the specifics of the project and credentials of the auditor. Remember any practitioner who holds itself out as a CPA is bound by the professional standards of the AICPA. Hence, if the IT Auditor is a CPA and '*holds itself out as a CPA*', then *both Objectivity and Independence* apply regardless of the circumstances. This means that the CPA can assist clients but cannot subsequently issue opinions that involve previous work. So, *one service or the other, but not both.*

While there are practice opportunities in all five use cases, use cases Two, Four, and Five stand out. The new CPA discipline ISC is a practice opportunity for CPAs and non-CPAs as well. Individuals in large CPA firms may practice in this area and not be CPAs. The need for 'an Adequate System of Internal Controls' will require continuous attention.

SOC Reports, which can only be prepared by CPAs, represent new practice opportunities for CPAs. For SOC Reports, the same professional standards that apply to financial auditing apply to SOC Reports.

Per AT-C Section 320, ".**02** ... a practitioner is required to comply with section 105, *Concepts Common to All Attestation Engagements*, and section 205, *Examination Engagements*". "... the practitioner is responsible for complying with all the requirements in sections 105 and 205. (Ref: par. .A2)"
—AICPA, SSAE 18, AT-C Section 320, p. 231

Today, there are CPA firms that focus on SOC Reports to the exclusion of traditional accounting, audit, and tax services.

Consider the distinction between IT Auditors and IT Consultants. Arguably, a good deal of overlap exists. Many advisory opportunities exist for IT Auditors and IT Consultants to collaborate and for IT Auditors to be IT Consultants, especially in the areas of Business Process Automation, Information Systems, Process Improvement, Internal Controls, IT Architecture, and Software Development. Since this book is directed to IT Audit, consider the variety of assistance and projects that exist in these areas and the expertise that IT Auditors can contribute to these projects. Figure 15.1 illustrates the relationship between IT

Figure 15.1 IT Auditor – Auditor or Consultant.

Audit and IT Consulting outside of the constraints imposed when independence is required.

Simply, IT Auditors can be Auditors or Consultants; they can provide IT assistance as Internal Auditors or as outsourced IT Consultants.

Professional Auditing Standards

Depending upon the IT Auditor's credentials and how Auditors hold themselves out, one or more of the following sets of professional standards may apply:

- For CPAs, https://us.aicpa.org/content/dam/aicpa/research/standards/codeof-conduct/downloadabledocuments/2009codeofprofessionalconduct.pdf
- For Members of ISACA, *IT Audit Framework (ITAF™) A Professional Practices Framework for IT Audit*, 4th Edition, ISACA, 2020.
- For Members of The Institute of Internal Auditors, the *International Standards for the Professional Practice of Internal Auditing (Standards)*, The IIA, 2017.

These Professional Standards share the Objectivity requirement. The primary difference among them is Independence. In the case of Internal Auditors, Objectivity, not Independence, is the professional standard. Internal Auditors are creatures of the businesses in which they operate; hence, they are not Independent, but they should be Objective.

Regardless of the activities of IT Auditors, they are expected to at least be Objective in their assessments, recommendations, and reports and in certain cases to be Independent of the Auditee.

Conducting IT Audits

As with other activities of this significance or magnitude, the first step is developing a Plan. Hence, these projects typically unfold in at least three major phases:

- Develop an IT Audit Plan
- Execute the IT Audit Plan
- Evaluate the Findings and Issue an IT Audit Report

Each Phase involves multiple steps, activities, and resources. And final reports may or may not be required.

In the case of an IT Audit in conjunction with a financial audit, the financial auditors typically dictate the nature and requirements of the IT Audit. The role of IT Auditors in this case is to perform the assessments and testing the financial auditors require in support of their financial and internal control opinions.

If the IT Audit is not in conjunction with a financial audit, then the IT Auditors develop their IT Audit plans and execute them. If the auditee is only seeking Internal Control assistance, an IT Audit Report may not be required. With or without a final report, IT Auditors develop their IT Audit Plans in conjunction with the auditee and its needs and requirements.

IT Audit Plans

A typical IT Audit Plans include:

- Identification of Project Scope and Objectives
- Statement of Work (SOW), including the procedures to be performed and the assessments to be made
- Project Results and/or Outcomes, including Recommendations
- Timing, Staffing, and Resource Requirements
- Audit Documentation Requirements

Scope and Objectives

Project Scope and Objectives may be as broad as the business' System of Internal Controls or as narrow as a specific topic, or incident, or project, such as a cybersecurity, software development, software implementation, or business process improvement. The Objectives could be as simple as assessing a situation and/or recommending internal control improvements, or as complex as detailed reporting including multiple findings and recommendations.

The ultimate Project Objective may be …

- Assessment oriented
- Problem Solution oriented
- Improvement Recommendations oriented

The nature of the work depends on the needs and requests of the auditee.

Statement of Work

An SOW identifies the activities that will be conducted, the procedures that will be performed, the areas that will be addressed in the Audit, and potential staffing and resource requirements.

These procedures will reflect the specific tasks required based on scope, objectives, and context, i.e., audit or advice. The larger the project the more likely project management will need project scheduling software where Work Breakdown Schedules (WBS) identify the specific activities that will be performed and their sequence and scheduling. This software typically includes Gantt Charts and Critical Path Analysis. The procedures can include researching, understanding existing business processes, changing existing business processes, revising or adding new business process controls, changing/revising current settings, testing, re-performance, validation, documenting, updating existing documentation, and so on.

For the uninitiated, multiple resources are available regarding these procedures and project management. The Institute of Internal Audit issued two GTAGs that address Conducting an Audit: *GTAG 11 Developing the IT Audit Plan* and *GTAG 12 Auditing IT Projects*, along with other GTAG's that focus on specific topics, such as Auditing Governance and Auditing Cybersecurity. Multiple resources are available that discuss auditing in great detail.

Project Results and Outcomes, Including Recommendations

Outcomes are the expected results of the work which may be confirmatory or may involve recommendations regarding new or revised operating procedures, devices, and/or Internal Controls. In any case from an Audit Planning standpoint, the desired outcomes should be identified, at least approximately, before the work begins. The exact results may drift during the project. The bigger the project, the more likely the project will encounter scope drift, also referred to as 'scope creep', generally expansive, although project scope can be reduced.

Timing, Staffing, Resourcing

Two challenging elements related to Timing, Staffing, and Resources are:

- Technical requirements that entail other expertise
- Sufficient time to remediate gaps and deficiencies

Depending upon the specifics of the IT Audit, special IT skills may be required to conduct the Audit. The firm conducting the IT Audit may have these skills in-house or may rely on outside experts for assistance. Either way these requirements need to be identified and their availability may affect the project schedule.

Project timing may be as soon as feasible, may be determined by a master schedule, or may be backward scheduled from an optimum completion data, such as prior to the beginning of a business's fourth quarter. Why before the fourth quarter? Because the business may need to demonstrate the remediation of deficiencies for at least one quarter before year-end. Timing may also hinge on staff availability and/or other auditee or auditor commitments.

Audit Documentation

Audit Project Documentation typically identifies the work that was performed, how the work was performed, and the outcomes or conclusions drawn from that work. Auditees may have specific formats for the documentation and/or the IT Auditor may adopt and/or adapt formats with which they are familiar.

A frequently used format for Business Process, Risk, and Control purposes is a Risk and Control Matrix (RACM) [Figure 3.1]. Per previous discussion, RACMs clearly identify at least the following items:

- Business Objectives, i.e., business objectives explicitly identifying desired outcomes and/or results.
- Risks to the Achievement of Business Objectives, i.e., conditions that will reduce or prevent the achievement of the Business Objectives.
- Controls to Remediate the Risks, i.e., controls that reduce the risk of not achieving the Business Objectives.
- Tests to Confirm the Internal Control Design is Suitable, Effective, and was In Effect during the Period being audited.

Executing IT Audit Plans

In terms of executing an IT Audit Plan, a variety of approaches are available:

- Assessing existing RACMs (or something similar).
- Developing new RACMs (or something similar).
- Identifying Conditions, Criteria, Causes, and Effects.
- Developing relevant Recommendations and/or Remediations.
- A Domain-based approach that involves procedures and techniques that are specific to the domain.

  For example, Penetration Testing for Cybersecurity vulnerabilities, or an Access Control review to confirm who has what kinds of access to different parts of a system, or reviewing a business process and evaluating the application controls in that business process, etc.

Using Risk and Control Matrices

If **Risk and Control Matrices** (RACMs) already exist, the IT Audit may be primarily a re-testing of the RACMs and updating them as appropriate. The revisions could involve adding additional Objectives, Risks, Controls, or Tests, revising what is already present, or deleting items that no longer apply. As a practical matter, the only way something might disappear is if a business activity disappears or a business process changes significantly requiring a new RACM. In a stable environment, the assignment is more likely to be a confirmation with minor revisions. If significant changes in business processes have occurred, the RACMs may need to be revised because the objectives, the process, or its artifacts have changed.

If RACMs do not exist, then an IT Audit will require significantly more work to identify the relevant business domains, the business processes, their business objectives, the risks to the achievement of these objectives, and the controls that remediate the risks to ensure the achievement of the business objectives.

For more information regarding RACMs, review the chapter on Internal Controls.

Alternate Approaches: Condition, Criteria, Cause, Effect, Recommendations

Alternate approaches are illustrated by ISACA in Figure 15.2.

This approach focuses on conditions, situations that are somehow broken, ineffective, or unsatisfactory, and asks: How can they be fixed or improved?

Domain-Based Approach

A Domain-Based Approach looks at major areas, such as Infrastructure, Access Control, Change Management, Cybersecurity, a major business process, such as selling or buying, or a major application, such as an ERP or a CRM system. This approach focuses on the systems that are involved and asks: How can this domain be improved? The typical focus here is confirming, improving, or upgrading the system of Internal Controls related to a specific domain; hence, the domain drives project context and content.

Issuing IT Audit Reports

Typically, an IT Audit Report will identify at least the following:

- Title, Author, Date
- Scope and Objectives
- Methods and Procedures
- Findings
- Recommendations
- Appendices as Needed

Figure 2—Five Attributes of an Audit Finding		
Attribute	**Description**	**Identifies**
Condition	Findings	The auditor findings. It is a statement of the problem or deficiency. This may be in terms such as control weaknesses, operational problems, or noncompliance with management or legal requirements.
Criteria	Requirements and baseline	Statement of requirements and identification of the baseline that was used for comparison against the auditor findings, based on the audit evidence.
Cause	Reason for the condition	While the explanation of the cause may require the identification of the responsible party, it is suggested that, unless required by audit policy, the report should identify the organizational business unit or person's title and not the individual's name. The same should be applied to the identification of the person representing the relevant point of accountability.
Effect	Impact of the condition	The answer to the question "so what?" It explains the adverse impact to the operational or control objective. By articulating impact and risk, the element of effect is very important in helping to persuade auditee management to take corrective action.
Recommendation	Suggested corrective action	While the corrective action should eliminate the problem or deficiency noted in the condition, the corrective action should be directed toward addressing the cause.

Source: ISACA®, IS Audit Reporting, USA, 2015

Figure 15.2 ISACA Audit Finding Example. Reproduced with the Permission of ISACA. "The Components of the IT Audit Report", ISACA *Journal Vol 1*, ISACA, p. 8.

If the IT Audit work includes a set of RACMs, these would typically be included in the report as part of the report or as an appendix to the report.

ISACA also offers the following list of potential components for an IT Audit Report (Figure 15.3).

ISACA's suggestion may be more than is needed. Feel free to adapt this outline to a project's specific requirements.

In terms of IT Audit reports, keep in mind the responsibility for a Suitable or Adequate System of Internal Controls rests with the Enterprise and its management. This does not necessarily mean management establishes the System of Internal Controls, but it does mean management is responsible for insisting on a Suitable System of Internal Controls and providing the necessary resources for the Enterprise to have and to maintain such an environment.

Remember the concept of Tone-at-the-Top. If management does not care about Internal Controls, being an Auditor, IT or otherwise, could be a difficult and lonely job.

Figure 1—IT Audit Report Components	
Report Component	**Source**
An appropriate and distinctive title	ITAF
Identification of the recipients to whom the report is directed	ITAF
Identification of the responsible party	ITAF
Table of contents	IS Audit Reporting
Introduction	IS Audit Reporting
Description of the scope of the audit engagement	ITAF
A statement identifying the source of management's representation about the effectiveness of control procedures	ITAF
A statement that professionals have conducted the audit engagement to express an opinion on the effectiveness of control procedures	ITAF
Identification of the purpose (objectives) of the audit	ITAF
Description of the criteria or disclosure of the source of the criteria	ITAF
A statement that the audit engagement has been conducted in accordance with ISACA IS audit and assurance standards or other applicable professional standards	ITAF
Further explanatory details about the variables that affect the assurance provided	ITAF
Findings, conclusions and recommendations for corrective action including management's response	ITAF
Auditor reply	IS Audit Reporting
A paragraph stating that because of the inherent limitations of any internal control, misstatements due to errors or fraud may occur and go undetected	ITAF
A summary of the (audit) work performed	ITAF
An expression of opinion about whether, in all material respects, the design and/or operation of control procedures in relation to the area of activity were effective	ITAF
Executive summary	IS Audit Reporting
Where appropriate, references to any other separate reports that should be considered	ITAF
Date of issuance of the audit engagement report. In most instances, the date of the report is based upon the issue date.	ITAF
Names of individuals or entity responsible for the report	ITAF
Appendix	IS Audit Reporting

Figure 15.3   IT Audit Report Components. Reproduced with the
Permission of ISACA. "The Components of the IT Audit Report",
ISACA Journal Vol 1, ISACA, p. 7

Chapter 16

Preparing System and Organization Controls (SOC) Reports

Chapter Contents:

Introduction to System and Organization Controls Reports

In April 1992, the AICPA introduced the Statement on Auditing Standards (SAS) 70, *Reports on the Processing of Transactions by Service Organizations*. SAS 70 was "the source of the requirements and guidance for CPAs reporting on controls at service organizations and for CPAs auditing the financial statements of entities that use service organizations to accomplish tasks that may affect their financial statements." [—https://www.journalofaccountancy.com/issues/2010/ aug/ 20103009.html] In 2011, SAS 70 was replaced by Statement on Standards for Attestation Engagements (SSAE) 16, which was subsequently updated to SSAE 18 in 2016. SSAE 18 is the current Professional Standard for System and Organization Control Reports (SOC Reports).

DOI: 10.4324/9781032689388-16

Over time, the focus and terminology of these reports shifted. In 2017, the AICPA redefined the SOC acronym, changing it from Service Organization Controls to System and Organization Controls. The redefinition was made to broaden these examinations beyond service organizations and beyond the types of controls being examined. This shift broadened SOC Reports beyond just Internal Control over Financial Reporting (ICOFR).

System and Organization Controls Reports (SOC Reports) are now available in multiple versions:

- SOC 1® – SOC for Service Organizations: ICFR
- SOC 2® – SOC for Service Organizations: Trust Services Criteria
- SOC 2®+
- SOC 3® – SOC for Service Organizations: Trust Service Criteria for General Use Report
- SOC for Cybersecurity
- SOC for Supply Chain

SOC 2® Reports include both Type 1 and Type 2 reports. The distinction between them, which is clearly laid out in the *SOC 2 Guide*, Table 1-1, pages 7 and 8, is the absence of Testing in Type 1 reports and the presence of Testing in Type 2 reports. A SOC 2+ is a SOC 2 for a Service Organization that implemented additional processes or controls to meet the requirements of a specific control framework; hence, the scope is beyond that of a normal SOC 2 examination.

For simplicity and comprehensiveness, the focus of this chapter will be a SOC 2 Type 2 Report.

The AICPA describes SSAE 16 reports as primarily an auditor-to-auditor communication and not intended for general distribution and thereby is referred to as a Restricted Use Report:

1.08 A SOC2 report is intended for use by those who have sufficient knowledge and understanding of the service organization, the services it provides, and the system used to provide those services, among other matters …

1.09 Without such knowledge, users are likely to misunderstand the content of the SOC 2 report, the assertions made by management, and the service auditor's opinion, all of which are included in the report. For that reason, a SOC 2 report … is **restricted** to use by users with that knowledge. **Restricting** the use of a service auditor's report in a SOC 2 examination is discussed beginning in paragraph 4.36 [Bold type added by author for emphasis.]

—SOC 2 Guide: Reporting on an Examination of Controls at a Service Organization Relevant to Security, Availability, Process integrity, Confidentiality, or Privacy, AICPA, October 15, 2022, p. 4

As an auditor-to-auditor report, they are only available to clients of service organizations, and user entities, and auditors of user entities. As Restricted Use reports, not general use reports, they are not available beyond the parties specifically named in the restricted use paragraph.

Also, keep in mind that SOC Reports are not certifications; they are merely reports. However, these reports are becoming more common and more important as businesses increasingly rely on external parties for IT Products and Services. CPA firms now exist that limit their services to SOC examinations and similar compliance services and do not provide traditional accounting, financial auditing, or tax services. These firms reflect the importance and increasing role of SOC Reports.

SOC Report Professional Standards

The preparation and issuance of SOC Reports is limited to CPAs. AT-C Section 320 summarizes the purpose of SOC Reports and identifies additional requirements placed on CPAs who perform SOC engagements. These requirements are in addition to the normal routine professional standards and requirements imposed on CPAs. Hence,

> Section 320: ".01 This section contains performance and reporting requirements and application guidance for a service auditor examining controls at organizations that provide services to user entities when those controls are likely to be relevant to user entities' internal control over financial reporting."
>
> —AICPA, SSAE 18, AT-C Section 320

> Section 320: ".02 In addition to complying with this section, a practitioner is required to comply with section **105, *Concepts Common to All Attestation Engagements***, and section **205, *Examination Engagements*.**" [Bold type added by author for emphasis.]
>
> —AICPA, SSAE 18, AT-C Section 320

CPAs are familiar with the key phrase in financial audit opinions 'fairly presents'. SOC extends this attestation to SOC Reports as well, with the following attestation: "fairly presents the service organization's system that was designed and implemented throughout the specified period." [—AICPA, SSAE 18, AT-C Section 320.07.i.]

Service Organizations and their Management are responsible for the following:

- An **adequate** System of Internal Controls
- An **effective** System of Internal Controls
- **Descriptions** of their System of Internal Controls
- **Assertions** regarding the Controls and their Control objectives

- That the description and assertions regarding the organization's system **fairly present** the service organization's System of Internal Controls
- That the System of Internal Controls is **suitably designed**
- That the System of Internal Controls achieved its objectives [, **was effective,**] during the period being audited. [Bold type and 'was effective' added by the author for emphasis]

—AICPA, SSAE 18, AT-C Section 320.08.
Management's description ...

IT Auditors may assist organizations in the development of a suitable System of Internal Controls; however, the System of Internal Controls is the responsibility of the organization and its management, notwithstanding the conflict of interest that assistance creates relative to issuing a SOC Report. The point is that the responsibility is that of the organization and its management, not of the IT Auditor. Without this recognition of and acceptance by the organization, SOC Reports cannot be issued. This responsibility is a fundamental pre-condition, the same fundamental pre-condition required for financial statement audits, i.e., the financial statements are the responsibility of the auditee, not the auditor.

A cautionary note: While this may be less likely to occur in financial statement audits, IT Auditors working with their clients may be inclined to assume more responsibility than is appropriate for an IT Auditor. In contrast, IT Consultants can be very involved in the design and implementation of a System of Internal Controls; however, they cannot issue SOC Reports for a variety of reasons, not the least of which are conflicts of interest and not being CPAs.

Regarding the distinction between SOC 2 Type 1 Reports and SOC 2 Type 2 Reports, see the following quotation from AT-C Section 320.08:

Type 1 report. See management's description of a service organization's system and a service auditor's report on that description and on the **suitability of the design** of controls.

Type 2 report. See management's description of a service organization's system and a service auditor's report on that description and on the **suitability of the design and operating effectiveness** of controls. [Bold type added by author for emphasis.]

—AICPA, SSAE 18, AT-C Section 320.08.
Type 1 report, Section 320.08. Type 2 report

Notice the difference between the two definitions, the absence of 'operating effectiveness' from Type 1 reports and its presence in Type 2 reports. The determination of operating effectiveness occurs only after Service Auditors have *tested* the design and the operation of the system of internal controls and concluded that the internal controls achieved their objectives throughout the span of time covered by the report.

For a comprehensive comparison of SOC 2 Type 1 and Type 2 Reports, see SOC 2 Guide: Reporting on an Examination of Controls at a Service Organization Relevant to Security, Availability, Process integrity, Confidentiality, or Privacy, AICPA, October 15, 2022, pages 7 and 8.

While this chapter focuses on SOC 2 Type 2 Reports, the AICPA also has provisions for SOC 3 – SOC for Service Organizations: Trust Services Criteria for General Use Report, SOC for Cybersecurity, and SOC for Supply Chain. Appendix A in the SOC 2 Guide compares SOC 1, SOC 2, and SOC 3 examinations and Appendix B compares SOC 2, SOC for Supply Chain and SOC for Cybersecurity examinations.

Management's Obligations

Management's obligations relative to a System of Internal Controls are the following:

- To acknowledge its responsibility to have a Suitable System of Internal Controls.
- To have a complete, accurate, and suitably presented description of its system of internal controls.
- To have a reasonable basis for its assertions, including suitability.
- To identify its control objectives.
- To identify the 'risks that threaten the achievement of its control objectives'.
- To have used 'suitable criteria' to confirm that its controls were 'suitably designed'.
- To confirm its controls 'operated effectively as of a specified date', for a Type 1 Report, or 'throughout the specified period' of the report, for a Type 2 Report.
- And the description and assertions must be provided to the Service Auditor and the Service Organization's customers.

Regarding the 'Suitability of the Criteria', Section 320.15 requires IT Auditors to evaluate whether management's description 'fairly presents' its System of Internal Controls. SSAE 18 identifies the following essential characteristics:

- Identify 'types of services provided' and 'classes of transactions processed.'
- The "automated and manual systems by which services are provided ... and by which transactions are

  - Initiated,
  - Authorized,
  - Recorded,
  - processed,
  - corrected as necessary, and
  - transferred to the reports ..."

- "The information used in the performance of [its] procedures ..."
- Addressing "significant events and conditions other than transactions".
  —AICPA, SSAE 18, AT-C Section 320.15, p. 237ff

In the case of SOC Type 2 Reports, Management's obligations also include:

- Relevant details of changes to the controls during the period covered by the report.
- The obligation 'Not to omit or distort' relevant information.

AT-C Section 320.16 identifies the suitability of the criteria used to evaluate the controls.

- Management must identify the 'risks that threaten the achievement of the control objectives'.
- In the case of a Type 1 Report, the identified controls by management, if they '**operated effectively**, provide reasonable assurance' that 'the risks would not prevent' the controls from achieving their objectives. [Bold type added by author for emphasis.]

Section 17 requires the controls to be '**consistently applied**' during the period covered by the SOC report. Intermittent controls are problems, as well as suspending, disabling, overriding, or otherwise interfering with controls.

Section 18 requires a 'written assertion' from management that "addresses all the criteria management used to evaluate the fairness of the presentation of the description, the suitability of the design of the controls, and in a type 2 engagement, the operating effectiveness of the controls." [—AICPA, SSAE 18, AT-C Section 320.18.] This section makes clear that management is responsible for the organization's System of Internal Controls.

The following section, Section 19, addresses materiality as a factor.

The service auditor's consideration of materiality should include the fair presentation of management's description of the service organization's system, the suitability of the design of controls to achieve the related control objectives stated in the description and, in the case of a type 2 report, the operating effectiveness of the controls to achieve the related control objectives stated in the description.
  —AICPA, SSAE 18, AT-C Section 320.19

Further with respect to Materiality:

Misstatements, including omissions, are considered to be material if there is a substantial likelihood that, individually or in the aggregate, they would

influence the judgment made by a reasonable user based on the financial statements. [Bold type added by author for emphasis.]
—*SOC 2 Guide*, AICPA, Oct 15, 2022, p. iv

Materiality, which applies to financial audits, applies equally to SOC engagements; however, the criteria of influencing a judgment by a reasonable user is now directed toward the reliance customers place on their service organizations and what is elsewhere described as 'shared responsibility.' Do customers, reasonable users, understand the limitations on services provided by their service providers and appropriately compensate for those limitations. Materiality requires knowledge of services that might cause harm due to misunderstandings. Please recall the discussion of Shared Responsibilities in the Cloud Services chapter. Shared Responsibility is intended to clearly identify issues for which Customers are responsible.

Section 21 specifically refers to an 'internal audit function'. A reminder that IT Auditors can, within limits, rely on the work of a Service Organization's Auditors and a reminder that an IT Auditor who prepares SOC Reports must be independent of the Service Organization's internal audit function; however, a CPA not involved in a SOC Report for the Service Organization could work with or be part of the Service Organization's internal audit function.

Scope of SOC Engagement

AT-C Section 320.25 Description of Evidence for SOC Report offers the following evidentiary list:

- Reasonable Control Objectives
- Evidence the Controls were implemented
- Identify Complementary User Entity Controls
  Again, recall Cloud Service Providers and the concept of 'Shared Responsibility'.
- Services provided by Subservice Entities
  The Standard provides two methods for handling services provided by Subservice Entities:

  - The Carve-out Method
  - The Inclusive Method

For more information regarding services provided by Subservice Entities, consult the definitions provided in AT-C Section 320.08.

Section 27 addresses the Service Auditor's Assessment:

- Assess that the controls were suitably **designed** to achieve their control objectives

Elsewhere the words 'adequate' and 'appropriate' are used when referring to the quality of the design of Internal Controls.

- 'Evaluate the Risks that threaten the achievement of control objectives'
- Evaluate the linkage between Controls and their Risks
- Determine that the Controls were implemented

For Type 2 Engagements, additional assessment is required:

- Test the Controls, their Design, Operating Effectiveness, and Continuous operation during the period covered by the report
- Understand changes that occurred in the Controls during the audit period and their 'significance' relative to the Controls and their Effectiveness

  Were the changes the result of deviations or in response to changes in the objectives or their risks or the environment in which the controls worked?

Section 30 requires reliable information from the Service Organization.

Section 31 identifies other procedures that may be performed by Service Auditors.

- 'How was the Control Applied?'
- 'Was the Control applied consistently?'
- 'How and by Whom was the Control applied?'

—AICPA, SSAE 18, AT-C Section 320.31

Section 31 also requires a 'method for selecting the items to be tested'.

Section 32 inevitably deviations will occur. Deviations require Service Auditors to 'investigate the nature and cause of any deviations'. This includes having an expected rate of deviation within which deviations are acceptable. Additional testing may be required to determine if the control objectives stated in the management's description 'operated effectively throughout the specified period'. The testing may indicate that 'the control did not operate effectively throughout the specified period'.

Section 33, Fraud, raises three questions:

- The system of controls was 'not fairly presented'
- 'The controls are not suitably designed'
- 'The controls did not operate effectively'

—AICPA, SSAE 18, AT-C Section 320.33

Section 34, Incidents of regulatory noncompliance, 'fraud or uncorrected mis-statements' may affect the service audit.

Section 36 discusses Written Representations regarding noncompliance and fraud 'that could adversely affect the fairness of' management's description.

SOC 2 Type 1 and Type 2 Reports

Because SOC 2 Type 2 Report are more extensive than SOC 2 Type 1 Reports, the outline below covers SOC 2 Type 2 Reports. The difference between a Type 2 and a Type 1 Reports is the testing of the System of Internal Controls.

Content of SOC 2 Type 2 Report

Section 40 outlines the content of SOC 2 Type 2 Reports. Below is a key word summary for Type 2 Reports:

a. 'Independent'
b. 'Appropriate addressee'
c. Identification of 'Management's description of the service organizations system' of internal controls
d. Relevant internal controls
e. Complementary user entity controls
f. Management's assertions
g. Service auditor's responsibilities
h. Statement regarding service auditor's examination
i. Internal control objectives
j. Inherent limitations regarding controls
k. Service auditor's test of controls
l. 'In all material aspects'
m. Restricted use report
n. Service auditor's signature
o. Practice location
p. Report date

> —For the complete text, see AICPA, SSAE 18,
> AT-C Section 320.40, p. 244ff

Section 41 outlines the content of SOC 2 Type 1 Reports, which is like Type 2 Reports but without testing.

Section 42 covers Modifications to Opinions:

- Was the presentation not fair?
- Were the controls not suitably designed?
- Did the controls not operate effectively?
- Did the controls not operate effectively throughout the period covered by the report?
- Was 'the Service Auditor … unable to obtain sufficient appropriate evidence'?

Section 320.A1, p. 253ff, provides 'Other Explanatory Material.'

Ancillary Professional Guidance Related to SOC Reports

Description Criteria (DC)

Description Criteria relate to the Service Organization's System description and subsequent evaluation.

The AICPA's Assurance Services Executive Committee (ASEC) issued criteria for the preparation of a service organization's description of its system.

1.41 The description criteria are used by management when preparing the description of the service organization's system and by the service auditor when evaluating the description. Applying the description criteria in actual situations requires judgment. Therefore, in addition to the description criteria, DC section 200 presents implementation guidance for each criterion.

—*SOC 2 Guide, AICPA*, Oct 15, 2022, p. 13

DC Section 200 lists the following nine Description Criteria (DC).

"DC1: The types of services provided

DC2: The principal service commitments and system requirements

DC3: The components of the system [referred to elsewhere as System Components] used to provide the services, including the following:

    a. Infrastructure
    b. Software
    c. People
    d. Procedures
    e. Data

DC4: For identified system incidents that (a) were the result of controls that were not suitably designed or operating effectively or (b) otherwise resulted in a significant failure in the achievement of one or more of those service commitments and system requirements, as of the date of the description (for a type 1) or during the period of time covered by the description (for a type 2), as applicable, the following information:

    a. Nature of each incident
    b. Timing surrounding the incident
    c. Extent (or effect) of the incident and its disposition

DC5: The applicable trust services criteria and the related controls designed to provide reasonable assurance that the service organization's service commitments and system requirements were achieved

DC6: If service organization management assumed, in the design of the service organization's system, that certain controls would be implemented by user entities, and those controls are necessary, in combination with controls at the service organization, to provide reasonable assurance that the service organization's service commitments and system requirements would be achieved, those complementary user entity controls (CUECs)

DC7: If the service organization uses a subservice organization fn 11 and the controls at the subservice organization are necessary, in combination with controls at the service organization, to provide reasonable assurance that the service organization's service commitments and system requirements are achieved, the following:

    a. When service organization management elects to use the inclusive method:

        i. The nature of the service provided by the subservice organization

        ii. The controls at the subservice organization that are necessary, in combination with controls at the service organization to provide reasonable assurance that the service organization's service commitments and system requirements are achieved

        iii. Relevant aspects of the subservice organization's infrastructure, software, people, procedures, and data

        iv. The portions of the system that are attributable to the subservice organization

    b. When service organization management decides to use the carve-out method:

        i. The nature of the service provided by the subservice organization

        ii. Each of the applicable trust services criteria that are intended to be met by controls at the subservice organization

        iii. The types of controls that service organization management assumed, in the design of the service organization's system, would be implemented by the subservice organization that are necessary, in combination with controls at the service organization, to provide reasonable assurance that the service organization's service commitments and system requirements are achieved (commonly referred to as complementary subservice organization controls or CSOCs)

DC8: Any specific criterion of the applicable trust services criteria that is not relevant to the system and the reasons it is not relevant

DC9: In a description that covers a period of time (type 2 examination), the relevant details of significant changes to the service organization's system and controls during that period that are relevant to the service organization's service commitments and system requirements"

—DC Section 200 2018 Description Criteria for a Description of a Service Organization's System in a SOC 2® Report (with Revised Implementation Guidance – 2022), AICPA, 2024, pp. 9–28

For more information regarding Description Criteria, see *DC Section 200 2018 Description Criteria for a Description of a Service Organization's System in a SOC 2® Report (with Revised Implementation Guidance – 2022)*, AICPA, 2024.

Trust Services Criteria "… are used to evaluate the suitability of design and operating effectiveness of controls stated in the description to provide reasonable assurance that the service organization's service commitments and system requirements were achieved." [*—SOC 2® Guide*, AICPA, October 15, 2022, p. 14.]

The Trust Services Categories are:

- Availability
- Integrity – Emphasis on Processing Integrity
- Security
- Confidentiality
- Privacy

—TSP Section 100 2017 Test Services Criteria for Security, Availability, Processing Integrity, Confidentiality, and Privacy (with Revised Points of Focus – 2022), AICPA, 2024, pp. 7 and 8

While the criteria are separate, significant overlap exists in their application to specific internal controls, such as access controls which involve all five of the Trust Services Criteria.

For more information regarding Trust Services Criteria, see *TSP Section 100 2017 Trust Service Criteria For Security, Availability, Processing Integrity, Confidentiality, and Privacy (with Revised Points of Focus – 2022)*, AICPA, 2024.

Other Specific Terms and Topics Related to SOC Reports

Boundaries

Every SOC engagement inevitably involves boundaries, which need to be clearly understood and communicated in SOC Reports to avoid misunderstandings by the users of the Service Organization's Services.

1.26 If management has determined that functions or processes related to the system are outside of the boundaries of the system identified as the subject matter of the examination, there may be a risk that intended users think those functions or processes were examined as part of the SOC 2 examination.

—SOC 2 Guide, AICPA, Oct 15, 2022, p. 9

Complementary User Entity Controls (CUECs)

Complementary User Entity Controls (CUECs) are internal controls that must be performed by users to ensure they benefit from the service organization's services. These controls 'complement' the services provided by the Service Organization. Recall the discussion about 'Shared Responsibilities' in the chapter on Cloud Services. SOC has a similar term, 'user entity responsibilities'. Either way, users need be aware of controls for which they are responsible either in addition to or in conjunction with the services provided by service organizations to fully benefit from the service organizations' services.

Deviations/Deficiencies/Misstatements

SOC examinations differentiate among Deviations, Deficiencies and Misstatements as follows:

Deviations are specific control failures. Deviations should have tolerable rates of deviation and expected rates of deviation for various tests.

Deficiencies are misstatements that result from controls that are not suitably, not appropriately, not adequately designed ... and did not operate effectively. If a control did not operate effectively, a variety of reasons may explain the ineffectiveness of the control, including an unsuitable design, improper implementation, inappropriate configuration, a changing environment in which the control operates, and/or a combination of these elements.

Misstatements are inconsistencies between control descriptions and description criteria, including omissions.

For further information about Deviations, Deficiencies and Misstatements, see *SOC 2 Guide*, AICPA, Oct 15, 2022, pp. 67 and 68.

Subservice Organization

A **Subservice Organization** is a supplier "... that performs controls that are necessary, in combination with controls at the service organization to provide reasonable assurance that the service organization's service commitments and system requirements were achieved." [—*SOC 2 Guide*, AICPA, Oct 15, 2022, p. 300.]

SOC 2 Guide Control Illustration

The SOC 2 Guide provides a helpful illustration, Table 16.1, of the information that should be included in a system description. [Note: In the SOC 2 Guide, this table is identified as Table 3-2.]

The table above is provided to give readers an example of the scope and detail recommended for SOC 2 Reports. In contrast, Risk and Control Matrices (RACMs), which are not SOC 2 Reports, may be more summarized; however, RACMs also include Business Objectives, Risks, as well as the Internal Controls established to reduce or remediate the Risks so that the Business will achieve its Business Objectives.

SOC Service Report Challenges

Obviously the first and potentially the biggest hurdle is management's commitment to and embrace of a Suitable System of Internal Controls. This is clearly management's responsibility, although the Service Organization's Management is reasonably more focused on its services than on a Suitable System of Internal Controls. The challenge for management is remembering its duty to its clients. The last thing that clients need is unreliable services that negatively impact the client's business operations let alone its financial statements.

The issuance of System and Organization Controls Reports (SOC Reports) are restricted to Certified Public Accountants (CPAs). Traditional accounting and auditing training focuses on financial, not on IT expertise, which means SOC Reports are outside the expertise and training of many accountants. The CPA Evolution initiative launched by the AICPA and NASBA (the National Association of State Boards of Accountancy) re-enforced the need for accountants to also be skilled in technology as well as accounting, auditing, and taxation. Furthermore, the CPA Evolution Initiative identified a new discipline, Information Systems and Controls (ISC). The new CPA exam, which launched in January 2024, recognizes the changes that automation has and will continue to have on businesses, on their operations, on their financial records, and on their financial reports, which are based on their operations. This new emphasis is designed to equip CPAs for the demands and consequences of increased automation. It also creates new careers opportunities for CPAs including issuing System and Organization Controls Reports (SOC Reports).

Table 16.1 Information about Controls to be Included in the Description of the System

Information to Be Included in a Description of a Control	Illustrative Control
1 What: The subject matter to which the control is applied	Requests for *changes to production, source, and object code*4 are initiated by preparing and submitting a change ticket to the Change Control Board for approval. The system automatically logs *changes made to production, source, and object code*. On a weekly basis, the change manager reviews the log of system changes and the approved change tickets to identify unauthorized and missing changes by determining that (1) there is an approved change ticket for each entry in the log and (2) all the changes identified in the approved change tickets have been recorded in the log. Any unauthorized or missing changes are entered into an incident record in the Incident Management System. Incident records are assigned to the application manager of the affected application for follow-up and resolution. The change manager tracks open records to resolution and prepares a weekly report to the vice president of application development.
Who: The party responsible for performing the control	Requests for changes to production, source, and object code are initiated by preparing and submitting a change ticket to the *Change Control Board* for approval. The system automatically logs changes made to production, source, and object code. On a weekly basis, the *change manager* reviews the log of system changes and the approved change tickets to identify unauthorized and missing changes by determining that (1) there is an approved change ticket for each entry in the log and (2) all the changes identified in the approved change tickets have been recorded in the log. Any unauthorized or missing changes are entered into an incident record in the Incident Management System. Incident records are assigned to the application manager of the affected application for follow-up and resolution. The *change manager* tracks open records to resolution and prepares a weekly report to the *vice president of application development*.

(Continued)

Table 16.1 (Continued)

Information to Be Included in a Description of a Control	Illustrative Control
How: The nature of the activity performed, including sources of information used in performing the control	Requests for changes to production, source, and object codes are initiated by *preparing and submitting a change ticket* to the Change Control Board for approval. The system automatically logs changes made to production, source, and object codes. On a weekly basis, the change manager *reviews the log of system changes and the approved change tickets to identify unauthorized and missing changes by determining that (1) there is an approved change ticket for each entry in the log and (2) all the changes identified in the approved change tickets have been recorded in the log.* Any unauthorized or missing changes are *entered into an incident record in the Incident Management System.* Incident records are assigned to the application manager of the affected application *for follow-up and resolution.* The change manager *tracks open records to resolution and prepares a weekly report to the* vice president of application development.
When: The frequency with which the control is performed, or the timing of its occurrence	Requests for changes to production, source, and object code are initiated by preparing and submitting a change ticket to the Change Control Board for approval. The system *automatically* logs changes made to production, source, and object code. On a *weekly basis,* the change manager reviews the log of system changes and the approved change tickets to identify unauthorized and missing changes by determining that (1) there is an approved change ticket for each entry in the log and (2) all the changes identified in the approved change tickets have been recorded in the log. Any unauthorized or missing changes are entered into an incident record in the Incident Management System. Incident records are assigned to the application manager of the affected application for follow-up and resolution. The change manager tracks open records to resolution and prepares a *weekly* report to the vice president of application development."

—*SOC 2 Guide*, AICPA, Oct 15, 2022, pp. 101–103.

Chapter 17

Modeling – An Essential Audit Skill

Chapter Contents:

Introduction to Audit Skills

Modeling is an essential skill for IT Auditors as well as for business analysts, designers, and software developers. IT Auditors need to know how to read models, often diagrams, how to construct models, and how to use models to understand, to illustrate, and to advise their auditees.

Models are basic analysis and design tools. They help IT Auditors understand and explain situations and processes. They provide basic evidence for IT Auditors regarding internal control design and their ability to reduce risks.

Models may be diagrams, or narratives, but they usually are a combination of diagrams and accompanying narrative, or diagrams as part of a narrative.

Business Models depict situations using diagrams, images, illustrations, and narrative. They may be:

- Structure-Oriented Models
- Process-Oriented Models

Structure Models focus on entities and transactions, how they are structured, and how various components are interrelated. Process Models focus on events, especially a sequence of related events that constitute a business process, where each event is a task, step, or activity, and a process is a string of related events, such as the buying, selling, and making things, or providing services.

DOI: 10.4324/9781032689388-17

In the IT Audit context, Structure Models focus on business structure. They can be organizational oriented, architecture oriented, data oriented, or decision oriented.

- Organization-oriented models show how an organization and/or its resources are structured and how various components relate to each other.
- Architecture-oriented models show how IT Architectures are structured, such as server or network architectures, which show various components and their interrelationships. Examples include network diagrams, data center layouts, application structure diagrams, and so on.
  Enterprise Architecture (EA) is a specific superset of IT design principles and practices.
- Data-oriented models show how Data is logically structured, how it is organized, how it is stored, and potentially how it is used.
- Decision oriented models describe Business Decisions and how they impact business process events, and their outcomes. These are particularly relevant to Internal Controls. For example, under what circumstances can credit limits be increased or decreased based on updated information, or which criteria determine successful testing, or under what circumstances are sales orders split into sub-orders, such as different shipment locations and/or times.

Process Models focus on business processes:

- How they begin, what initiates them.
- Their actions, their steps, the sequence of steps, and the decisions that occur as the processes proceed to their conclusions.
- They show the conclusion(s), the outcomes, the results of business processes.

Familiar basic diagrams for Structure and Process diagrams are:

- Flowcharts
- Entity Relationship Diagrams (ERD)
- Decision Trees

These diagrams can be:

- Conceptual Models
- Physical Models
- Logical Models

Conceptual Models are abstract or ideal situations, whereas Physical Models relate to entities and events in the real world, and Logical Models focus on logical relationships among elements.

Modeling Context

The heyday of modeling was the 1970s and 1980s, culminating in the mid-1990s with UML, a Unified Modeling Language. The idea behind UML was to consolidate various modeling methodologies into a single language. Well-known modelers then included Yourdon, Marco, Constantine, Orr, Jackson, Shlaer, Mellor, and the 3 Amigos (Grady Booch, Ivar Jacobson, and Jim Rumbaugh). Each had their own techniques and methodologies.

To understand the breadth of modeling, consider Object-Oriented Models, which have a different approach:

- Behavior Diagrams
- Interaction Diagrams
- Structure Diagrams

Also, consider an Agile approach, which focuses on before, during, and after development.

- Before development, 'What problem are we trying to solve?'
- During development, 'How might we build a solution to solve that problem?'
- After development, 'What about this, what could possibly happen?'
    —Agile Alliance, https://www.agilealliance.org/glossary/three-amigos

Hence, many different approaches and techniques.

For many senior analysts, developers, and coders, the IBM X-20-8020 Flowchart Template was our starting point. Today, some of its symbols live on while others no longer make sense. Arguably, the most common symbols were rectangles, diamonds, terminal events, documents, off-page connectors, and straight lines. Because of their universality, they live on. The punched card, the perforated tape, and the display symbol became historical artifacts. However, the IBM Template, Figure 17.1, left an indelible mark on diagramming.

Modeling Objectives

As noted above, modeling generally serves multiple objectives, including at least:

- Analysis
- Design
- Illustration
- Documentation

As an analysis tool, models are developed by analysts and designers to show visually conceptual, hypothetical, or physical models. These may be described

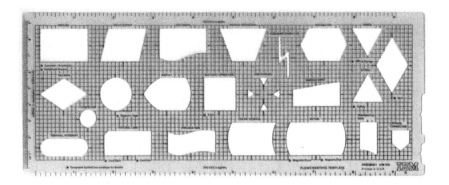

Figure 17.1 IBM Flowcharting Template.

as current state and future state, where current state models portray things as they are, and future state models describe or define different future realities. Implicit in current state and future state models is the notion of change, ideally improvement. The future state models define the future, and ideally, a path or roadmap from the current state to the future states.

As a design tool, models provide a white space to design, to layout, the subject matter being modeled. Like an architect laying out a room or a building, auditors are designing physical or logical situations, such as physical process flows, physical entities, logical data flows, data storage, and so on.

As an illustration tool, models may be used to illustrate different approaches to something. For example, the architect may propose different floor plans, different exteriors, different interiors, different traffic patterns, different hardware, etc.

As a documentation tool, models are used to describe situations, circumstances, and approaches to handling situations. Visual models may accompany narrative descriptions. For example, an architect could describe a proposed building and supplement that description with an actual model of the building, traditionally a cardboard or plastic model, but today, it is more likely a computerized three-dimensional model. The model is designed to document the architect's plans, thoughts, and images with respect to the proposed building.

For IT Auditors, models may accompany narratives and lists to show or illustrate business entities or business processes and to identify the internal controls designed to regulate those entities and processes, especially different situations that can be encountered by a process and how the process will handle these alternatives. For example, a model might illustrate different payment methods that are available to customers, or illustrate different outcomes when customers return products.

Modeling Techniques

Structure diagrams show relationships among items, for example the relationships among customers, their orders, and the objects they order, whereas Process

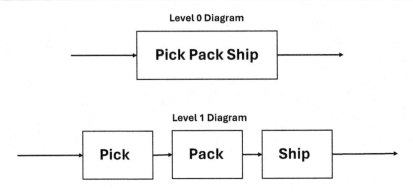

Figure 17.2 Simple Example of Decomposition.

diagrams show the steps, step-by-step, in a particular process such as customers ordering things from suppliers, payment arrangements, assembling and shipping orders and getting paid for those orders.

A frequent modeling question is levels of detail or granularity. For example, Customer records could be shown as high-level entities without details, or they could be shown with details such as addresses, payment mechanisms, contacts, and preferences. In the same way, pick-pack-ship could be shown as a single step in the process or be broken into three separate steps: picking, packing, and shipping. These examples demonstrate the technique of decomposition. In a highly summarized diagram, the objective is to emphasize the process rather than the individual steps in the process; however, a complete picture of the process may require multiple diagrams showing successive levels of detail. This process of showing the model in increasing levels of detail is referred to as decomposition and is illustrated in Figure 17.2.

The specific set of symbols used by an IT Auditor may vary as long as users understand what the diagrams intend to show.

Modeling Types/Methods

As noted above, while there are many modeling techniques, several stand out because they are frequently used.

- Flowcharts
- Relationship Diagrams
- Hierarchies
- Fishbone Diagrams
- Decision Trees

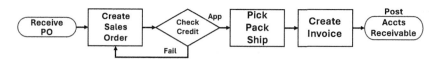

Figure 17.3 Process Flow Diagram Sale by a Supplier to a Customer.

Flowcharts show succession. The horizontal axis is typically the time axis. The diagram shows the succession, the progress, of related events. Figure 17.3 is a simple example.

Relationship Diagrams show relationships. Figure 17.4 shows four generations.

Hierarchies are an approach to showing relationships between superordinates and subordinates. Organization charts are good examples of hierarchies, but this method can also apply to product lines, or product groups, and their constituent products within each other. For an example, see Figure 17.5.

Fishbone diagrams can show succession or relationships. They generally have the shape of a fish skeleton and can be used to show a succession of choices, such as the operation of a configurator where current choices are affected by previous choices. Fishbone Diagrams can also be used to show related topics. For example, a fishbone diagram could be used to portray topics in an article or book.

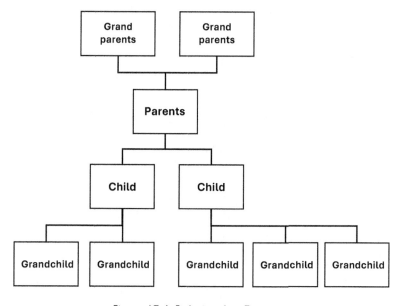

Figure 17.4 Relationship Diagram.

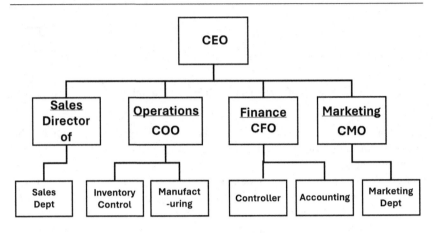

Figure 17.5 Hierarchy Diagram.

In the case of Figure 17.6, imagine Chapters, Topics, Subtopics, and Sub-subtopics across the entire diagram; the Fishbone diagram could quickly get very complex.

Decision trees show the interrelationships of decisions. An excellent example of this is a configurator where successive choices determine subsequent choices.

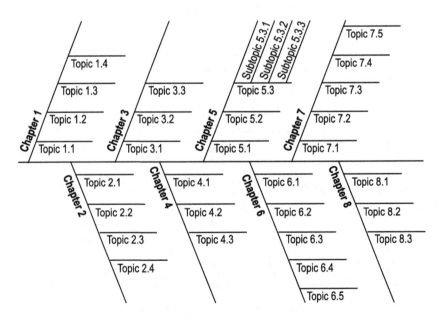

Figure 17.6 Fishbone Diagram.

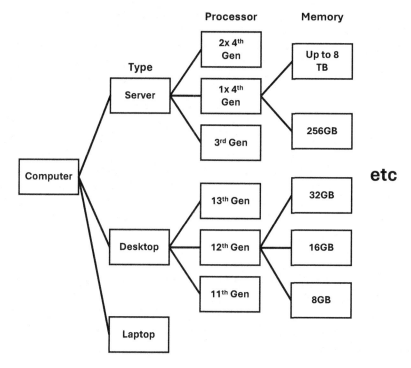

Figure 17.7 Decision Tree.

In the case of Figure 17.7, notice how choices on the left determine choices on the right. The first decision is which kind of computer to get. The second choice is which type of processor to get. The third choice is which kind of memory to get. Typically, the number of choices to configure a computer could be a dozen or more.

A challenge in modeling is the summary-detail problem or put slightly differently how much detail to put into a model. Hierarchical is one technique to deal with levels of detail whereby the highest layer or order model is a highly summarized model, and sub-models within the main model drill into details and distinctions among the details.

IT Audit and Modeling

Modeling is an essential tool and skill for IT Auditors.

Early in the book, Risk and Control Matrices were introduced. These are Internal Control Models based on Business Objectives, Risks to achieving the Business Objectives, and the Internal Controls implemented to remediate the Risks so that Enterprises achieve their Objectives. RACMs can be supplemented with narratives, diagrams, and procedure manuals.

Hence, IT Auditors need to know how to prepare models, how to 'read' models, and how to revise and/or generate their own models.

For more information about Modeling, many books and online resources are available. This chapter is far from exhaustive, but it identifies some of the significant types of diagrams that IT Auditors are likely to encounter.

A Final Note

At the beginning of this chapter, UML (Unified Modeling Language) is mentioned. It is a property of The Object Management Group. "The Object Management Group® Standards Development Organization (OMG® SDO) is a global, open membership, non-profit consortium. Our members collaborate to craft technology standards that offer measurable value to a diverse range of vertical industries." [— https://www.omg.org/index.htm]. Its products include BPM+ (Business Process Management Plus), SYSML (Systems Modeling Language™) and UML™ (Unified Modeling Language™). For more information, see https://www.omg.org/index.htm.

Among other OMG standards, the OMG's Business Process Model and Notation (BPMN™), version 2.0.1, is an ISO standard, ISO 19510:2013. OMG Systems Modeling Language (SysML®), version 1.4, is ISO 19514:2017, and its Unified Modeling Language (UML™), version 2.4.1, is ISO 19505-1:2012 and 19505-2:2012.

Chapter 18

Technology Trends and Their Potential Impact on IT Auditing

Chapter Contents:

This chapter is intended to introduce trends and technologies that are likely to have a significant impact on Businesses and on IT Auditing.

Abstraction

Physical devices and processes have already been replaced by services, especially cloud-based services. Whereas one used to be able to see, touch, and point to servers, storage, and ancillary devices, they have become services that were provisioned and used without regard to their physical aspects. These devices have been **Virtualized**; they have been **Abstracted**.

This change is significant on several levels.

As auditees moved from physical environments to virtual environments, physical elements became cloud services. Auditees were left dealing with physical items only to the extent on what remained under their control. Entire data centers were replaced by Cloud Service Providers (CSPs), such as AWS, Azure, and Google Cloud. From the auditee perspective, the physical embodiments went away, at least a large part; however, they didn't really go away, they just went behind a wall. This change left auditees increasingly relating to services instead of physical devices. The Physical items had been **Abstracted** with direct and indirect consequences.

DOI: 10.4324/9781032689388-18

In this process, the auditee's needs changed from skill and experience related to physical devices to skill and experience needed to manage an abstracted environment where servers, storage, and networking are readily available via Cloud Service Provider consoles. Instead of buying and maintaining hardware, auditee's now needed expertise to provision and maintain their virtual resources.

With fewer on-premises Infrastructure, the auditees needed fewer technical resources and the skill set changed from managing physical environments to managing virtual environments. The change involved both the quantity of resources needed and the type of resources needed.

Depending upon corporate culture, the previous resources were either reassigned or laid off, and Enterprises turned to outsourced resources to fill their technical gaps. Instead of FTEs (Full Time Equivalents), auditees needed smaller amounts of technical expertise measured in hours or days to manage their virtual compute environments. In this process, auditees reduced their in-house resources dedicated to managing their environments.

Likewise, IT Auditors found themselves in a different situation. Not only were they concerned about the remaining physical infrastructure, but they were also now concerned about the new virtual services provided by outside vendors, the Cloud Service Providers (CSPs). This change reshuffled Auditors objectives and expanded their examinations beyond previous audits. This imposed new demands on IT Auditors as well as on their auditees.

Auditors lost direct access to many physical elements they previously dealt with. Their Audits shifted from Internal Controls related to physical items to Internal Controls related to logical items, in this case online services. While the packaging changed, the underlying principles remained. The issues related to Availability, Accuracy and Correctness, Completeness, Consistency and Timeliness, Confidentiality, Integrity, Reliability, and Validity remained.

In the same way that the auditee's needs changed, IT Auditors need to upskill for the new environments. As IT Audit firms seek to fulfill their obligations, their personnel needs change, especially in the areas of technical skills and outsourced technical support.

Indirect consequences of this change include loss of expertise and corporate memory as well as need for new skills and expertise. This change affected both the businesses and their auditors. Without being disparaging, auditees and their auditors became 'dumber' in some respects, which is not as bad as it seems. The problem is how to maintain skill and knowledge related to basics as their manifestations changed, as the 'packaging' changed.

On a positive note, the change freed auditees and auditors alike to focus on the bigger picture, i.e., what we are trying to accomplish instead of how the technology works.

This change forces everyone to see the world differently through a different lens from a different perspective. Virtualization now defines the world, at least major segments of it. Consider the emergence of the Graphical User Interface

(GUI), which shielded users from command-line programming. The virtual world similarly requires different knowledge and expertise.

As mentioned above, nothing went away, it just went 'underground'. This means the rules are still there; only the manifestations changed. This explanation is obviously very simplified, but the result is that average users will know less and less about the technology on which they depend.

In terms of the future, users will become accustomed to using virtual services, and will, in the process, lose touch with the physical elements with which they previously interacted. Consider a simple example of doors and locks. We see a door and realize it needs to be locked. But what if the door is invisible? We forget about the door let alone locking it. All of which is to say, we lose touch with the reasons for the controls and countermeasures. This loss is not confined to just users, it also affects IT Auditors and their auditees as well.

This change, this transition shifts certain client responsibilities to their service providers. That shift makes things both easier and more difficult for clients. The result is easier in the sense that clients do not have to worry about infrastructure and physical assets. The result is more difficult because clients become more dependent on third parties over which they have little control and limited transparency regarding these vital services.

This transition also impacts IT Audit and IT Auditors. Audit checklists and Audit procedures need to be revised and IT Auditors need to upskill.

On a positive note, this transition has created practice opportunities for IT Auditors who are CPAs, System and Organization Controls Reports (SOC Reports).

Agility

Agility, at least in the IT space, grew out of software developers' dissatisfaction with traditional software development methods, which took too long to produce physical results. Their dissatisfaction resulted in the adoption of an iterative approach in contrast with the former highly structured step-by-step method. Regardless of one's evaluation of the two methods, a slower, planned pace was replaced with a quicker, interactive, more reactive approach to software development and business as well. This change sped up the world. An example of this speeding up is Fast Fashion. Instead of two, three, or four seasons a year, clothiers are introducing new clothing continuously instead of in seasons. To accomplish this, apparel companies need agility to design, fabricate, and distribute apparel quickly.

Speeding up our business lives and our personal lives is not limited to Agile. Adaptability, Flexibility, and New, Continuous Change became hallmarks of the 21st century. Consider an affordable telephone call that can connect two parties anywhere in the world instantly. Consider commercial aviation, which can take us anywhere in the world in 24 hours or less. Operations are now 24 hours a day, seven days a week, 52 weeks a year; in other words, continuous. We can easily buy things online any time, day or night. Fast and continuous have changed our lives. Availability, a central control theme, is now a business mandate. A cruise is now less a mode of transportation and more a leisurely way to see the world in comfort. If you are in a hurry, the airplane is the obvious choice.

Agility also impacts IT Audit. Agility is certainly helpful, no question about that, but at the same time IT Audit cannot forget methods and tools that are artifacts of the traditional Waterfall Methodology. These methods and tools can be used to illustrate, analyze, design, and document processes and controls for IT Audits. IT Auditors need to know, or at least be familiar with both approaches to be able to adequately design and evaluate initiatives, projects, and developments that use these approaches.

Continuous Improvement

The father of Continuous Improvement is William E. Deming and his work in Japan after the Second World War. Deming's message to the Japanese recovering from the devastation of WWII was that improving quality reduces expenses, increases productivity, and increases market share.

> When W. Edwards Deming first popularized the idea of continuous improvement, it was a broad philosophy where many different approaches contributed to a general culture of innovation. Today, continuous improvement is a foundational concept in a variety of project management philosophies like lean, agile, six sigma, and total quality management [TQM].
> — https://www.atlassian.com/agile/project-management/
> continuous-improvement

> Continuous improvement is an ongoing process of identifying, analyzing, and making incremental improvements to systems, processes, products, or services. Its purpose is to drive efficiency, improve quality, and value delivery while minimizing waste, variation, and defects. The continual improvement process is driven by ongoing feedback, collaboration, and data.
> — https://kanbanize.com/lean-management/improvement/
> what-is-continuous-improvement

Kanbanize further identifies six benefits of Continuous Improvement as follows:

1. "Increased Efficiency
2. Improved Quality
3. Cost Savings
4. Employee Engagement

5. Enabling Transformation
6. Supporting Innovation"
— https://kanbanize.com/lean-management/improvement/
what-is-continuous-improvement

COBIT's fifth domain, Monitor, Evaluate, Assess (MEA), embraces Continuous Improvement.

While IT Auditors are not specialists in Continuous Improvement, IT Auditors must remember that Continuous Improvement animates business operations including increasing automation across the Enterprise, especially automating processes that were previously manual processes. These forces place greater importance on Application Controls since automation is replacing unautomated business processes and their manual controls.

CMMI

Closely related to Continuous Improvement is Maturity. The term 'Maturity' was popularized by Carnegie Mellon University. Originally, CMMI referred to the Carnegie Mellon Maturity Index; today, CMMI abbreviates Capability Maturity Model Integration. The underlying idea is the maturing of business processes so that incidents are no longer Ad Hoc affairs but are subject to predefined policies, procedures, practices, and standards. As these procedures mature, organizations can reflect on their effectiveness and revise them to make them more effective. The colloquial version of this approach is 'learning from our experiences'.

CMMI is a methodology for IT Auditors to consider, especially its emphasis on continual learning and improvement, which is good for both IT Auditing and the subjects of IT Audits and IT assistance.

A note in passing, ISACA acquired the CMMI® Institute in 2016. This combined the global leader in capability improvement with the professional association for IT Governance, Assurance and Cybersecurity. At the time of the acquisition, Mr. Matt Loeb, ISACA's CEO said: "Our acquisition of CMMI Institute will help us to broaden our focus on helping professionals and their organizations optimize their use of technology, increase value for stakeholders and improve business performance." [— www.businesswire.com/news/home/20160303005950/en/ISACA-Acquires-Global-Capability-Maturity-Leader-CMMI®-Institute] Businesswise.com goes on to say: "ISACA and CMMI Institute share a vision for advancing organizational performance that centers on driving excellence in the IT, information systems governance, data management governance, software, and systems engineering functions in organizations across a spectrum of industries." [— www.businesswire.com/news/home/20160303005950/en/ISACA-Acquires-Global-Capability-Maturity-Leader-CMMI®-Institute] CMM dates back to 1991 when Carnegie Mellon's

Software Engineering Institute (CMU SEI) released the first version of the Software Development Capability Maturity Model (CMM).

Not to be left out, the U. S. Department of Defense implemented CMMC (Cybersecurity Maturity Model Certification) in 2020, and recently updated their model to CMMC Model 2.0. This is a quick way of saying maturity models have become established beyond IT.

Convergence – Coalescence

Abstraction, Speed, Continuity, Continuous Operation, and Continuous Improvement are converging; they are coalescing. They define the 21st century. In the process, they have led to some interesting 'Silicon Valley' concepts including 'Minimally Viable Product' (MVP), 'Good Enough to Ship', Disruption, and 'Disrupting the Disruptor'. The clamor in the marketplace has become intense as vendors scramble for market share and survival.

Convergence is present in several different ways. Convergence first appeared when analog telephone technology, POTs (Plain Old Telephone System), was superseded by digital communication. Voice Over IP (VOIP) moved telephone communications from the analog realm into the digital realm, leading to teleconferencing. The next step in this convergence will be immersive technologies, such as Augmented Reality and Virtual Reality, where everyone in a conference will 'feel' as though they were in a single room. Convergence is not limited to communications, virtual cloud services converge Infrastructure elements into a console that can provision these elements as parts of a single platform, and this is only the beginning.

From the perspective of IT Audit, this convergence or coalescence re-enforces the need for skilled IT Auditors who are well-grounded in modern technologies as well as traditional concepts and methods.

Artificial Intelligence

Artificial Intelligence leaped from the R&D Department to consumer awareness seemingly overnight. The AI race then began in earnest. No one wanted to be left behind. Never mind the years of research and investigation that preceded ChatGPT's release on November 30, 2022. The company that launched ChatGPT, OpenAI, was founded on December 10, 2015, roughly seven years from start to release. OpenAI's companion product, DALL-E, was released on January 5, 2021, roughly 5 years in development.

Alan Turing, the British polymath who was instrumental in the efforts to decode the German Enigma machine during World War II, asked why machines could not reason in his 1950 paper 'Computing Machine and Intelligence' in *Mind* 49: pp. 433-460. In Turing words' "Can machines think?" In "The History of Artificial Intelligence," the roots of Artificial Intelligence as we know it today were traced back to the mid-1950s to the Logic Theorist, a conference that debuted at the Dartmouth Summer Research Project on Artificial Intelligence (DSRPAI) in 1956. [— sitn.hms.harvard.edu/flash/2017/history-artificial-intelligence/] The point is that while AI sprung into public view in 2022, work on Artificial Intelligence dates back to at least the mid-1950s. So, AI was in the pipeline for almost seven decades before ChatGPT sprang to public attention.

OpenAI jumped back into the public conversation in November 2023 when the Board of Directors fired its CEO, who was reinstated only a day or two later. At the same time, the composition of the Board of Directors was changed. Note OpenAI's mission statement: "OpenAI is an AI research and deployment company. Our mission is to ensure that artificial general intelligence benefits all of humanity." [— https://openai.com/about, 2024.] Among the precipitating factors for these changes was a struggle between 'benefitting humanity' and commercializing AI ahead of the competition.

As the saying goes, 'You ain't seen nothin' yet'. What is in store for us may be beyond our wildest dreams. Without regard to hyperbole, Artificial Intelligence will profoundly affect our personal and business lives for generations to come. Anything written now will be an underestimation by the time you read this. The hope is that our 'fears' are not an understatement as well.

Will Artificial Intelligence (AI) be a boon, a boondoggle, or both? AI will undoubtedly help IT Auditors do their work and will tax their ability to do their work. It will at the same time assist and complicate the work of IT Auditors. It will further **abstract** business processes and decision-making.

Something to keep in mind. When will Artificial Intelligence (AI) become normative; when will Artificial Intelligence become an authoritative source. Today, AI is at least a helpful curiosity. At some point it will become authoritative but when and to what extent remains to be seen in the same way that Encyclopedias and Wikipedia eventually became authoritative. Between now and then, we are responsible for our use of AI. If AI makes a mistake, it is our mistake. If it is helpful, great. Remember Dr. George E. P. Box's statement that "All models are wrong, but some are useful". [— George E. P. Box, Norman Draper, *Empirical Model-Building and Response Surfaces*, John Wiley & Sons, 1987.] A reasonable interpretation of Dr. Box's statement is something to the effect that 'All models are incomplete', where incomplete says the models are not the same as what they model.

For further comments on AI, see The Epilog – The unfinishable Chapter.

Technology Trends and IT Audit

Technology Trends can and will both help and challenge IT Audit.

On the helping side, Remote Monitoring and Management software (RMM) has become a boon for IT Departments and IT Auditors. At a minimum, this software allows auditors to catalog all devices and software on a network and to varying degrees manage those devices and software, remotely. At the same time, this software presents opportunities for malicious activity. An attacker could use this software to discover the devices and software on your network and plan their attacks accordingly including being able to take over various devices and systems. The SolarWinds® Orion® breach is an example of RMM software and a mundane supply chain attack using an Orion software patch. In this case, patches for Orion®, an infrastructure monitoring and management platform, was an unwitting vehicle to deploy malware. High-tech software that was beneficial became destructive.

The **abstraction** of physical computing into digital virtual services will allow Enterprises to get out of the hardware and software business by moving their workloads off on-premises resources to cloud-based services. This will both potentially extend capabilities, but at the same time 'dumb us down' in the process. To survive in this transition, IT Auditors need to focus on the basics, such as Availability, instead of worrying about specific interventions and countermeasures. IT Auditors should focus on the various measures Cloud Services Providers (CSPs) use to ensure continuous operation. This gets us out of batteries, air conditioning, and physical access controls into redundant fault-tolerant measures that CSPs employ to ensure continuous operation.

This change is both subtle and immensely significant. These types of changes will continue and will be profound. For example, an Artificial Intelligence may take over the management of remote cloud computing resources such that additional resources are acquired as needed, reconfigured as needed, as well as responding to specific client requests.

In these situations, what do IT Auditors audit? How do they Audit emerging realities? This is complexity piled on complexity piled on more complexity.

Suggestions

Rather than recommendations, suggestions seem more appropriate and more responsive to continually changing conditions and demands.

- Remember Basics, such as Availability, Accuracy/Correctness, Fault Tolerance, etc.
- Think critically at a higher level of **Abstraction**.
- Evaluate new technology in terms of both benefits and risks and decide how to manage the risks.
- Business Objectives, Risks, Controls, and Tests of Controls remain the basics of IT Audit.

Details will remain important but do not lose sight of the big picture, of the underlying controls and countermeasures required for businesses to achieve their business objectives. Remember everything flows from Business Objectives.

Chapter 19

Professional Guidance

Chapter Contents:

COBIT2019

COBIT, which originally stood for Control Objectives for Information and Related Technologies, is published by ISACA (Information Systems and Control Association). COBIT was originally developed to define a generic set of IT Governance and IT Management practices. COBIT 2019, the current version of COBIT, identifies 40 distinct objectives organized into five domains as listed below:

Evaluate, Direct and Monitor (EDM)

    EDM01   Ensured Governance Framework Setting and Maintenance
    EDM02   Ensured Benefits Delivery
    EDM03   Ensured Risk Optimization
    EDM04   Ensured Resource Optimization
    EDM05   Ensured Stakeholder Engagement

Align, Plan and Organize (APO)

    APO01   Managed the I&T Management Framework
    APO02   Managed Strategy
    APO03   Managed Enterprise Architecture
    APO04   Managed Innovation
    APO05   Managed Portfolio
    APO06   Managed Budget and Costs

DOI: 10.4324/9781032689388-19

APO07   Managed Human Resources
APO08   Managed Relationships
APO09   Managed Service Agreements
APO10   Managed Suppliers
APO11   Managed Quality
APO12   Managed Risk
APO13   Managed Security
APO14   Managed Data

Build, Acquire and Implement (BAI)

BAI01   Managed Programs
BAI02   Managed Requirements Definition
BAI03   Managed Solutions Identification and Build
BAI04   Managed Availability and Capacity
BAI05   Managed Organizational Change Enablement
BAI06   Managed IT Changes
BAI07   Managed Change Acceptance and Transitioning
BAI08   Managed Knowledge
BAI09   Managed Assets
BAI10   Managed Configuration
BAI11   Managed Projects

Deliver, Service and Support (DSS)

DSS01   Managed Operations
DSS02   Managed Service Requests and Incidents
DSS03   Managed Problems
DSS04   Managed Continuity
DSS05   Managed Security Services
DSS06   Managed Business Process Controls

Monitor, Evaluate and Assess (MEA)

MEA01   Managed Performance and Conformance Monitoring
MEA02   Managed System of Internal Control
MEA03   Managed Compliance With External Requirements
MEA04   Managed Assurance

—ISACA, COBIT 20-19 Framework Governance and Management
Objectives, ISACA, 2018

ITIL 4th Edition, 2019

ITIL, which originally stood for Information Technology Infrastructure Library, was developed by the British Government to standardize IT management practices across the Government. Like COBIT, ITIL focuses on Value creation. ITIL identifies 34 practice areas, which are organized into three sets of practices as shown below:

5.1 ITIL Management Practices

    5.1.1   Architecture Management
    5.1.2   Continual Improvement
    5.1.3   Information Security Management
    5.1.4   Knowledge Management
    5.1.5   Measurement and Reporting
    5.1.6   Organization Change Management
    5.1.7   Portfolio Management
    5.1.8   Project Management
    5.1.9   Relationship Management
    5.1.10 Risk Management
    5.1.11 Service Financial Management
    5.1.12 Strategy Management
    5.1.13 Supplier Management
    5.1.14 Workforce and Talent Management

5.2 Service Management Practices
    5.2.1   Availability Management
    5.2.2   Business Analysis
    5.2.3   Capacity and Performance Management
    5.2.4   Change Control
    5.2.5   Incident Management
    5.2.6   IT Asset Management
    5.2.7   Monitoring and Event Management
    5.2.8   Problem Management
    5.2.9   Release Management
    5.2.10 Service Catalogue Management
    5.2.11 Service Configuration Management
    5.2.12 Service Continuity Management
    5.2.13 Service Design
    5.2.14 Service Desk
    5.2.15 Service Level Management
    5.2.16 Service Request Management
    5.2.17 Service Validation and Testing

5.3 Technical Management Practices
    5.3.1   Deployment Management
    5.3.2   Infrastructure Management
    5.3.3   Software Development and Management
                 —ITIL® Foundation ITIL 4 Edition, Axelos, 2019, pp iv, v

GTAG

Global Technology Audit Guides (GTAGs) are published by The Institute of Internal Audit (https://www.theiia.org/). While COBIT and ITIL are intended to be comprehensive covering IT 'end-to-end', GTAGs are intended to delve deeper into specific topics as listed below:

GTAG – Global Technology Audit Guides

1. Information Technology Risk & Control, 2nd
2. Change & Patch Management Controls, 2nd
3. Continuous Auditing: Implications for Assurance, Monitoring and Risk Assessment
4. Management of IT Auditing, 2nd
5. Auditing Privacy Risks
6. Discontinued
7. Information Technology Outsourcing, 2nd
8. Auditing Application Controls
9. Identity and Access Management
10. Business Continuity Management
11. Developing the IT Audit Plan
12. Auditing IT Projects
13. Fraud Prevention and Detection in an Automated World
14. Auditing User-developed Applications
15. Information Security Governance
16. Data Analysis Technologies
17. Auditing IT Governance
Auditing Smart Devices
Assessing Cybersecurity Risk
Auditing Identity and Access Mgmt
Auditing Network & Communications
Auditing Insider Threat Programs
Auditing Smart Devices
IT Controls
Understanding and Auditing Big Data

Notice that one GTAG was withdrawn and The IIA stopped numbering the GTAGs after the publication of number 17. The more recent GTAGs and Practice Glides (PGs) are titled but not numbered.

Note: During the preparation of this book, the Institute of Internal Auditors (The IIA) dropped its numbering scheme.

Comparing COBIT and ITIL is significant in two dimensions:

- First, seeing the correlation between two frameworks developed for different purposes.
- Second, seeing the differences between the two frameworks.

Below are two mappings, first mapping ITIL to COBIT, second mapping COBIT to ITIL. The two mappings show the commonalities and the differences between the two frameworks based on their terminologies. Notice that one framework covers a topic in a single element while the other framework splits the topic into several subtopics. Also, notice that each framework contains elements that are not in the other framework. Coming from different perspectives and having different backgrounds, differences are inevitable, which are listed at the end of the two comparisons.

Aligning ITIL to COBIT

COBIT 2019		ITIL 4th Edition	
EDM01	Ensured Governance Framework Setting and Maintenance		
EDM02	Ensured Benefits Delivery		
EDM03	Ensured Risk Optimization	5.1.10	Risk Management
EDM04	Ensured Resource Optimization	5.2.6	IT Asset Management
EDM05	Ensured Stakeholder Engagement		
APO01	Managed the I&T Management Framework		
APO02	Managed Strategy	5.1.12	Strategy Management
APO03	Managed Enterprise Architecture	5.1.1	Architecture Management
APO04	Managed Innovation		
APO05	Managed Portfolio	5.1.7	Portfolio Management
APO06	Managed Budget and Costs	5.1.11	Service Financial Management
APO07	Managed Human Resources	5.1.14	Workforce and Talent Management
APO08	Managed Relationships	5.1.9	Relationship Management
APO09	Managed Service Agreements	5.2.15	Service Level Management
APO10	Managed Suppliers	5.1.13	Supplier Management

(Continued)

COBIT 2019		ITIL 4th Edition	
APO11	Managed Quality		
APO12	Managed Risk	5.1.10	Risk Management
APO13	Managed Security	5.1.3	Information Security Management
APO14	Managed Data		
BAI01	Managed Programs	5.1.8	Project Management
BAI02	Managed Requirements Definition	5.2.2	Business Analysis
BAI03	Managed Solutions Identification and Build	5.3.3	Software Development and Management
BAI04	Managed Availability and Capacity	5.2.1 5.2.3	Availability Management Capacity and Performance Management
BAI05	Managed Organizational Change Enablement	5.1.6	Organization Change Management
BAI06	Managed IT Changes	5.2.4	Change Control
BAI07	Managed Change Acceptance and Transitioning	5.2.4 5.2.9 5.2.17 5.3.1	Change Control Release Management Service Validation and Testing Deployment Management
BAI08	Managed Knowledge	5.1.4	Knowledge Management
BAI09	Managed Assets	5.2.6	IT Asset Management
BAI10	Managed Configuration	5.2.11	Service Configuration Management
BAI11	Managed Projects	5.1.8	Project Management
DSS01	Managed Operation	5.3.2 5.2.10	Infrastructure Management Service Catalogue Management
DSS02	Managed Service Requests and Incidents	5.2.5 5.2.7 5.2.13 5.2.14 5.2.16	Incident Management Monitoring and Event Management Service Design Service Desk Service Request Management
DSS03	Managed Problems	5.2.8	Problem Management
DSS04	Managed Continuity	5.2.12	Service Continuity Management
DSS05	Managed Security Services	5.1.3	Information Security Management
DSS06	Managed Business Process Controls		
MEA01	Managed Performance and Conformance Monitoring	5.1.5 5.2.7	Measurement and Reporting Monitoring and Event Management
MEA02	Managed System of Internal Control		
MEA03	Managed Compliance With External Requirements		
MEA04	Managed Assurance		
		5.1.2	Continual Improvement

Aligning COBIT to ITIL

ITIL 4th Edition		COBIT 2019	
5.1.1	Architecture Management	APO03	Managed Enterprise Architecture
5.1.2	Continual Improvement		
5.1.3	Information Security Management	APO13 DSS05	Managed Security Managed Security Services
5.1.4	Knowledge Management	BAI08	Managed Knowledge
5.1.5	Measurement and Reporting	MEA01	Managed Performance and Conformance Monitoring
5.1.6	Organization Change Management	BAI05	Managed Organizational Change Enablement
5.1.7	Portfolio Management	APO05	Managed Portfolio
5.1.8	Project Management	BAI01 BAI11	Managed Programs Managed Projects
5.1.9	Relationship Management	APO08	Managed Relationships
5.1.10	Risk Management	EDM03 APO12	Ensured Risk Optimization Managed Risk
5.1.11	Service Financial Management	APO06	Managed Budget and Costs
5.1.12	Strategy Management	APO02	Managed Strategy
5.1.13	Supplier Management	APO10	Managed Suppliers
5.1.14	Workforce and Talent Management	APO07	Managed Human Resources
5.2.1	Availability Management	BAI04	Managed Availability and Capacity
5.2.2	Business Analysis	BAI02	Managed Requirements Definition
5.2.3	Capacity and Performance Management	BAI04	Managed Availability and Capacity
5.2.4	Change Control	BAI06 BAI07	Managed IT Changes Managed Change Acceptance and Transitioning
5.2.5	Incident Management	DSS02	Managed Service Requests and Incidents
5.2.6	IT Asset Management	EDM04 BAI09	Ensured Resource Optimization Managed Assets
5.2.7	Monitoring and Event Management	DSS02 MEA01	Managed Service Requests and Incidents Managed Performance and Conformance Monitoring
5.2.8	Problem Management	DSS03	Managed Problems
5.2.9	Release Management	BAI07	Managed Change Acceptance and Transitioning
5.2.10	Service Catalogue Management	DSS01	Managed Operation
5.2.11	Service Configuration Management	BAI10	Managed Configuration

(Continued)

ITIL 4th Edition	COBIT 2019	
5.2.12 Service Continuity Management	DSS04	Managed Continuity
5.2.13 Service Design	DSS02	Managed Service Requests and Incidents
5.2.14 Service Desk	DSS02	Managed Service Requests and Incidents
5.2.15 Service Level Management	APO09	Managed Service Agreements
5.2.16 Service Request Management	DSS02	Managed Service Requests and Incidents
5.2.17 Service Validation and Testing	BAI07	Managed Change Acceptance and Transitioning
5.3.1 Deployment Management	BAI07	Managed Change Acceptance and Transitioning
5.3.2 Infrastructure Management	DSS01	Managed Operation
5.3.3 Software Development and Management	BAI03	Managed Solutions Identification and Build
	EDM01	Ensured Governance Framework Setting and Maintenance
	EDM02	Ensured Benefits Delivery
	EDM05	Ensured Stakeholder Engagement
	APO01	Managed the I&T Management Framework
	APO04	Managed Innovation
	APO11	Managed Quality
	APO14	Managed Data
	DSS06	Managed Business Process Controls
	MEA02	Managed System of Internal Control
	MEA03	Managed Compliance with External Requirements
	MEA04	Managed Assurance

TOGAF

TOGAF®, in contrast with COBIT and ITIL, views the world through the lenses of Enterprise Architecture. The **TOGAF**® model is expressed in Figure 19.1.

TOGAF® views Enterprise Architecture in terms of Business Requirements as an eight-step cycle:

- A. Architecture Vision
- B. Business Architecture
- C. Information Systems Architectures
- D. Technology Architecture

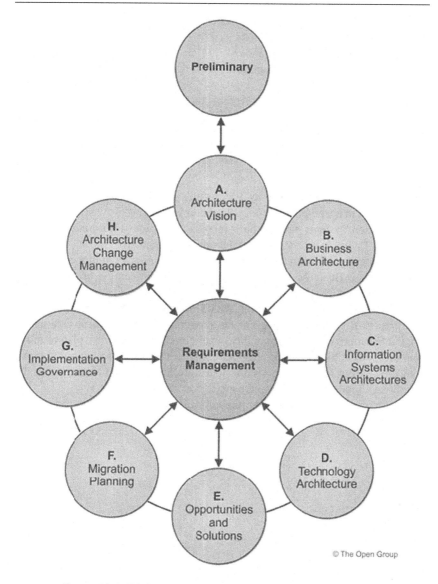

Figure 19.1 TOGAF Diagram. Reproduced with Permission of The Open Group (TOG). https://www.opengroup.org/togaf.

E. Opportunities and Solutions
F. Migration Planning
G. Implementation Governance
H. Architecture Change Management

TOGAF® envisions three types of Architectures:

- Business Architectures
- Information Systems Architectures
- Technology Architectures

Business Architectures include an Enterprise's business goals and objectives, and strategies to accomplish these goals and objectives.

Information Systems Architectures include the various Information Systems adopted by Enterprises to automate their goals and objectives.

Technology Architectures include the specific technologies employed by Enterprises and their Business systems including some combination of on-premises Infrastructure and cloud-based computing assets.

Given three types of architectures, what Opportunities and Solutions exist for Enterprises? Migration Planning creates a roadmap to convert these Opportunities and Solutions into a viable reality, where roadmaps provide a plan to move from the Current State to different Future States. The changes required to move from the Current State to the Future States are implemented according to the Enterprise's Implementation Governance.

The Enterprise Architecture is ultimately adjusted and revised in response to changes in the Business, its Business Environment, its Information Systems, and Technology.

Epilogue – The Unfinishable Chapter

Artificial intelligence (AI) is arguably the biggest, potentially the most significant thing to impact society since its beginnings. AI has introduced existential questions into daily conversation. 'How will AI affect my future?' 'Will I have a job?' 'What will that job be?' 'How will AI affect my life?' AI is not only a helpful assistant but how will it shape the future and my life in particular?

In terms of massive use of AI, we are still at the beginning. How this will play out over the next several years and decades remains to be seen. Hence, this chapter is unfinishable. But there are reasonable questions that can be asked of AI. Below is a list from the perspective of IT Audit.

- How will IT Audit determine if an AI is 'suitable' for an Enterprise?
- How will IT Audit determine if the guidance provided by the AI was accurate, reasonable and suitable?
- How will IT Audit evaluate the actions of an AI?
- How will IT Audit determine if the AI made up something without support or evidence, if it 'hallucinated' and was what it created suitable for the Enterprise?
- How will IT Audit determine if malicious behavior was occurring?
- How will IT Audit confirm AI's Conclusions? AI's Predictions? AI's Prescriptions?
- How will IT Audit evaluate an AI?
- How will IT Audit evaluate an AI's algorithms?
- How will IT Audit evaluate the Data upon which the AI was trained?
- How will IT Audit evaluate the interaction of AI's algorithms with post-training Data?
- Does AI require ongoing supervision?
- If so, who will supervise the AI?
- What guardrails will be built into AI?
- How will IT Audit confirm those guardrails and their effects on the AI?
- Will the AI be incapable of *escaping* those guardrails?

- How will any such instances be discovered, resolved, and blocked if an escape occurs?
- What impact will AI have on Sensitive Data, on Confidential Data, on Privacy? Will businesses be able to keep information confidential and private or will the AI 'leak' everything? Will the AI add sensitive and/or confidential information to its training set? This data will become accessible beyond the business from which it originates?

The next edition of this book may well include entire chapters devoted to AI and IT Audit's policies, procedures, practices and standards regarding AI and its implementation in business.

Will AI add significant new dimensions to IT Auditing? Absolutely yes.

By Way of Reminders,

- Remember that the standard established for a System of Internal Controls is Adequate, Appropriate, Suitable.
- Remember that SOX expanded the CPAs opinion beyond financial statements that 'fairly present' to include assertion that the Business' System of Internal Controls is suitable and effective.
- Remember that Business Automation is constantly increasing.
- Remember that assets that were previously physical have been transformed into services with both positive and negative effects. This is Abstraction, the replacement of physical elements with virtual services, which IT Audit will examine.
- Remember the roles of Service Level Agreements (SLAs) and Cloud Service Providers' (CSPs) 'Shared Responsibilities'.
- Remember that Business Objectives determine Risks and Internal Controls.
- Remember that the test criterion for the Design of Internal Controls is Suitability.
- Remember that Effectiveness is a two-pronged test: were the Internal Controls Effective and were they in Effect during the period being Audited.
- Remember Basic IT Good Practices. They were developed by IT to ensure integrity and reliability. No one wants to be blamed for something that could have been prevented or at least controlled. These are General IT Controls, illustrative but not inclusive.
- Remember the importance of Application Controls. They control business process. They control both Enterprise operations and its business processes.
- Remember System and Organization Controls (SOC). They are management's responsibility. They are the basis for IT Audit's assertions regarding a service provider's Internal Controls and their Suitability.

Index

Printed in the United States
by Baker & Taylor Publisher Services